P9-BJA-379

Pelagius

A RELUCTANT HERETIC

Pelagius

A RELUCTANT HERETIC

B. R. REES

THE BOYDELL PRESS

© B. R. Rees 1988

All Rights Reserved. Except as permitted under current legislation
no part of this work may be photocopied, stored in a retrieval system,
published, performed in public, adapted, broadcast,
transmitted, recorded or reproduced in any form or by any means,
without the prior permission of the copyright owner

First published 1988 by The Boydell Press, Woodbridge
Reprinted in hardback and paperback 1991

The Boydell Press is an imprint of Boydell & Brewer Ltd
PO Box 9, Woodbridge, Suffolk IP12 3DF
and of Boydell & Brewer Inc.
PO Box 41026, Rochester, NY 14604, USA

ISBN 0 85115 503 0 (hardback)
ISBN 0 85115 294 5 (paperback)

British Library Cataloguing in Publication Data
Rees, B. R.
    Pelagius: a reluctant heretic
    1. Pelagianism   2. Church history
    I. Title
    273′.5   BT1450
    ISBN 0-85115-503-0
    ISBN 0-85115-294-5 pbk

Library of Congress Cataloging-in-Publication Data
Rees, B. R. (Bryn R.)
    Pelagius, a reluctant heretic/B. R. Rees
        p.   cm.
    Bibliography: p.
    Includes index
    ISBN 0-85115-503-0
    1. Pelagius 2. Pelagianism   3. Heretics,
    Christian—Biography   I. Title
    BT1450.R44   1988   88-7350
    273′.5—dc19   ᴸ4889

BT
1450
• R44
1988

This publication is printed in acid-free paper

Printed in Great Britain by
St Edmundsbury Press Ltd, Bury St Edmunds, Suffolk

Contents

CAMROSE LUTHERAN COLLEGE
LIBRARY

For my dear wife, Zena

Preface

My interest in Pelagius was first awakened when the premature death of my friend and colleague at Birmingham, Donald Dudley, made it necessary for me to take over his course of lectures on Augustine in 1973, and, a few years later, I found myself volunteering to give an enlarged and more intensive version at Lampeter. When I was invited to deliver the Donald Dudley Memorial Lecture at Birmingham in 1982, I could think of no more appropriate a subject than the Pelagian controversy. The more I studied the history of that controversy and the part played in it by Pelagius, Augustine and others the more conscious I became of the need for an up-to-date account which would acquaint students of church history and doctrine as well as the general reader with the results of scholarly research over the past three decades. I must also admit that I was hopeful that I might be able to redress at least some of the effects of the bad press which Pelagius had received over the centuries and was still receiving in some quarters.

I was encouraged to go ahead with my self-imposed task by Gerald Bonner, and the extent of my indebtedness to him will be obvious to my readers, although, to save him embarrassment, I have to add that I did not consult him at any point and so he is not directly responsible for any of the views which I have expressed or for errors of which I may have been guilty. I am also greatly indebted to many friends at Cardiff who have helped me in various ways: to Robin Attfield, Ceri Davies and Peter Walcot for reading my typescript and making invaluable comments on its style, content and presentation; to Michael Jarrett, Morfydd Owen and John Percival for lending me their own copies of publications which would otherwise have been difficult to obtain for my extended use; to Tom Dawkes and Brian James for helping me to find my way around the Humanities Library at Cardiff and for advice on bibliographical matters, and to their junior colleagues in the Inter-Library Loans section and at the issues counter for their patience and co-operation in supplying my needs; and, last but by no means least, to Carmen Larreta and Bonny Harvey for typing different parts of my book at different times over and above the call of duty, and to Jean Walcot, who has relieved me of much of the burden of compiling an index by transferring the data to her word-processor and producing the final version.

Finally, I wish to acknowledge the financial assistance which I have received from the Leverhulme Trust through the award of an Emeritus Fellowship for the years 1984–6 enabling me to visit other libraries and to obtain secretarial assistance, and to the publishers, their printer and their reader for making this a much better book than it would have been without their expertise.

My greatest debt of all is to my dear wife, who has put up with my constant and, I am sure, often boring chatter about Pelagius over the past six years and has done everything in her power to ensure that I would have the health and strength to persevere to the end.

Cardiff   B. R. REES
March 1988

Introit

'I have become a great theologian in a short time,
and you are going to see the evidence of it.'

BLAISE PASCAL[1]

Pascal made this claim, no doubt with tongue in cheek, soon after beginning his Socratic cross-examination of the learned doctors of the Sorbonne in order to establish the precise difference between them on the subject of divine grace and its relation to free will; but it was not long before he found himself totally disillusioned with their sophistry and decided to abandon the reasons of the mind for those of the heart.[2] I make no such claim even in jest; indeed, I have to confess that there have been times when my own modest attempt to comprehend the issues and ramifications of the first great debate on the same subject has left me feeling just as nonplussed as Pascal and rather like poor old Kaspar must have felt when asked to explain the causes of the Battle of Blenheim. Small wonder! Confusion has surrounded both Pelagius and Pelagianism ever since, and even before, the heresiarch's condemnation. For centuries now the adjective 'Pelagian' has been a convenient term of abuse in the Christian Church and Pelagius himself a bogyman for upright clerics to evoke when wanting to frighten wayward members of their flock. John Cassian, Vincent of Lérins and Faustus of Riez in the fifth century, Erigena in the ninth, Alexander of Hales, Peter Abelard, Duns Scotus and Thomas Aquinas in the twelfth and thirteenth, William of Ockham in the fourteenth, Melanchthon and Arminius in the sixteenth, John Wesley in the eighteenth, Teilhard de Chardin in the twentieth – all in turn have been dubbed 'Pelagian', 'Semi-Pelagian' or 'Synergist', treated as victims of the same disease and consigned to ecclesiastical quarantine, and even that 'battered liberal' Erasmus did not enjoy complete immunity from it. Christians in the West seem to have been peculiarly susceptible to attacks of the virus: in fourteenth-century England Archbishop Thomas Bradwardine detected a Pelagian hiding beneath every academic gown, just as Reinhold Niebuhr in twentieth-century America saw Pelagians in every pew: Pelagianism has often been described as 'the English disease', and we are told that by the early years of the present century the United States had 'gradually made its way, from

---

[1] *Les Provinciales*, ed. L. Cognet, *Garnier Frères*, 1965, i. 8.
[2] Unamuno, 23, comments that Kant too 'reconstructed with the heart that which with the head he had overthrown'.

being the most Calvinist, to being the most Pelagian of Christian nations.'[3]

Pelagianism is indeed an ever-recurring temptation and has survived all the onslaughts of its adversaries to challenge Arianism for the dubious honour of having been the most persistent of Christian heresies. How many members of the average congregation today realise that not a few elements of the services which they attend are still being criticised as 'Pelagian'? Anglicans, for example, if challenged on the subject, might well reply, 'Oh no! we are using the *ASB*!' But it is precisely the *Alternative Service Book 1980* which came under fire a few years ago from a Professor of Ecclesiastical History on the grounds that much, too much, of its liturgy is Pelagian.[4] Prayers, it is claimed, asking God for some moral of spiritual improvement are in fact calculated to urge the worshipper only to *self*-improvement, and even in the *ASB* version of the famous Franciscan prayer 'Pelagius prevails'. The author of the article referred to, summarised in *The Times* under the heading 'Old Heresy clouds New Liturgy', is clearly not only against the *ASB* but also against Pelagius, and for the traditional, Augustinian reason that no good human action is possible without the grace of God to inspire and sustain it. One is reminded of the comment of a writer already quoted that, in the modern Church, 'the hymns may assume predestination, but the sermons are Pelagian'. The same writer, concluding his sketch of the influence of Pelagianism on the Church and the Church's resistance to it, sums up with the statement that 'any movement towards Pelagianism is bound in the end, so long as Christianity survives, to be resisted'.

But even Passmore feels obliged to admit that 'not a few modern readers will sympathise with Pelagius in this debate, seeing in him the blunt Englishman [*sic*] cutting through the tortuosities of North African sensuality and sensibility.'[5] It is an incontrovertible fact that many good Christians over the intervening centuries have suspected that, despite the bad press which Pelagius has received, there may have been more than a grain of truth in his teaching. 'Pelagius', writes R. F. Evans, who has done as much as anyone in recent years to dispel the clouds of misunderstanding, 'is one of the most maligned figures in the history of Christianity. It has been the common sport of the theologian and the historian of theology to set him up as a symbolic bad man and heap upon him accusations which often tell us more about the theological perspective of the accuser than Pelagius.' Giants like Harnack and Karl Barth have sometimes passed hasty and misleading judgements on him for advancing views which were not his at all, the former dismissing him as '*im tiefsten Grunde gottlos*', and others have followed suit by crediting – or,

---

[3] Passmore, 115. More recently an Anglican clergyman has remarked: 'Pelagius lives on, not in official formularies or in academic theology. British Christians tend to a theology of self-help and morality' (M. Jackson, 244). Reinhold Niebuhr once described F. R. Tennant's *The Concept of Sin* as 'the most elaborate of modern Pelagian treatises' but Passmore regarded it as 'not a particularly original book' (109).

[4] Hall, 2ff. For a broadly similar view of liturgical translations used in the Roman Catholic Church cf. Cooper, 43, 50, a reference which I owe to a former student, Tom Dawkes.

[5] Passmore, 95, 100, 114.

rather, debiting – him with all the tenets of Pelagianism *per saturam*.[6]

Small wonder then that this kind of radical misunderstanding has spread to lesser mortals deriving their knowledge from secondary sources and concerned to draw analogies with fields far removed from theology, like a reviewer of a book entitled *The Benn Heresy*, who has commented that 'Benn himself refers approvingly to Pelagius, that ancient Briton who thought that good works were sufficient for entry to heaven without necessarily believing in God.' Now it may well be that Mr Tony Benn sees himself as a latter-day Pelagius in the field of politics and Pelagius as a kindred spirit in that of theology, both of them pursued and persecuted by the misguided and often malicious mouthpieces of the establishment whose personal prejudices inhibit them from penetrating to the essential truth underlying the arguments of their opponents. But one doubts if he would be so naïve and ill-informed as to think that Pelagius held that belief in God was not essential in a Christian: Pelagius lived in the Roman Empire of the fourth and fifth centuries, not in the Britain or America of the twentieth century whose theological climate nurtures rumours of God dead and myths of God incarnate.

No, Pelagius was not *gottlos*; he was 'fundamentally a Christian moralist', and he wanted, above all else, 'to be an orthodox theologian of the Christian Church and to be known as such'.[7] As for Pelagianism, Gerald Bonner has rightly emphasised that recent research – to which, incidentally, he has made a significant contribution – has demolished the monolithic view of it: the Pelagians were not 'a party with a rigidly defined doctrinal system; they were a mixed group, united by certain theological principles which nevertheless left the individual free to develop his own opinions upon particular topics'.[8] What was to become a notorious heresy began as an ascetic movement but, since Jerome and Augustine in the fifth century, theologians have lumped both heresy and movement under the same name and treated Pelagius as the eponymous founder of both. From the early fifth to the late twentieth century he has fallen a victim to over-simplification and culpable misinterpretation of the evidence offered by his writings and used against him by his opponents, and, as a result, the very real and profound differences separating him from Augustine and the Church have been obscured. The two protagonists have been seen as black and white, the one a symbol of heresy and the other of orthodoxy, the one condemned and degraded, the other canonised and exalted. But the question which both sought to answer is perennial: 'at stake is a much more basic conception of what the very nature of human existence is according to Christianity. Set in the context of human freedom, the Pelagian controversy asked the perennially radical question of the quality of human behaviour, and the sources of good and evil in this world.'[9] It is a question which is as important today as it was when it became the subject of debate between Christians for the first time and Pelagius and Augustine

[6] R. F. Evans, 1968(a), 66f.; on Pelagius' 'poor press' in modern times see Phipps, 131f.
[7] Ibid., 42, 92.
[8] Bonner, 1970, 31.
[9] Haight, 32.

clashed with each other in a battle which was to end in tragedy for Pelagius.

But what of the man himself, his life and personality? 'A cultivated and sensitive layman . . . an elusive and gracious figure, beloved and respected wherever he goes, . . . silent, smiling, reserved':[10] these vivid phrases of R. G. Collingwood suggest a rich store of information and anecdote of the kind we associate with the *Lives* of many VIPs of the ancient world. The reality is very different: there is no *Life* of Pelagius, and hard facts about his life are at a premium. We possess seven works which have survived more or less intact and are generally agreed to have come from his own pen – a commentary on the Pauline Epistles, a confession of faith and five letters which are, in fact, minor treatises[11] – as well as several more attributed to him at one time or another, a number of isolated fragments and Augustine's numerous quotations from his two major treatises now lost. In none of these is there even a trace of autobiographical detail, which well accords with our general impression of a modest, retiring man who would have shrunk in distaste from the degree of publicity, not to say notoriety, thrust upon him by posterity. The pen-pictures contributed by his contemporaries, who can hardly claim to be objective, leave us with little more than an indication that he must have had a distinct tendency to obesity. He is said to have possessed 'the torso and strength of a wrestler and a fine, corpulent figure', 'the shoulders of a Milo', 'broad shoulders and a stout neck'; 'he displays his fat even upon his forehead'; and, not surprisingly, 'he moves along at the stately pace of a tortoise'.[12] Due allowance must obviously be made for the extravagance of theological polemic.

What do we know about his birth and death? In short, precious little. We know the date and place of neither; but it is reasonably certain that he was born not long after 350 in Britain and died not long after 418 somewhere in the countries adjoining the Eastern Mediterranean, just possibly in Egypt.[13]

---

[10] Collingwood and Myres, 308.

[11] R. F. Evans, 1968(b), argues that only four of the letters attributed to Pelagius by Plinval, 1943, 1947, were actually works of Pelagius: *On the Christian Life* (PL 40, 1031–46); *On Virginity* (PL 30, 162–8) (CSEL 1, 225–50); *To Celantia* (PL 22, 1204–29) (CSEL 56, 329–56); *On the Divine Law* (PL 30, 105–16). The *Letter to Demetrias* (PL 30, 15–45; 33, 1099–1120), though attributed to various authors at various times, is now accepted as an authentic work of Pelagius. It has sometimes been suggested that the quality of the Latin text, which is higher than that of his other works, may imply that Pelagius was assisted by someone else, the most obvious candidate being his faithful *amanuensis*, Annianus of Celeda, described by Orosius as his 'armour-bearer' and by Jerome as his 'voice' and 'shadow'. Annianus also translated the sermons of John Chrysostom, adding two Epistles of his own, one of which, prefixed to Matthew, shows some resemblances in its phraseology to the *Letter to Demetrias* (see Garnier in PL 48, 626–30).

[12] Jerome, *Letters* 50, 4 (PL 22, 515) (CSEL 54, 392); *Dialogue against the Pelagians* I, 28 (PL 23, 522); Orosius, *Book in Defence against the Pelagians: On the Freedom of the Will*, 31 (PL 31, 1200) (CSEL 5, 657); Jerome, *Dialogue* III, 16 (PL 23, 586).

[13] While I cannot find any firm evidence to prove that he spent his last years in Egypt, I agree with J. Ferguson, 1956, 114, and 1980, 117, and Wermelinger, 210, that the traditional assumption that he went to Egypt from Palestine is preferable to any other, since Cyril of Alexandria did not at first assent to his condemnation and he may have joined Melania and Pinianus on their second journey to Egypt (Wermelinger, 251). Syria would have been the obvious place of asylum after John's successor in Jerusalem, Praylius, had withdrawn support for his cause there; but if he did go there, it is strange that Marius Mercator did not mention it.

Augustine, Paul Orosius, Prosper Tiro of Aquitaine and Marius Mercator, all contemporaries, and Gennadius of Marseilles, a near-contemporary, refer to him as *Brito, Britto, Britannicus* or *Britannus*,[14] and only Jerome as *Scotus* or *Scottus*, that is to say, 'Irish',[15] but this may have been no more than a current term of abuse. J. B. Bury, however, took Jerome's reference seriously and combined it with his additional phrase 'from the locality of the Britons' to produce a compromise to the effect that he was an Irishman who came from a family which had settled in western Britain,[16] and Heinrich Zimmer attributed the very high regard in which the Irish came to hold him later to his having been born in Ireland.[17] But Britain is by far the strongest candidate for the honour, if such it be, of having provided him with his birthplace, even if all efforts to pinpoint its precise location have been characterised by ingenuity rather than conviction. It remains as uncertain as that of Homer and almost as keenly competed for: at different times the main contenders have emerged as the south-west, south-east and north of England and, of course, Wales, that traditional stronghold of dissent.[18] As for speculations that his name was a hellenised form of Muirchu (Irish) or Morgan (Welsh), they deserve only to be buried along with many other 'pure fantasies about his background'.[19]

It is reasonably certain then that he hailed originally from Britain but we can only guess why he left it for Rome; Souter once made the interesting suggestion that he did so because of a difference of opinion with his father[20] but he may have done so simply to further his career, as did many other young men of his time, including Augustine, who left Africa for the same reason. It is probable that he came of good family and had been given a sound education, *pace* Jerome and Orosius, in classical literature and philosophy, which he was to extend by wide reading in the Church Fathers after his arrival in Rome in the early eighties of the fourth century. There have been speculations that he spent some time in Gaul or Palestine before moving on to Rome but these are unsupported by factual evidence,[21] and the idea that the law was his first choice of career, though attractive and promoted by Plinval and R. F. Evans as helping to explain the legalistic tone of much of his

[14] Augustine, *L*, 186, 1 (PL 33, 816) (CSEL 57, 45); Orosius, *Book in Defence*, 12 (PL 31, 1182) (CSEL 5, 620); Prosper, *Chronicle*, year 413 (PL 51, 591), *Poem on the Graceless*, i. 13 (PL 51, 94); Marius Mercator, *Footnotes to Words of Julian* (PL 48, 111A); Gennadius, *On Famous Men*, 43 (PL 58, 1083 – *v.l.* in *codice Çorbeiensi*).

[15] *Commentary on Jeremiah* III, pref. (PL 24, 758) (CSEL 59, 151).

[16] Bury, 1904, 26ff.; 1905, 296.

[17] In his *Pelagius in Irland*; see 122, n. 100.

[18] For discussions of Pelagius' origin see H. Williams, 1912, 200ff.; Souter, 1922–31, 1ff.; Plinval, 1943, 57ff.; J. Ferguson, 1956, 39ff.

[19] Bonner, 1972, 32. Ferguson, 1956, 40, 1980, 115, is reluctant to accept the argument advanced by Souter, 1922–31, 2, that the not infrequent appearance of the names Pelagius and Pelagia before Pelagius' time rules out the need to invent a Latin name to represent his Celtic one. For earlier examples of the names Pelagius and Pelagia in Greek see Pape-Benseler II, 1159, and for Libanius' fellow-pupil Pelagius, who became consular governor of Syria in the second half of the fourth century, *Der Kleine Pauly* IV, 593; there was also a martyr-saint Pelagia in the late third/early fourth century (Livingstone, 389f.).

[20] Souter, 1907, 423ff.; 1915, 180; 1922–31, 3.

[21] H. Williams, 1912, 199f.

teaching, is based solely on Jerome's remark that the 'monk' who had criticised his attack on Jovinian in 393 or 394 'had abandoned the law and turned his attention to the Church'.[22] Jerome is not the only contemporary to describe him as a 'monk'[23] but it is a description which he himself does not recommend to his supporters.[24] 'This apparently simple and insignificant question has sharply divided scholars' with Bury, N. K. Chadwick and Hugh Williams, for example, in the Ayes lobby and Plinval and Grosjean in the Noes.[25] Certainly he never belonged to a religious community in the formal sense, and perhaps we should dub him 'honorary monk' in view of his undoubted adoption of an ascetic way of life. Both Orosius and Pope Zosimus were later to speak of him as a layman,[26] and he was never ordained, as was his friend Celestius – by the Church in the East after his condemnation by that of the West – nor does he ever seem to have sought ordination, thus revealing an apparent lack of total commitment which was hardly likely to endear him to professionals like Jerome and Augustine.

In sum, all we are able to say with any conviction about his origins and early life is that he was a Briton, was born sometime in the early part of the second half of the fourth century, emigrated to Rome in the early eighties and was neither a monk nor a priest. The rest is buried in the quicksands covering his 'prehistory', and we can now struggle out of these on to rather firmer ground. Having arrived there, we shall first give a blow-by-blow account of the origins and course of the Pelagian controversy, then examine in greater detail the case for and against Pelagius, and end by tracing the aftermath of his condemnation as the first major heresiarch of the Western Church and its confirmation by the Church in the East. This happened at the Council of Ephesus in 431, which included in its canons one which placed under threat of arbitrary excommunication anyone who failed to dissociate himself from

[22] *Letters* 50, 2. Plinval, 1943, 63ff., and R. F. Evans, 1968(a), 31, both accept this view but Ferguson, J., 1956, 43f., has reservations, pointing out that 'though his skill in controversy may indicate some legal training, he is not referred to as a lawyer like his associate Celestius'. The question whether Pelagius was really the target of Jerome's letter will be discussed in c. I.

[23] Augustine refers to him as a monk in *PP*, xx. 36 (PL 44, 342) (CSEL 42, 92) and in *H*, 88 (PL 42, 47); Mercator in his *Footnotes to Words of Julian*, pref. 2 (PL 48, 111).

[24] *On the Divine Law*, 9 (PL 30, 115), assuming with R. F. Evans that Pelagius was the author of this tract, which he cites as *On the Law*.

[25] Hanson, 1968, 144, n. 2.

[26] Orosius, *Book in Defence*, 4 (PL 31, 1177) (CSEL 5, 607), 5 (PL 31, 1117) (CSEL 5, 609); Zosimus, *Letter on the Case of Pelagius*, 3 (PL 20, 657; 45, 1721) (CSEL 35, 104). Passmore, 121, describes him as 'that indomitable layman', and Ferguson, 1956, 144ff., discusses his concern for the vocation of a layman and for the importance of the laity in the Church. Celestius, on the other hand, 'is said to have reached the priesthood in Asia' (*L* 175, 1; 176, 4) (PL 33, 760, 764) (CSEL 44, 654, 667). Mercator, *Memorandum on the Name of Celestius* i. 2, records that this happened at Ephesus 'by fraudulent means' but Garnier denies that he was ever a monk (PL 48, 72f., 282). Orosius' *Book in Defence*, described by Plinval, 1943, 283, as '*un pamphlet assez mince, mais le plus amusant des pamphlets religieux*', is certainly 'no theological masterpiece and like the writings of Marius Merce or oversteps the bounds of the tolerable but it is carefully composed throughout and is no mere hotch-potch of quotations' (Wermelinger, 67). The same writer (ibid.) questions whether Augustine ever read his *Book in Defence* and suggests that his 'independent stance' on the delicate matter of the doctrine of grace at a time when it was not yet settled excited general displeasure in Africa.

'the opinions of Celestius', that is, Pelagianism. In a sense it was no more than a *quid pro quo* for the action of Pope Celestine in declaring Nestorius a heretic in 430 in response to a dossier on him received from Cyril of Alexandria and accompanied by a request that the Western Church should give its opinion on Nestorianism. Thus, as a matter of courtesy rather than a result of reasoned debate, the Eastern Church overruled the earlier decision of the Synod of Diospolis, which came under its jurisdiction, in favour of Pelagius.

It may be useful at this point to add a note of explanation on the relationship between the Eastern and Western Churches at the time of the Pelagian controversy. By the end of the fourth century the tetrarchy formally established by Diocletian in 293, by which the western and eastern parts of the Roman Empire were each given their own Augustus and Caesar but with the intention that they should maintain unity of government throughout the Empire, remained in existence only in theory, since the two sons of Theodosius I in practice ruled East and West with equal rights. This *de facto* political division resulted in a corresponding separation of the Catholic Church into two components in East and West. Though the Church in the West, which included North Africa, and that in the East, which included Egypt, remained in communion with each other, their theological interests reveal a marked difference for historical and cultural reasons. Whereas in the late fourth and early fifth centuries the Eastern Church continued to grapple with metaphysical problems such as the nature of God and the relation of the Son to the Father, the Western Church became more concerned with the practical questions of the relationship of Rome to the other provinces and the formulation of a doctrine of salvation which would be wholly consistent with traditional teaching. The importance of the Pelagian controversy in both of these connections cannot be overestimated.

I

A FAMOUS VICTORY

'What they fought each other for
I could not well make out.
But everybody said, quoth he,
That 'twas a famous victory.'

ROBERT SOUTHEY[1]

Augustine tells us that, possibly around 405, Pelagius had heard a bishop in
Rome, believed by some to have been Paulinus of Nola, quoting the famous
sentence from the tenth book of the *Confessions*, 'Give me what you command,
and command what you will' – *da mihi quod iubes, et iube quod vis*. 'This', he
comments somewhat ruefully, 'was more than he could stomach and, contradicting it with some show of anger, he almost went to law with the man who
had referred to it.'[2] But the doctor of grace knew nothing of this at the time
and, in any case, had other fish to fry then; and so Pelagius continued
unimpeded with his vigorous campaign to reform the moral standards of
Christians in Rome. Indeed, we are tempted to wonder if we would ever have
heard of Pelagianism without the rude intervention of Alaric the Visigoth,
who unwittingly sealed the fate of it. For it was the imminence of Alaric's
attack on the capital city which drove Pelagius in 409 to join the general
exodus from Italy and make his way, perhaps via Sicily, to Africa, where
Augustine saw him but did not converse with him,[3] and thence to Palestine.
But before he left Rome, he had completed his commentary on the Pauline
Epistles and had made known in it his views on grace and free will and

---

[1] 'After Blenheim', *The Golden Treasury*, ed. F. T. Palgrave, Oxford 1929, 214.
[2] *GP* xx. 53 (PL 45, 1026); the offending sentence is in *C*, X, xxix. 40 (PL 32, 796) (CSEL 33,
256). Courcelle, 1947, 270ff., 1963, 580, suggested that the bishop concerned may have been
Paulinus of Nola, who was a friend of Pelagius during the latter's stay in Rome as well as a
correspondent of Augustine but was 'not a fighter' (Frend, 1984, 678) and did not get involved in
the controversy between the two men. Martinetto, 83ff., argued that Pelagius' first reactions to
Augustine's doctrine of grace appear in his Pauline commentary and his treatise *On the Hardening
of Pharaoh's Heart*. This is almost certainly true of the commentary, though Wermelinger, 22,
reminds us that Pelagius does no more than mention many interpretations with which he does
not himself agree; but the date and authorship of the treatise, held by Plinval to have been
written by Pelagius c. 397–8 and published by him on behalf of G. Morin in 1947, 137ff. (PLS 1,
1506–39), are still uncertain.
[3] *PP* xxii. 46 (PL 44, 346) (CSEL 42, 100).

1

baptism as well as many other topics around which the Pelagian controversy was to centre.[4]

In Palestine he was confronted first by Jerome and, a little later, by the Spanish priest Paul Orosius, himself a refugee from the barbarians, who had escaped from his native country, as he was later to claim, 'with the help of a cloud which suddenly enwrapped me'.[5] He was 'the man who gave to the Mediterranean world the remains of the first Christian martyr, St Stephen',[6] presented to him by Avitus, a fellow-presbyter from Bracar, to take back there on his return, though, in the event, he had to leave them at Minorca on his return journey. At this time, however, on his arrival in Palestine, it was he who brought Pelagianism into the open and first linked the names of Pelagius and Celestius as 'joint sowers of the heresy in Africa',[7] though Pelagius had played no part in the controversy there. After some initial skirmishing Pelagius was charged with heresy before Bishop John of Jerusalem at the Synod of Diospolis in 415, only to be acquitted after dissociating himself from the more extreme views of Celestius. Thus encouraged, he wrote his two major treatises, now lost, *On Nature* and *On Free Will* to clarify his own views and, he hoped, to justify them. But his real troubles were only beginning: both Jerome in Palestine and Augustine in Africa remained unconvinced of his innocence and identified him as the teacher of Celestius, using his pupil merely as a front man to conceal his own responsibility for the new heresy.

Dissatisfied with the outcome of the Synod of Diospolis and egged on by Augustine, whose case had been strengthened by synods held at Carthage and Milevis, the African bishops now appealed to a higher authority, that of Pope Innocent I. After some delay, not unreasonable if, as he claimed, he knew of no Pelagians in Rome at the time, he ruled that Pelagius and Celestius be excommunicated unless they renounced their heretical opinions. 'The case is closed', cried Augustine in triumph – *causa finita est*;[8] but his elation was premature, since both men appealed against the decision. The exact sequence of events which followed is somewhat blurred but the events themselves stand out clearly. Innocent's successor, Zosimus – the former had died in the meantime – re-opened the case, only to pronounce an ambiguous

---

[4] Souter at one point (1922–31, 4f.) claims that internal evidence establishes that it was not written before 'about 405' and recalls that, according to Marius Mercator (*Memorandum on Celestius* ii. 1 in PL 48, 83), it was in circulation before 410, the year when Alaric finally entered Rome; but elsewhere (ibid. 188ff.) he suggests a dating between 404 and 409, and Duval, 1980, 526, prefers one between 406 and 410. The date generally accepted for Rufinus of Aquileia's translation of Origen's commentary on Romans, on which Pelagius drew extensively, is 405–6 (Murphy, 192ff.; Hammond, 403ff.). So, since Pelagius may well have left Rome in 409, it is safest to date his commentary between 405/6 and 409.

[5] *History against the Pagans* iii. 20, 194 (PL 31, 839) (CSEL 5, 183).

[6] Hunt, 211; cf. H. Chadwick, 1976, 190; Wermelinger, 89.

[7] Bonner, 1972, 45.

[8] *S* 131, x. 10 (PL 38, 734); Bonner, 1963, 343, n. 1, warns that this famous phrase has often been misquoted and that too much should not be made of it in the present context, since it was clearly one of which Augustine was very fond.

verdict, which could have been regarded as something of a 'climb-down'[9] and was certainly little to the taste of the African bishops. They returned to the attack, and the Emperor Honorius now intervened from his retreat in Ravenna, mainly in the interests of public order, which he saw as threatened by riots in the city of Rome allegedly activated by the Pelagians remaining there and a physical attack on a retired official, Constantius, who had openly opposed the views of Celestius as being without scriptural support – *sine scriptura*.[10] He issued an imperial rescript banishing Pelagius, Celestius and all their adherents, though it is doubtful if the two leaders were still in Rome at the time. Almost simultaneously, over two hundred African bishops in council passed a series of canons against what had by now become known as Pelagianism, and Zosimus in his *Epistula Tractoria* of 418 finally condemned both Pelagius and Celestius of heresy and excommunicated them. Celestius continued to contest this decision in Rome and Constantinople without success but Pelagius, after an unsuccessful appeal at Jerusalem, was forced to leave Palestine and 'vanishes from history, his face set eastward, elusive to the last'[11] – though some romantics have seen him marching westwards to die in Britain. The heresy which bore his name was again condemned, somewhat summarily, as 'the opinions of Celestius' at the Council of Ephesus in 431 along with Nestorianism, the Church in the East at last setting its seal of approval on the earlier decision of that in the West.

From the tangled web of charge and counter-charge which led to this outcome and which may never be completely unravelled, one fact at least stands out: to the end, Pelagius never saw himself as a heretic, much less as a heresiarch. He was at heart a moral reformer who, as he became familiar with Christian society in Rome at the turn of the fourth century, became also more and more critical of its moral standards and responded to the general laxity and extravagance he saw around him by preaching the need for simple and virtuous living based on man's freedom to choose for himself what he would, and would not, do. By his teaching, writing and example he attracted to himself, like Jerome before him, a circle of Christians of like beliefs, many of them rich and influential. He and they naturally sought to express themselves by formulating the principles on which their beliefs were founded, and it is to this period of his life that some of his extant letters and his Pauline commentary, 'the earliest extant work of a British author',[12] belong. Other members of the movement expressed themselves in different ways and with differing emphases, so that it became increasingly difficult for their opponents to disentangle the views of Pelagius from those of his associates. But, at the time of his arrival in Palestine, there was one stalwart of the Church awaiting

---

[9] J. Ferguson, 1956, 110; Wermelinger, 127ff., discusses possible reasons for Innocent's reluctance to condemn Pelagius and Celestius outright at this stage.

[10] Prosper, *Chronicle*, year 418 (PL 51, 592).

[11] Collingwood and Myres, 309.

[12] M. R. James, *The Cambridge History of English Literature* I, 1908, 65, cited in Souter, 1922–31, ix.

him there who was never in any doubt as to the extent of his responsibility for this new heresy which had reared its ugly head.

In a letter to an old friend, Domnio, living in Rome, Jerome had referred as long ago as 393 or 394 to a certain monk who had been publicly attacking him for his treatise *Against Jovinian*.[13] The identification of this 'monk' as Pelagius was first made by Plinval in 1943[14] and, thereafter, generally accepted by scholars.[15] But it was R. F. Evans who first made a comprehensive review of the evidence for it, citing twelve heads under which Pelagius could be compared with the unnamed monk of the letter written by Jerome.[16] More recently, he has been strongly challenged by Yves-Marie Duval on the grounds that (a) most of the points of the comparison used by him could be shared by Pelagius with others on Jerome's black list and are no more than *'clichés de polémique'*; (b) there is no sound evidence for connecting the 'jealousy' of Pelagius attributed to Jerome by Augustine and Julian with a time earlier than around 414 and 415; and (c) Jerome's own statements on 'jealousy' similarly cannot be referred to the earlier period in the later part of the fourth century when the correspondence between Domnio and Jerome took place. In sum, it is not a pen-picture of Pelagius which is contained in Jerome's letter; it is a *'portrait-robot de l'hérétique'*, an identikit picture of the typical heretic as Jerome saw him.[17]

Duval is justified in claiming that the references which have been cited from Augustine, Julian and Jerome himself, in order to establish a clash between Pelagius and Jerome in, say, 394 and to identify it as the cause of the ill will which existed between them later, must be subjected to a much closer examination than anyone before his paper has seen fit to give to them. But his case for disputing the identification of Pelagius with the monk referred to in Jerome's letter on the grounds of the contents of the letter itself is much less convincing, however ingenious and carefully argued. The pen-picture which it gives us just does not read like an identikit picture of a typical heretic: it reads – and *feels* – like a portrait of an actual, living individual whom Jerome knew personally and had been able to identify from Domnio's letter. Domnio may well have named Pelagius in his letter, which has not survived, and the fact that Jerome does not repeat the name proves nothing: it was accepted practice, as Duval admits, for those engaged in theological controversy at that time not to name names, and Jerome himself names Pelagius only once in the course of all his attacks upon him, and that in a letter written probably in 418 not long before his own death and at a time when the battle was as good as

[13] *Letters* 50 (PL 22, 512–16) (CSEL 54, 388–95).
[14] Plinval, 1943, 50ff.
[15] E.g. J. Ferguson, 1956, 44f., 77f.; Myres, 1960, 22, nn. 10, 11; 24, nn. 15, 16; Hammond, 426, n. 1; Kelly, 1978, 187ff.; Wermelinger, 46f., 49f. Brown, 1972, 221, n. 4, on the other hand, is less confident, though he accepts that R. F. Evans has made 'a somewhat stronger case' than Plinval.
[16] R. F. Evans, 1968(a), 31ff.
[17] Duval, 1980, 530ff.

over.[18] Nor is his previous acquaintance with Pelagius in dispute: he refers to their former relationship in his *Commentary on Jeremiah* as something which he realises that he must take care not to appear to be damaging.[19] And there does not appear to be a single instance elsewhere in the ample repertory of his invective where he employed the tactical device which Duval attributes to him on this occasion.

If the identification of Pelagius with the unnamed monk of the letter to Domnio is correct, as is probable, *pace* Duval, then it has the considerable advantage of helping to explain Jerome's attitude to Pelagius on the latter's arrival in Palestine, because there would be an old score to settle between them, and they would have crossed swords on a previous occasion. The main issue then had been the supreme merit of celibacy: 'Jerome condemns marriage' was how he summed up the burden of Pelagius' criticism. What exactly had Pelagius said, and done, to give offence? In the letter there is more abuse than argument, and we learn little from it about the real issues. Pelagius is referred to as 'a certain gossipy monk, a wanderer around the streets, the cross-roads and the highways, a pettifogger, a sly detractor, who with a beam in his own eye strives to remove the mote from another's.' 'He delivers harangues against me', complains the aggrieved Jerome, 'and gnawing at the books I wrote against Jovinian, tears them and pulls them apart.' This scoundrel, ignorant as he is of the works of Aristotle and Cicero, dares to criticise one who is well versed in philosophy, the Christian Fathers and the scriptures; he is one who acknowledges no teacher but claims to be inspired and instructed by God himself. Jerome goes on to cast aspersions on such a man's sense of vocation, his constant association with women, his habit of instructing them in the privacy of their bedchambers instead of coming out into the open and conducting a debate by correspondence with views set out in writing and supported by argument. If he would but venture to do this, he would soon find out his mistake in attacking such an adversary; he would hear in reply across the many seas, lands and peoples which separated them the echo of Jerome's cry: 'I do *not* condemn wedlock, I do *not* condemn marriage.'[20]

At the same time Jerome proceeded to clarify his views on marriage in more moderate terms in a letter to his friend Pammachius at Rome, insisting that his earlier remarks on the subject should not be taken to indicate that he condemned it for those who chose it because they felt unable to pursue the higher course of celibacy.[21] There was nothing unusual in such a position, and many other Christians, including Pelagius, would have agreed with it; it was the intemperate, indeed vitriolic, tone of his treatise *Against Jovinian* which had excited criticism. In it his polemic had been sustained and reinforced by

---

[18] *Letters* 152 (*RB* 27, 1910, 1–11) (CSEL 56, 364) – a letter to Riparius, in which Jerome more than made up for any previous reticence on his part occasioned by his preference for correcting the Pelagians rather than dishonouring them (*Commentary on Jeremiah* IV, 1, 3).
[19] *Commentary on Jeremiah* IV, pref. (PL 24, 785) (CSEL 59, 222).
[20] *Letters* 50, 5 (PL 22, 516) (CSEL 54, 394).
[21] *Letters* 49, 5 (PL 22, 511f.) (CSEL 54, 357).

personal abuse, libel and misrepresentation of the kind once described by N. H. Baynes as 'ecclesiastical Billingsgate':[22] for example, he refers to Jovinian as 'a debauched preacher', 'an old serpent' and 'a dog returned to his vomit', fastening on him the nickname 'Christian Epicurus' which many others were to adopt later. His language was so virulent that even his old friends reacted in the opposite way to which he had intended, and Pelagius was only one of many who rose to defend Jovinian, though not accepting his extreme views. Jerome had good cause to be sorely disappointed with the outcome of this controversy: it had been a thoroughly unpleasant episode in his battle-scarred career as a defender of the faith and one which he would doubtless have preferred to be forgotten.

We can well imagine his annoyance when, nearly twenty years later, this same Pelagius turned up in Palestine to disturb the relative peace of his retreat like Banquo's ghost at the feast, and when he began to curry favour and join forces with another old antagonist of his, Bishop John of Jerusalem. Pelagius and Jerome were soon at odds with each other again in 413, when both were invited to send letters of advice to a young girl named Demetrias, who came from a rich and influential Roman family with which both men had been closely associated in Rome. To Demetrias, who had recently decided to take the vow of virginity and become a nun at the age of fourteen, each wrote after his own fashion, Jerome taking the opportunity to warn her not to bother her head too much with theological problems raised by adherents of Origen, a snide reference to Pelagius,[23] and Pelagius to stress the importance of the part played by the human will in enabling individuals to choose and perform right actions and so to win salvation, and of the existence in human beings of 'a kind of natural sanctity'.[24]

The reference to Origen reveals that there was another old controversy from his past which Jerome suspected Pelagius of trying to revive to his discredit. He had certainly been an admirer of Origen in his earlier days; but he had insisted in his *Defence against Rufinus* written in 401 that his admiration for Origen was confined to the latter's work as an exegete of the scriptures and

[22] I owe this quotation to Bonner, 1972, 82, n. 176.
[23] *Letters* 130 (PL 22, 1107–24) (CSEL 56, 175–201).
[24] *Letter to Demetrias*, 4, 25ff. (PL 30, 19; 33, 1101); this 'natural sanctity' is often linked by Pelagius to *conscientia*, to which, however, he gives 'a wider connotation than our own "conscience"' (Ferguson, 1956, 142). The letter also made a great stir among Augustine's circle. He had written to congratulate Proba and Juliana on Demetrias' vocation as soon as they had told him of it (*L* 150 in PL 33, 645) and had also, in 414, addressed to Juliana his treatise *On the Good of Widowhood* (PL 40, 429–50) (CSEL 41, 303–43), the latter part of which contained a warning against listening to the 'tittle-tattle of certain men, enemies of the grace of God, who are trying to defend freedom of the human will' (xvii. 21). Juliana does not seem to have been altogether happy with the suggestion that a family like hers could ever be tainted with heresy, and so, after receiving a copy of the *Letter to Demetrias*, he and his friend Alypius write to her again in 417 to explain the grounds for their earlier anxiety, urging her to avoid all 'teachings contrary to grace' and identifying Pelagius as the author of the letter on the evidence of another letter of Pelagius, though he had earlier asked *her* to identify him. Juliana did distance herself from Pelagius after his condemnation, and the *Letter to Demetrias* was one of the documents used against him by the African Councils: as Wermelinger points out, 205, n. 353, Augustine's refutation of *Letter to Demetrias*, c. 11, in his own letter to Juliana (*L* 188, in PL 33, 849ff.) (CSEL 57, 120ff.) (ii. 4) was wholly in the spirit of the fifth canon of the Council of Carthage in 418.

6

did not extend to his dogmas.[25] As a result of the recriminations which followed this debate, he had forfeited the friendship not only of Rufinus but also of John of Jerusalem. So, without too great a concern for theological niceties, he now launched into a vigorous attack on Pelagius in his *Dialogue against the Pelagians*, in his letters to friends and even in his *Commentary on Jeremiah*, on which he was currently engaged and in which he attacked Pelagianism twenty-two times, apart from making several references in his preface to its founders, including, of course, Pelagius. This man is a 'huge, bloated, Alpine dog, weighed down with Scottish oats, . . . able to rage more effectively with his heels than with his teeth'.[26] Had he, Jerome, not long ago pulverised the arguments of Rufinus just as he had demolished those of Jovinian? It was intolerable that an upstart monk, semi-educated and himself under the shadow of heresy, should now try to disinter the bones of old adversaries and use them to embarrass him. He must be quashed once and for all — 'battered with the club of the spirit', as he typically put it,[27] and along with him all those whose discredited causes he was espousing — John of Jerusalem, still a thorn in his flesh, Rufinus Tyrannius of Aquileia, who had died in Sicily in 410,[28] and the last fading traces of the ghost of Origen, 'that insane allegorist',[29] whose works had been rejected and condemned by the Church at Rome in the person of Pope Anastasius in 400 acting under pressure from Theophilus, Patriarch of Alexandria.[30]

Thus it was Jerome who first took up the cudgels and openly challenged Pelagius to combat, just as he had done in about 394, but at that time without success: by accusing him of fostering Origenism through his own misunderstanding of Jerome's *Commentary on Ephesians* as a work packed with borrowings from Origen, Pelagius was impugning his authority as an orthodox teacher of the Church, especially now that Origenism had been formally condemned not only in Alexandria, Syria and Palestine but also by Rome. As always, attack was Jerome's best method of defence, and he concentrated his attack on pinning the label of Origenist on Pelagius in turn on the grounds that, by teaching that a baptised Christian was able to live without sin, if he so willed, he was simply preaching Origenism. It was this doctrine of *impeccantia*, 'sinlessness', that Pelagius was called upon to renounce at a diocesan synod called by John of Jerusalem in 415. He acknowledged that this was what he taught but, when asked how he could reconcile it with divine grace, cleverly skated over the thin ice by quoting the scriptures on the necessity of grace and anathematising anyone who denied that grace was essential.[31] His accuser, Orosius, was thrown out of his stride but the same charge appeared as one of

---

[25] *Defence against Rufinus* I, 11–17 (PL 23, 397–492); cf. *Letters* 84, 2 (PL 22, 744f.) (CSEL 55, 121f.).

[26] *Commentary on Jeremiah* III, pref. (PL 24, 758) (CSEL 59, 151).

[27] Ibid.

[28] *Life of Tyrannius Rufinus* II, 20 (PL 21, 191); cf. the *Notitia* of Schoennemann (PL 21, 15) and Hammond, 372ff.

[29] Kelly, 1975, 316, with the relevant passages in n. 43.

[30] *Life* II, 19 (PL 21, 277–85); Schoennemann's *Notitia* (PL 21, 14).

[31] *PP* vi. 16; xiv. 37; xv. 38; xxx. 54 (PL 44, 329f.; 342f.; 350f.) (CSEL 42, 68f.; 93f.; 106ff.).

the seven items in a *libellus* drawn up against Pelagius by two exiled Gallican bishops, Heros and Lazarus, at the Synod of Diospolis in December of 415.[32] Here again he reiterated his defence and qualified his teaching on *impeccantia* by adding that it was only possible if a man's efforts were combined with the help of divine grace.

The Synod was satisfied with this explanation but not Jerome: he continued to equate Pelagius' 'sinlessness' with Stoic *apatheia*, that is, the ability of man to rise above the passions, and to repeat his charge that here was conclusive proof that Pelagius was an Origenist, since it was Origen who had tried to adapt such pagan ideas to Christian thought. But Origen was no Stoic: 'although there is much knowledge of Stoicism and an evident debt to the Stoic theodicy, it is a mistake to overestimate this Stoic element in his mental furniture and to label him a Stoic'.[33] For example, in his treatise in eight books *Against Celsus*, 'the only large-scale work by Origen that survives intact in Greek',[34] he makes great use of Stoic arguments to refute Celsus' attack on Christianity, mainly because he first assumed him to be an Epicurean; but he insisted that reason by itself was not enough if one wanted to attain to a true knowledge of God. 'Human nature', he wrote, 'is not sufficient to find God unless it is helped by God who is the object of the search; and he is found by those who, after doing all they can, admit that they need him.'[35] Pelagius would have agreed with this statement but, try though he did, he was unable to dislodge his opponent from his entrenched position by arguing that his doctrine was not the equivalent of Stoic *apatheia* and that he was not harking back to Stoic teaching on the equality of sins either. The cunning old man knew that in Origenism he had as good a stick with which to beat Pelagius as any other; by this time there were few theologians who could not be accused of revealing at one time or another one of the countless heads of this 'hydra of heresies'.[36] So, for Jerome, Pelagianism was, in his own words, nothing but 'a new heresy springing out of an old'.[37]

[32] Ibid. i. 2; iii. 5, 9; iv. 12; v. 13; vi. 16; xii. 27 (PL 44, 320f.; 322f.; 325; 326f.; 329f.; 336) (CSEL 42, 52f.; 56f.; 63f.; 64; 68f.; 80f.). Neither of the two accusers seems to have appeared in person before the Synod, one being ill and the other excused attendance, and it is uncertain to what extent they were involved in the composition of the indictment. Their absence perhaps indicates that they were no more than front-men for Jerome and Orosius, and they were clearly right out of their theological depth; in addition, they had already been discredited by the circumstances of their expulsion from Gaul, a factor which must have had some effect on the attitude of the judges to their prosecution of a man of high standing like Pelagius. The indictment, which had to be translated into Greek sentence by sentence for the benefit of the Synod, is discussed in detail by Wermelinger, 71ff.; see my Appendix II.
[33] H. Chadwick, 1966, 107.
[34] J. W. Trigg, 215.
[35] I owe this quotation to H. Chadwick, 1966, 82f.
[36] Theophilus' phrase in his Festal Letter of 402, quoted in Cross, 993, s.v. *Origenism*.
[37] *Commentary on Jeremiah* V, xxv. 3 (PL 24, 834) (CSEL 59, 301); cf. II, x. 23, IV, 24ff. (PL 24, 751, 817) (CSEL 59, 139, 268). But, as R. F. Evans, 1968(a), 6, points out, 'Jerome's attacks are never wholly deficient in truth'; in his *Commentary on Jeremiah* II, x. 23 and *Dialogue against the Pelagians* I, 32 (PL 24, 751; 23, 525) (CSEL 59, 110, 127) he cites two sentences from Pelagius' *Book of Testimonies*, known to Augustine under the title of *Book of Chapters* and to Gennadius under that of *Book of Selections*, to the effect that 'all men are governed by their own free will' and 'man can be without sin' (PL 48, 594ff., *Tituli* LXXII and C).

Now, as he struggled to free himself from the clutches of his Scylla, Pelagius found himself being dragged down into the bubbling cauldron of his Charybdis. His treatises *On Nature* and *On Free Will*, written to defend his position on sin and 'sinlessness', attracted the adverse attention of Augustine, since in them he had too little to say about divine grace and too much about the human will. Thus his Odyssey had taken him from Rome to Africa and from Africa to Palestine, and events that took place in all three combined to bring about his downfall. But it was in Rome that the course of his future had been mapped out: it was there that he had first fallen foul of Jerome, it was there that he had first clashed with Augustine's doctrine of grace and had written his commentary on the Pauline Epistles, it was there that he had made friends with Celestius, already branded as a heretic by the Council of Carthage in 411. There too he had made the acquaintance of another associate who was to play just as important a rôle in his personal drama, though himself dead by the time the controversy got under way; this was Rufinus the Syrian, 'that mysterious and somewhat sinister figure',[38] the third of the Pelagian musketeers, held by some to have been the real founder of the heresy.

For Rufinus of Syria's involvement in the heresy we have two pieces of evidence. In his *Book of Footnotes on Words of Julian*[39] Marius Mercator, a friend and disciple of Augustine, wrote: 'This most stupid but none the less hostile criticism of the orthodox faith was first introduced into Rome in the papacy of Anastasius of sacred memory (that is, between 399 and 402) by a certain Rufinus, a Syrian by race, who, not daring to promote it on his own, was clever enough to hoodwink a British monk named Pelagius into doing so, having given him a thorough grounding in the aforesaid unholy and foolish doctrine.' Rufinus of Syria was the man referred to by Celestius when defending himself at Carthage as 'the holy priest Rufinus . . ., whom he had heard deny the transmission of sin',[40] and also the author of a *Liber de Fide* written probably between 399 and 402.[41] Is there sufficient evidence in its contents to prove that it had a strong influence on Pelagius?

The scribe who contributed the following gloss to the Leningrad manuscript of the *Liber de Fide*, probably in the sixth century, had no doubt that Rufinus was a Pelagian: 'The book is Pelagian and full of the blasphemies of the Pelagians, for, under the pretext of conducting a debate with the Arians,

---

[38] Bonner, 1972, 19. Wermelinger delivers the *coup de grâce* to those who have attempted to identify this Rufinus with Rufinus of Aquileia and to Marrou's invention of a third Rufinus (1969, 465ff.) on the grounds that Rufinus of Syria could not have been the priest who travelled to Rome from Palestine c. 399/40 at the behest of his master Jerome, because it was unthinkable that one of Jerome's pupils could have held Pelagian ideas. Rufinus of Bethlehem is without doubt the Rufinus of Syria who wrote the *Liber de Fide*.

[39] Pref., 2 (PL 48, 111).

[40] *OS* iii. 3 (PL 44, 387) (CSEL 42, 168).

[41] Bonner, 1970, 36ff., sets out the arguments in favour of this dating: M. W. Miller, 8ff., dated the *Liber de Fide* to 413–28 but had been misled by the arguments of Altaner, refuted by Refoulé, 1963(a) (cf. de Blic, 518f.). The *Liber de Fide* is in PL 48, 451–88.

he has injected into it the poisons of his own heresy.'[42] This is the judgement of a man writing with hindsight long after the event, and it is evident from the book itself that its author's main targets were the trinitarian heresies of Arianism, Eunomianism and Sabellianism: 'in a work of sixty-one chapters only cc. 29–41 and 48 can be regarded as indubitably Pelagian, and not all the doctrine there expressed can be called unorthodox.'[43] The villain of the piece is Origen, who is subjected to virulent attacks again and again. It is only after firing a salvo at Origen's theory of the pre-existence of souls that the author turns aside, as it were, to direct a volley at the traducianists, whom he then dismisses as stupid and mad for asserting that 'Christ destines unbaptised children to the punishment of everlasting fire'.[44] Of grace and predestination Rufinus has nothing to say, and his views on Adam and the Fall were to be subsequently modified or rejected by Pelagius and even Celestius.

On the other hand, on the subjects of original sin and infant baptism he provides 'a manual of Pelagianism'.[45] When he writes that 'infants receive baptism not on account of their sins but in order that they may through baptism be, as it were, created in Christ and become partners in his heavenly kingdom', that 'infants who are not born in sin yet merit the grace of baptism that they may be co-heirs of Christ's kingdom', and that 'if infants are baptised because of Adam's sin, then those born of Christian parents ought not to be baptised at all',[46] Rufinus is anticipating some of the commonplaces of Pelagian teaching which Augustine was to reject again and again in his arguments against Pelagius and his associates. But it must be pointed out that Pelagius himself never explicitly denies that infants needed baptism for the remission of their sins; on the contrary, he will re-affirm his acceptance of such a need in his *Liber de Fide* submitted to Pope Innocent in 417, and, elsewhere he will ask, 'Who can be so impious as to deny to an infant of any age the common redemption of the human race?.'[47] It was Celestius, not Pelagius, who was to continue to maintain to the very end – in *his Liber de Fide* submitted to the Pope at the same time as that of Pelagius – Rufinus' central thesis that infants were baptised not on account of inherited sins but in order that they might gain entry into the kingdom of heaven.[48] This does not make Rufinus *ipso facto* the founder of Pelagianism; but it was to this topic that Augustine devoted much of his second sermon delivered at Carthage in 413,[49] just as he had directed most of the earlier part of his *On the Merits and Forgiveness of Sins and Infant Baptism* in 411/12 to a refutation of Rufinus' *Liber de Fide*.[50]

Whatever we may think of the claim that Rufinus was the real founder of

---

[42] PLS 1, 1099; Miller, 36, n. 4.
[43] Bonner, 1970, 37.
[44] *Liber de Fide* 41 (PL 48, 477f.).
[45] Bonner, 1970, 43; see also his comments in 1972, 25, 30, 36.
[46] *Liber de Fide* 40, 48 (PL 48, 477, 482).
[47] *OS* xix. 21 (PL 44, 395) (CSEL 42, 181).
[48] *Liber de Fide* 19 (PL 48, 503).
[49] *S* 294 (PL 38, 1335–48); *PP* xi. 25 (PL 44, 335) (CSEL 42, 79).
[50] This suggestion was first made by de Blic, 518f., and later taken up by Refoulé, 1963(a), 47.

Pelagianism – a subject to which we shall return later – it was certainly Rufinus and Celestius, not Pelagius, who were the first targets of Augustine's anti-Pelagian campaign. He did not openly attack Pelagius until 415, when he wrote his treatise *On Nature and Grace* as a riposte to Pelagius' *On Nature*. Earlier, in *On the Merits and Forgiveness of Sins and Infant Baptism*, Pelagius is not mentioned until the third book, in which Augustine argues against the views expressed in his commentary on the Pauline Epistles, only just received and described as 'containing very brief expository comments': but he is still reluctant to believe that the views on original sin which he has found there are those of Pelagius himself, whom he refers to as 'a holy man, as I am told, who has made no small progress in the Christian life'.[51] Nor is there any reference by name to Pelagius in the second anti-Pelagian treatise, *On the Spirit and the Letter*, also written in 412 and aimed at 'a not very troublesome group of men',[52] though this work too is in part an answer to Pelagius' commentary. In 413 he addresses a letter to Pelagius as 'My lord greatly beloved and brother greatly longed for', and the letter is couched in the most friendly terms, even if we allow for the extravagant phraseology of contemporary epistolography.[53] In 414, writing to a Sicilian lawyer, Hilarius, to enlighten him on matters on which a debate had already begun among Sicilian Christians, such as the possibility of sinlessness and the fate of infants dying without baptism,[54] he still makes no explicit connection between those who were causing his correspondent such deep anxiety – among them, no doubt, the man known as the 'Sicilian Briton' or 'Sicilian Anonymous'[55] – and Pelagius himself, now far away in Palestine.

Yet, only three years later, in his treatise *On the Proceedings of Pelagius*, he was trying to convince his readers that he had identified Pelagius as a heretic as long ago as 412, and that his cordial letter of 413 contained many hidden meanings, including a warning that he must amend his ways or else: 'lord', he claims, was no more than a conventional form of address for one Christian to use in writing to another, 'brother' meant that this was how he was bound to regard a fellow-Christian, and 'greatly longed for' indicated only that he had wanted to see Pelagius in person to discuss his opinions and statements with him.[56] These explanations may well be justified; but, as Augustine goes on to argue, the sting of his letter comes in the tail, and the one remark which can be fairly described as 'coded', if we accept his explanation for it, is concealed in the final sentence: 'At the same time, I must warn you rather to pray for me that *the Lord may make me* the kind of man you already suppose me to be.' This, he maintains, is a clear hint of the absolute

---

[51] *MFS* I, i. 1 (PL 44, 185) (CSEL 60, 3). Wermelinger, 23, remarks that the emphasis on infant baptism in this work has often led to its being cited by the second half of its full title – *On Infant Baptism*.

[52] *SL* ii. 3 (PL 44, 202) (CSEL 60, 156).

[53] *L* 146 (PL 33, 596) (CSEL 44, 273f.).

[54] *L* 157 (PL 33, 674–93) (CSEL 44, 449–88).

[55] Morris, 1965, 37ff., argues that he was a Briton but Bonner, 1972, 5f., does not accept this view, preferring to call him 'the Sicilian Anonymous'.

[56] *PP* xxvi. 51; xxvii. 52; xxix. 53 (PL 44, 349f.) (CSEL 42, 104ff.).

necessity of divine grace. If such it indeed was, then Pelagius certainly missed the hidden meaning intended; otherwise, would he have produced this very letter at the Synod of Diospolis as a testimonial from Augustine to his good standing?

Opinions will always differ as to the intention of Augustine's letter to Pelagius in 413 and as to his attitude to Pelagius prior to 415; probably his initial hesitation was prompted partly by the fact that he saw in Pelagius an ally against the Manichees, partly by the high reputation which Pelagius had won among his many influential supporters in Rome. But by the time he came to write his *Retractations* in 426–7 Augustine himself was in no doubt at all. In the relevant passage he explains that he had not mentioned Pelagius or others by name in his first anti-Pelagian treatise simply because he still hoped at that time that this would be the best way to correct them without alienating them further; again, he had mentioned Pelagius by name in the third book of that treatise 'with considerable commendation because his life and conduct were praised by many'.[57] At this stage he had been concerned only to refute certain statements made by Pelagius in order to show him the error of his ways and had been reluctant to attack him personally; but when he continued to defend his views 'with persistent animosity' and after his 'disciple' Celestius had been condemned for holding similar opinions, a more direct line of attack was called for and from now on no holds were barred.

There had been a similar hardening of Augustine's heart against the Donatists, who had by no means been finally disposed of when the real dangers of Pelagianism became fully apparent to him. Thus, at the very time when he was able to justify his *volte-face* in accepting the necessity to exercise *disciplina* in dealing with one obdurate group of dissidents, the man now acknowledged as leader of the African Church found himself being confronted by another – indeed he might well have quoted the great Roman poet whom he had once so admired: *primo avulso non deficit alter!*[58] Is it surprising if he lost his patience with this new coterie, which went so far as to question the importance of infant baptism by insisting that infants were not baptised for the remission of sins? They were now getting perilously close to the central issue of the Donatist controversy, though it had been the re-baptism of adults which had been the main bone of contention for them. In the eyes of Pelagius adult baptism and the grace which it bestowed upon the repentant sinner stood at the very heart of Christian belief; but he too placed no more emphasis on infant baptism than had the Donatists. It was not relevant to his teaching

---

[57] *R* II, 33, ed. Bogan, II, 60 (PL 32, 644) (CSEL 36, 171), supported by *L* 157 (PL 33, 674–93) (CSEL 44, 449–88), probably written in 413; cf. *L* 186 (PL 33, 815–32) (CSEL 57, 45–80), addressed to Paulinus of Nola in 417. In case the word *Retractations* may mislead the reader, it should be explained that it comes from the Latin *retracto*, not *retraho*, and means 're-examinations'. Wermelinger, 270f., maintains that the predominance of the Pelagian controversy in the work suggests that it could be regarded as a book of vindication against Pelagian ideas.

[58] Vergil, *Aeneid* VI, 143 – omitting, of course, the adjective *aureus*, 'golden', hardly appropriate in this case.

on man, and he was content to declare himself an agnostic as to the fate of those who died unbaptised: 'I know where they do not go but where they do go I do not know.'[59]

Augustine too had once dismissed this problem almost in despair and was to agonise about it to the end of his life. But he had set himself to carry out an exhaustive examination of all the available evidence, had resolved the question to his own satisfaction at least and had made his definitive judgement available in his seven books *On Baptism against the Donatists*, begun around 400 and completed probably some years later. The purpose of baptism, as he saw it, was to counteract a specific effect of original sin, and it was therefore imperative that it be administered as soon as possible after birth, since 'except by becoming a member of the Body of Christ there is no hope of salvation.'[60] He had been startled in 411 to learn that the Pelagians were claiming that by baptism children gained sanctification, not remission of sins.[61] It had thus become clear to him that the gravamen of the charges against Celestius lay in his denial of the need for infant baptism as an antidote for the transmission of original sin, and he believed Celestius to be a pupil of Pelagius. We have seen that there is no evidence that Pelagius held precisely the same views on infant baptism as had been advanced by his associate, who had displayed a strange lack of tactical finesse in pressing such views in Africa, where the subject of infant baptism was one of special importance to Christians. But it seemed to Augustine that, when cornered, Pelagius either would or could not give a straight answer and that his arguments against original sin in his book *On Nature* would have the effect of undermining one of the most cherished practices of the Church. Augustine had been made painfully aware at Carthage in 413 that his own views were still in danger of being misunderstood when, in order to pacify his congregation, he had found it necessary to fall back on Cyprian, the martyred bishop of that city, as his authority. This priceless jewel still needed protection from careless handling by men who did not appreciate its value. The plain fact is that, where infant baptism was concerned, Pelagius and Augustine were on entirely different wavelengths: what was of little significance to the one was absolutely crucial for the other.

Around 415 then, Augustine's attitude to Pelagius altered. But the reason he gives for it, namely, his reading of Pelagius' *On Nature*, has been called into question,[62] since it contains nothing new when compared with his commentary on the Epistles of Paul. In other words, *On Nature* was not so much a sudden shock as the last piece in a jig-saw with which he had been wrestling for three years, the final proof that Pelagius' unorthodox position on a number of matters fundamental to the Christian faith, like grace, original sin and

---

[59] *OS* xxi. 23 (PL 44, 395f.) (CSEL 42, 182). Contrary to the view expressed by Augustine, Pelagius did not teach that there was a middle place for infants dying unbaptised between heaven and hell, nor did he attempt to distinguish between the kingdom of God and eternal life; see Refoulé, 1963(b), especially 248f.

[60] *S* 294, x. 10 (PL 38, 1341).

[61] *MFS* III, vi. 12 (PL 44, 192f.) (CSEL 60, 139).

[62] R. F. Evans, 1968(a), 82ff.

baptism, must now be subjected to a frontal assault and no longer by oblique hints and warnings. Nor was it only the orthodox faith which was being threatened; it was the personal authority of Augustine himself as a spokesman of the Church. In this book Pelagius was using quotations from respected Catholic writers, including Augustine, and, in particular, seemed to be employing as ammunition against him statements from his early work *On Free Choice*, written against the Manichees in the years between 388 and 395.[63] In fact, the citations were used because Pelagius agreed with them but, always on the alert for the smallest signs of a Manichean revival, he also thought that he had found some in Augustine's teaching on original sin and predestination elsewhere in this book, since the former he saw as restoring to evil its Manichean status and the latter as the virtual equivalent of Manichean fatalism.

It has often been suggested that Augustine never entirely freed himself from the influence of some aspects of the Manicheism of his youth, and he may well have been conscious of being open to suspicion on that score even now, when he was at the zenith of his career. We can imagine his annoyance when he found that Pelagius was not above encouraging such a suspicion and charging him, the erstwhile hammer of the Manichees, with crypto-Manicheism. Had he to prove again that he had broken with this devilish creed years ago? Already, on at least one occasion, that of his consecration as bishop in 395, the old charge had sparked off a scandal, when the senior bishop of Numidia had refused for a time to preside at the ceremony and the Donatists had not been slow to use this refusal against him.[64] Towards the end of his life Julian of Eclanum, the last of his Pelagian adversaries and in many ways the most hostile and the most able, was to torment him with this same charge, and he was forced to clarify his position *vis-à-vis* both Pelagianism and Manicheism.[65] Now this trouble-maker Pelagius was accusing both Jerome and himself of neo-Manicheism, just as they in turn were doing the same to him.

Why was Manicheism still so important? What was there about this strange, Gnostic heresy that made it so popular as a smear-word in the early fifth century? 'For a sensitive man of the fifth century', writes Peter Brown, 'Manicheism, Pelagianism and the views of Augustine were not as widely separated as we would now see them: they would have appeared as points along the same great circle of problems raised by the Christian religion.'[66] And Gerald Bonner describes Augustine's earlier polemic against the Manichees as 'a highly important preparation for theological discussions which were not envisaged at the time when he wrote'.[67] Problems were then

[63] *NG* lxi. 71 – lxx. 84 (PL 44, 282–90) (CSEL 60, 286–99).

[64] *LPet* III, xvi. 19 (PL 43, 366f.); *CD* IV, lxiv. 79; III, lxxx. 92 (PL 43, 545f., 591f.) (CSEL 52, 557ff., 495).

[65] *TLP* II, ii. 2ff. (PL 44, 572f.) (CSEL 60, 461ff.) lists the similarities and differences between Manichees, Pelagians and Catholics. It is ironical that at the outset of the controversy the only common ground between Augustine and Pelagius was their opposition to Manicheism as defenders of free will.

[66] Brown, 1967, 370.

[67] Bonner, 1963, 194.

raised and argued about which were to develop into major issues in the debate with the Pelagians and, in the course of this debate, Augustine 'defined Pelagius' terms for him', just as Pelagius 'made him (Augustine) re-think his assumptions as no-one else could have done . . . and presented him with a new perspective on evil'.[68] Ever since his youth Augustine had been preoccupied, almost obsessed, with the problem of evil: 'Where then is evil, and whence has it come, and by what path has it crept in hither? What is its root, and what its seed?', he asks in his *Confessions*, reiterating the same questions again and again.[69] In his account of his own spiritual and intellectual pilgrimage he traces the slow and often painful steps by which he arrived at his final solution, one of them being his temporary attachment to Manicheism. No doubt it had first appealed to him because of its dualism of good and evil, which corresponded to his experience as a young man, tugged this way and that by bodily desires and repugnance to the actions to which they led him. Evil seemed to him at that time, as it did to the Manichees, to be a powerful force dragging him down into the depths of degradation, in other words, to be the root of all sin. But further examination revealed that this could not be the right answer: 'like many other simple explanations, it raises as many problems as it resolves.'[70] The idea of a god whose powers were limited in the struggle against evil was not to Augustine's taste, and he abandoned it after nearly nine years of adherence for his own interpretation of Neoplatonism. Evil, he now came to see, could not be substance but must be privation of good, a corruption of God's creation, permitted by him to exist for his own good but inscrutable purposes. Augustine's debate with the Manichees had all-important consequences for his concept of man, since it made him realise that, whereas Adam had been created good, he had also been created with free will, thus making him liable to sin through the wrong exercise of that free will; Adam fell because he turned away from good and from God *by his own choice*, and his sin was a voluntary act of evil.

Here we reach the main battleground on which Augustine and Pelagius were to fight. The very arguments for man's responsibility, exercised by use of his free will, which Augustine had deployed against the Manichees, were now being adapted by Pelagius to suit his own case that man had the power to save himself, always provided that he had accepted the saving grace of baptism *of his own choice*. Augustine's reply was to insist upon the sole power of grace to act upon man: the Pelagians, he wrote, are a new brand of heretics, 'certain pseudo-monks who, under the pretence of defending the freedom of the will, dispute the grace of God and endeavour to overthrow the foundation of the Christian faith'.[71] So the controversy came to centre around two different interpretations of free will and grace, with each party to it accusing the other of over-emphasising one of these at the expense of the other. 'The

---

[68] G. R. Evans, 1982, 148.
[69] *C* VII, v. 7 (PL 32, 736) (CSEL 33, 147).
[70] Bonner, 1963, 197.
[71] *PP* xxxv. 61 (PL 44, 355) (CSEL 42, 116).

two men disagreed radically on an issue that is still relevant, and where the basic lines of division have remained the same: on the nature and sources of a fully good, creative action.'[72] And so a debate which began almost coincidentally between a dedicated defender of Christian orthodoxy and an equally single-minded reformer of Christian morals will lead to a public examination of some of the most profound issues affecting the faith which both sincerely professed.

By 415 Augustine had finally realised that the time had come to direct his artillery at Pelagius across the no man's land which separated them. His 'pupil' Celestius had been condemned but he himself had escaped to Palestine and was there carrying the fight to Jerome; a letter from Sicily warned that Pelagianism was rife there,[73] an appeal had come from Spain for help in resisting new doctrinal errors which had spread to that region and were joining forces with Priscillianism,[74] and the Spanish priest Orosius had arrived in Africa, seeking advice on the same subject, possibly with the encouragement of the African bishops.[75] When Orosius moved on to Palestine, he went armed with two letters from Augustine to Jerome. These letters,[76] each of them virtually a minor treatise, are of the highest importance, not least because they show Augustine's deep concern for the human implications of issues raised in his debate with Pelagius, though the latter is not referred to by name. The first issue is that of infants dying unbaptised and condemned to eternal punishment through no fault of their own, if Augustine's theory of predestination were correct, an issue which was to trouble him to the end of his days; he was no *tortor infantium*. He now sought Jerome's help with this problem and, in order to justify his own position, set it in the context of his views on the origin of the soul, which he rightly perceived to be the starting-point of any doctrine of transmitted sin. What if Jerome still adhered to his earlier view, that is, of separate creation by God of each soul on conception?[77] If so, it was imperative that he and Jerome should be seen to be in agreement on a subject which was fundamental to his whole case against the Pelagians and that no trace should remain of the rift which had grown between the two great doctors of the contemporary Church since their

[72] Brown, 1967, 371.

[73] *L* 156, replied to in 157 (PL 33, 673–93) (CSEL 44, 448–88).

[74] Orosius, *Enquiry or Memorandum to Augustine on the Error of the Priscillianists and Origenists* (PL 42, 665–70) (CSEL 18, 151–71); see *R*, II, 44, ed. Bogan, II, 70 (PL 32, 648f.) (CSEL 36, 183). In reply Augustine wrote his treatise *Against the Priscillianists and Origenists* in 415 (PL 42, 669–78) but in it he reveals little knowledge of the Spanish heresy, and his principal account of it was not to appear until he addressed his book *On the Heresies* to the deacon Quodvultdeus in 429.

[75] Avitus, *Letter to Palchonius* (PL 41, 805f.); see Davids, 23f.

[76] *L* 166, 167 (PL 33, 720–41) (CSEL 44, 545–609); the letters were entitled *On the Origin of the Soul of Man* and *On the Opinion of the Apostle James* respectively.

[77] Jerome, *Defence against Rufinus* II, 4 (PL 23, 389). The main alternative to creationism in Augustine's day was traducianism, the belief that a child's soul was transmitted to it by its parents along with its body, and we shall have occasion later to observe how difficult Augustine found it to choose between these two theories of the soul's origin. As an orthodox Christian the third possibility was not open to him, namely pre-existence or reincarnation, since it was mainly associated with Gnosticism and Origen, both of them anathematised by the Church.

disagreement of many years earlier. But if he had any fears that the old man had to be alerted to the need for the strongest possible, concerted action against Pelagius, now that he had passed into his sector of the battlefield, he had misread Jerome's attitude to Pelagianism, which, as we have seen, had already led him into a bitter war of attrition by 415. In fact, Jerome's reply did not arrive until 416 and was very brief, merely explaining his failure to reply earlier.[78]

Thus it was that the two most articulate and influential personalities in the Western Church joined forces against Pelagius and that both saw not only the Church but also their own reputations to be at stake. The exasperated Jerome had never been one to pull his punches when in the ring with his opponents or even, for that matter, with his friends when they offended him. All the eloquence and violence of his invective were now aimed at these pestilential Pelagians and especially at the man whom he believed to be their leader. By 417 Pelagianism had become for him 'an unceasing, obsessional pre-occupation',[79] no doubt aggravated by an attack upon his monastery at Bethlehem in 416, commonly held to have been instigated by Pelagians. For his part, Augustine must have found this heresy not only dangerous but also a tiresome distraction from the manifold tasks of a bishop, already quite enough to tax him in weakened health. Nor should it be forgotten that though, unlike Jerome, kindly and patient by nature, he too was a man who never failed to push his views to their logical conclusion. In pressing his case on the need for salvation even if it meant applying coercion, on the eternal damnation of infants dying unbaptised, on the absolute necessity for regeneration through baptism within the Church, on the exclusive power of divine grace to save or destroy, on a form of predestination which limited the number of the saved right from the moment of creation – in all the multifarious aspects of the Christian faith on which his brilliant and comprehensive mind touched and fastened through his long career, he was impelled to adopt extreme positions in order to buttress his own arguments and demolish those of his opponents.[80] The fundamentals of his life's work were now being challenged by one who lacked his practical experience and his unrivalled knowledge and under-standing of Christian scriptures and doctrine.

Pelagius, as the main target of Augustine's last and greatest counter-attack on the enemies of the faith, was out-manoeuvred and out-gunned from the start and, at the last, driven from the field with ignominy and branded as a heretic and an outcast. In the words of George Orwell, taken from the original preface to *Animal Farm* which was suppressed at the time when he wrote it: 'Anyone who challenges the prevailing orthodoxy finds himself silenced with surprising effectiveness.'[81] In the words of Augustine himself, pronounced against the Donatists, '*Securus iudicat orbis terrarum*': 'the verdict of the world is

---

[78] *Letters* 134 (PL 22, 1161f.) (CSEL 56, 261ff.).
[79] Kelly, 1975, 324.
[80] Cf. Bentley-Taylor, 232f.
[81] I owe this reference to Thorpe, 6.

17

conclusive.'[82] These 'palmary words of St Augustine' became 'the shadow of a hand upon the wall' for Cardinal Newman, when he took his final step towards Rome, and were later recast and expanded in his own uncompromising terms: 'the deliberate judgement, in which the whole Church at length rests and acquiesces, is an infallible prescription and a final sentence against such portions of it as protest and secede.'[83]

It was indeed 'a famous victory'; but if we are to begin to appreciate its significance for the Western Church at this point in its history, we must try to set it in its historical context – the process of Christianisation of the Roman Empire which had begun with Constantine's adoption of Christianity as the official religion of that Empire and had gained a slow but steady momentum in the course of the fourth century. The old pagan order, though now deprived of imperial patronage, had not been completely swept away but still 'survived in an uneasy synthesis with the new: people and institutions and much of cultural life were still rooted in the pagan past'.[84] Yet this 'façade of continuity', as Peter Brown has explained, 'only masks an important change' in that 'the secular traditions of the senatorial class, traditions which one might have assumed to be intimately bound up with the fate of their pagan beliefs, came to be continued by a Christian aristocracy'.[85] The Christianisation of the Roman Empire must be seen not simply as a result of imperial pressure or a change of taste and attitude but rather as part of a prolonged and complex process of development.

In dealing with such a complex and, in terms of documentation, elusive process it is not easy to trace the precise steps by which it took place or to evaluate the relative importance of the many factors which contributed to it. But it is generally agreed that the legislative measures introduced by the Emperors in order to repress paganism, though often necessary and at least partially and temporarily effective, were much less influential in the long term than the less obvious pressures exerted by the need for social conformity. Among these was the practice of mixed marriages between pagan and Christian, which the Church had long ceased to discourage because it usually seemed to work out in its favour; but while giving full weight to the influence upon their husbands of the growing number of educated women converted to Christianity, we must not overemphasise this factor, since, as Brown has rightly warned us, 'we do not know when they became Christian', and it would be unwise to ignore 'the immense *esprit de corps* of a Roman *gens*'.[86] The appeal of the more extreme forms of asceticism emanating from the East and increasing in popularity in the West also needs to be taken into account, as do the effect of miraculous cures, the emotional appeal of stories of martyrdom and, not least, the tendency to syncretism which had for so long been one of

[82] *LParm* III, 24 (PL 43, 101) (CSEL 51, 131).

[83] *Apologia pro Vita Sua*, Everyman's Library 1949, 120f.

[84] Frend, 1984, 554; I am greatly indebted to him for his excellent account of the process of Christianisation in Pt. III, c. 16.

[85] Brown, 1972, 168.

[86] Ibid. 174.

the most prominent features of Roman religion. But perhaps most important of all was the classical culture of the age, shared by pagan and Christian alike, which provided a common ground enabling them to live together and, in the end, to accept Christianity as the only available means of ensuring that the Roman state could supply the religious foundation demanded both by its past traditions and by its present circumstances. Thus, in late-fourth-century Rome, 'the conventional good man of pagan Rome had imperceptibly become the conventional good Christian "believer"';[87] but there were many who began to be concerned with the problem of deciding what exactly was the kind of behaviour and way of life and what were the moral standards which should distinguish the true Christian from the conforming pagan.[88] Sincere and thoughtful Christians in Rome were anxiously seeking for an answer to this question, and many derived fresh inspiration from the pilgrimages which they undertook and which brought them under the influence of practices and ideals that recalled the spirit of total dedication characteristic of their predecessors when faced with persecution and martyrdom. To lead them in their search and point them in the right direction they needed gurus, spiritual mentors of high moral standing and steeped in the scriptures, and among those who answered their call were Jerome and Pelagius, both of whom found their way to Rome by different routes before the end of the fourth century. Jerome's last stay in Rome was a brief one – from 382 to 385 – and he left under a cloud; but Pelagius stayed longer and became the leader of a large and influential circle of loyal adherents comprising not only educated aristo-crats, many of them women, but also clerics who were later to form the nucleus of the opposition to his final condemnation in 418.

As we have seen, Pelagius' central message, though at first addressed to a comparatively limited audience, had profound implications for the Church as a whole: it was 'firmly based on a distinctive idea of the Church'[89] as a perfect religious institution consisting of perfect Christians wholly dedicated to the observance of the strict code of behaviour enjoined by its founder and followed by his apostles. In a treatise *On the Christian Life*, now generally accepted to have been written by Pelagius himself, he insists that 'God wanted his people to be holy',[90] an injunction spelt out by one of his followers in terms whose meaning is unmistakable: 'Surely it is not true that the Law of Christian behaviour has not been given to everyone who is called a Christian? . . . There can be no double-standard in one and the same people.'[91] The members of Pelagius' Church were to be *integri*, 'perfect, authentic, without moral blemish';[92] there was no place in it for nominal Christians, camp-

---

[87] Ibid. 193.

[88] Markus, 1974, 123, reminds us that Eusebius had long before deplored 'the hypocrisy of those who had crept into the Church' (*Life of Constantine*, iv. 54) and that Augustine himself 'around 400 . . . was worried about the influx of half-converted, "feigned" Christians, as he called them'.

[89] Brown, 1972, 194.

[90] *On the Christian Life*, 9 (PL 40, 1038; 50, 392).

[91] *On Riches*, vi. 3 (PLS 1, 1387).

[92] *Letter to a Young Man* (*Humanae referunt litterae*), 3 (PLS 1, 1378).

followers who had crept into its shelter under pressure from the need for political or social conformity. Their baptism had presented them with the unique opportunity to become 'authentic Christians' once and for all by abandoning their old pagan ways and leading a new life: it had 'placed a glass wall between the past and the present'.[93] This unique opportunity they had squandered by lapsing into their old, comfortable habits of self-indulgence and careless pursuit of Mammon.

But the blame for this lapse was not theirs alone: their established leaders in the Church were at least as culpable, since it was they who had misled their flock by encouraging them to accept standards of Christian behaviour which were no more than second-rate. It was at this point that Pelagius clashed with Augustine and other leaders of the Church, and we have noted his indignation when he heard the tenth book of the *Confessions* read out in Rome. What he heard convinced him that its author had betrayed a great tradition of Western Christianity. 'It is Pelagius', maintains Brown in a memorable sentence, 'who had seized the logical conclusions of this tradition: he is the last, the most radical, and the most paradoxical exponent of the ancient Christianity – the Christianity of discontinuity.'[94] Brown goes on to argue that it was still possible to find a place in late-fourth-century Italy for a Christianity of discontinuity, and it was Augustine's great hero Ambrose who had pointed the way ahead. But the Church which set out to put such a Christianity into practice would be a minority Church, a Church of the *élite* and for the *élite*, a leaven in the lump. And the emergence and survival of such a minority Church was a possibility that neither the leaders of the established Church nor the representatives of the imperial government could afford to countenance. They were bound to see it as a fresh source of division at a time when what Rome needed most of all, especially after its shattering experience at the hands of the Goth, was security and solidarity. The established Church was to be the main agency of those who sought to supply this need, and any challenge to its integrity must be resisted and crushed. Thus the final defeat of Pelagius and his followers was not only a rejection of what the Church judged to be a heresy in theological terms but an elimination of what was identified as a potentially dangerous source of schism in the body social and politic.

<hr />

[93] Brown, 1972, 195.

[94] Ibid. 200. Not the least of the debts owed to Brown by students of Pelagius and Pelagianism are his three seminal papers on the Christianisation of the aristocracy and the patrons and other supporters of Pelagius. The extent of my personal indebtedness to Peter Brown's publications both in this chapter and elsewhere in my book is indicated by the number of times I have quoted from them, realising that their elegance and succinctness defy any attempt at paraphrase.

II

THE 'TRUE' SPOKESMAN

'Religious history, like all history, is written by the victors, who naturally present their own favourites as the "true spokesmen for the founding revelation".'

PETER L. BERGER[1]

So it was in the aftermath of the battle between Pelagius and his opponents, when the noise of conflict began to die down and the protagonists had sheathed their swords. Both Jerome and Augustine left behind them a great corpus of their works, among them the latter's fifteen anti-Pelagian treatises, all intact and only one unfinished; we have also at our disposal writings by Prosper of Aquitaine, Paul Orosius and Marius Mercator, all contemporaries of Pelagius who were opposed to his teachings and exerted a considerable influence on the later historians of the Church. Of his own works only a handful have survived, along with a number of quotations embedded in Augustine's treatises, sermons and letters and selected by him solely in order to refute them. But enough remains to ensure that he has not lacked supporters over the intervening centuries, many of whom have denied that he was a heretic. Are they any better placed to judge a heresy of the early fifth century than we are to adjudicate on the resounding controversy which followed the publication of *Essays and Reviews* in the middle of the nineteenth?

A heresy is a product of a particular period of history, and to try to detach it from its historical context is a very risky business. The word itself, derived from the Greek noun *haeresis*, which had the primary meaning of 'choice', came to be applied to philosophical schools as having chosen a certain 'way of thought'.[2] In the New Testament it is found in the Acts of the Apostles describing the Sadducees and Pharisees as parties or divisions within the Jewish religion, and Josephus uses it in the same sense.[3] But already – in Acts, Corinthians and Galatians – it is also being used *in malam partem* of the Nazarenes as a religious sect whose ringleader is identified as Paul,[4] and from Ignatius onwards it is used more and more to describe theological error. In Christian terminology of the second century a *haeresis* is no longer a 'choice' but a '*wrong* choice', and a heretic is one who has followed a '*wrong* way of

[1] Berger, 146.
[2] Dionysius of Halicarnassus, *On Literary Composition*, 2; he is referring to Stoicism in this instance.
[3] Of Sadducees: Acts 5, 17; Josephus, *Jewish Antiquities* 13, 171. Of Pharisees: Acts 15, 5; 26, 5; Josephus, *Life*, 10, 12, 171 and elsewhere.
[4] Acts 24, 5; cf. 24, 14 and 28, 22; 1 Cor. 11, 19; Gal. 5, 20.

thought', thus encouraging a division in the ranks of the Church. Pelagius was deemed to be a heretic because he had made a wrong choice in the considered view of the ecclesiastical establishment of his day, and no amount of retrospective judgement, short of formal rehabilitation, can ever alter that verdict. 'Not to say what the Church says' is 'the real criterion of heresy'.[5]

Strictly then, Pelagius was, and is, a heretic in the eyes of the Catholic Church, and his condemnation as such is an unquestionable datum of history, whatever we in the more permissive atmosphere of the late twentieth century may think, or argue, to the contrary. But whether his condemnation was justified is another matter and one which we are entitled to subject to the closest examination – even if we accept the warning that contemporary scholarship is tending to become so enamoured of ancient heretics for various reasons, not all of them theological, as to be capable of turning 'into an article of interpretive faith' the words of the American poet, 'Truth forever on the scaffold, Wrong forever on the throne.'[6] 'Heresy', the *Concise Oxford Dictionary of the Christian Church* tells us, 'is the formal denial or doubt of any defined doctrine of the Catholic faith.'[7] Can it be with justice applied to Pelagius? If so, it is the duty of those who hold that view to justify it by establishing beyond reasonable contradiction that there was such a defined doctrine and that he either denied or doubted it.

In these times it is not sufficient to repeat Augustine's claim that 'the verdict of the world is conclusive'; too often history has shown that verdict to be wrong and to represent no more than the last gasp of a corrupt and effete establishment. Just recently we have celebrated the five-hundredth anniversary of the birth of Martin Luther. How many of his contemporaries would have credited the possibility that the time would come when Church and State would vie with each other in claiming him as their own 'true spokesman'? Perhaps only one, Erasmus. Living as he did in the very centre of a maelstrom of charges and counter-charges of heresy, he could still maintain: 'We are not obliged to believe everything in the writings of the Christian fathers, and if we are in error, we are not necessarily heretics: not every error is heresy';[8] and in defending his own sturdiest opponent, Luther himself, 'They simply cry heresy, but no author is free from heresy, whether ancient or modern.' Again, in his controversial interpretation of the parable of the wheat and the tares, he concludes: 'Let them grow together until the harvest', identifying the tares with the heretics whom others wanted to root out altogether.[9] Pelagius, of course, was a heretic in the eyes of Erasmus, who 'did take seriously the consensus and avowed that save for its authority he might

[5] Robinson, 28.

[6] James Russell Lowell, 'The Present Crisis' in *Complete Poetical Works*, Boston 1925; I owe this reference to Henry, 126.

[7] Livingstone, ed., 237.

[8] The Leiden edition of Erasmus, ed. Leclerc, 1703, repr. 1963, V, 1172F–1173A; cf. 1172A and Bainton, 1977, 322.

[9] *Erasmi Epistolae*, ed. P. S. and Mrs Allen, 1906–58, III, 939; Leiden ed. IX, 1015–94; see Bainton, 1977, 193, 253f.

easily have been a Pelagian or an Arian' but 'adhered to it only on theological matters which he considered insoluble or inconsequential'.[10] Can we, endowed with the hindsight of the fifteen centuries which separate us from Pelagius, hope to determine whether the questions which he raised are for us insoluble or inconsequential? We can at least take our cue from a Christian as wise and humane as Erasmus and beware of condemning Pelagius out of hand merely because the 'true' spokesmen so condemned him at the height of the Pelagian controversy, even if it was they who won the overwhelming approval of the Councils of the Church. 'What councils?' Erasmus once asked; 'there were Greek Councils which did not know Latin at all.' 'Don't listen to the Greeks', rejoined a friend; 'they were heretics too.'[11] Yes, there are heretics and heretics, and a man can even be a 'heretic in the truth': 'because his pastor says so, or the assembly so determines, without knowing other reason, though his belief be true yet the very truth he holds becomes his heresy.'[12]

We do not lack modern theologians of considerable distinction to reinforce the need for caution in differentiating between heretics, pseudo-heretics and 'heretics in the truth'. 'All exploration, whether in the theological or socio-logical field', said John Robinson, 'involves the risk, indeed the certainty, of mistakes. But it is at least arguable, from the study of church history, that more damage has almost always been done *in the long run* by the suppression of opinion than by any error given rein by freedom',[13] *Experto credite.* He goes on to illustrate his point by summarising the notorious cases of John Macleod Campbell, found guilty of heresy by the Church of Scotland in 1831, and of Bishop Pike, accused of heresy in 1966. And John Macquarrie has pointed out that Campbell's book *The Nature of the Atonement*, which appeared twenty-five years after his deposition from the ministry of his Church, is now recognised as 'one of the classics of Scottish theology'.[14] The lesson which he proceeds to draw from this unhappy episode and its ironical outcome is that it is not enough to detect and expose in an alleged heresy a contradiction of some particular formulation but that it is also necessary to show that it is in conflict with 'the reality of faith that this dogmatic formulation sought to express' and is 'excluded as a possible reinterpretation or re-expression of the faith.'[15] If heresy *is* suspected, then the best way to combat it is by a clear and affirmative statement of the true position of the Church, thus correcting bad

[10] Bainton, 1977, 239f. Erasmus agreed with Luther that salvation is by faith alone and that man cannot be perfect but he disagreed in wishing to give man credit for good deeds done.

[11] *Epistolae* II, 465; cf. Leiden ed. IX, 752f. and Bainton, 1977, 167.

[12] John Milton, *Areopagitica* in *Complete Prose Works* II, Yale and Oxford 1959. T. H. Huxley, *Science and Culture* xii, in his essay 'The Coming of Age of the *Origin of Species*' says much the same in different words: 'Irrationally held truths may be more harmful than reasoned errors.'

[13] Robinson, 29, quoting from the evidence which he gave to the committee appointed to examine the case against Bishop Pike and which was incorporated in its report. It is interesting to note in the context of Pelagianism that it was Reinhold Niebuhr, one of the most severe critics of its appearance in modern theology, who wrote of 'residual awareness of the possibility of error in the truth in which we believe, and of the possibility of truth in the error against which we contend', a quotation which I owe to Professor David Greenwood.

[14] Macquarrie, 1975, 45.

[15] Ibid., 46.

theology with good. Schleiermacher, he reminds us, held that 'there are in fact only a few basic heresies, and what makes any one of these a heresy is that when the implications of the position are followed out, the whole Christian faith collapses.'[16]

In all fairness, it must be added that Macquarrie is careful to distinguish in his discussion of heresy and the criteria which may be properly employed in identifying it between the situation today and that which faced the Church in its first five centuries. Thus it may be that in the case of some great heresies of the past the issues have never since been 'wrought out so clearly and argued with such amplitude for stakes that were incalculably high.'[17] Yet it would not be irrelevant to comment that Campbell's 'error' was in teaching 'that God's reconciling grace is offered to all men and not just to a predestined few',[18] and that this, as we shall see, was something on which Pelagius rightly insisted and which Augustine wrongly rejected as a result of his misinterpretation of scripture. But it was only one of the issues of principle about which they were in fundamental disagreement. The questions which we must endeavour to answer are: Was the teaching of Pelagius such that, if its implications were followed out, it would have caused the collapse of the whole Christian faith? Was it in conflict with 'the reality of faith' and so 'excluded as a possible reinterpretation or re-expression' of it? Was a serious attempt made to 'correct bad theology with good'? Was Pelagius, to use a definition of heresy in the twelfth century, 'a heretic who not only fell into error but, on being shown his error, persisted in it'?[19] It may help us to try to establish how Pelagianism was seen by the Church of the early fifth century against the background of earlier heresies.

The main preoccupation of the early Fathers was to resist the attacks of paganism and the insidious teachings of Gnosticism in its many forms, and the identification of heresy was at this stage a concomitant of the process of formulating Christian doctrine, indeed was often indispensable to such a formulation. Controversy revolved around two focal and related issues – the nature of the Godhead and the interrelation of the three persons of the Trinity: Monarchianism and its variations (Adoptionism, Modalism, Sabellianism and Patripassianism), Docetism and Montanism were all, in a sense, no more than skirmishes leading up to the all-out battle with Arianism, the principal heresy denying the divinity of Jesus, which was to rage throughout the fourth century and to threaten to tear the Church from limb to limb, leaving its scars unhealed until the seventh century, when the Lombards were finally converted to orthodoxy. As for Apollinarianism, the first great christological heresy, denying the full manhood of Jesus, it was eventually forbidden as a form of public worship in 381, by which time heresy had become a crime against the state.

By the time of Pelagius then, there were two accepted doctrines which had

---

[16] Schleiermacher, 95f., quoted in Macquarrie, 47.
[17] Murray, 44, quoted in Macquarrie, 44.
[18] Macquarrie, 45.
[19] Moore, 3.

24

been hammered out against the heretics and laid down by the Church in black and white, those of the Incarnation and the Trinity. No one could, or did, accuse Pelagius of denying these two fundamental doctrines; on the contrary, his teachings show that he lost no opportunity of attacking any who had done so, and not even Augustine claimed that his christology was other that orthodox.[20] As for Origenism, we have seen that Jerome's attempt to cast its dark shadow over him was either sincere but misguided or a deliberate, tactical riposte to the revival of insinuations that he himself was tarred with the same brush. Manicheism too was a blunt stick which could be used to beat Jerome and Augustine with as much, or as little, justification as Pelagius. By now 'Manichee' had become 'an imprecise term of general abuse',[21] and Jerome admits that 'any grave and pale ascetic' was likely to be so labelled.[22] But it was still a force to be reckoned with in the later fourth century and, despite the increasing severity of the laws directed against it and particularly of the Edict of Theodosius in 382, it could still command considerable support in Africa and some even in Rome – 'for Rome hides several of them', in Augustine's words.[23] When Orosius was sent by bishops in Spain to consult Augustine on how best to combat the threat of Priscillianism, this Spanish heresy was closely linked with Manicheism by them because they saw it as a fresh manifestation of the Manichean menace.

Priscillianism has the doubtful distinction of being the first heresy of the West, preceding Pelagianism by a few decades. 'In the seventies of the fourth century', writes Henry Chadwick in his definitive study of it, 'the Spanish churches were stirred by a new voice: a devout cultivated layman named Priscillianus began to ask his fellow Christians to take their baptismal renunciation more seriously and to give more time to special spiritual study.'[24] 'Priscillian's call is strongly ascetic', he comments, 'addressed not merely to isolated individuals, but to the faithful willing to give an unreserved dedication to Christ their God.' Priscillian, in other words, like Pelagius, wanted reform within the Church, not apart from it, and the response was encouraging, quickly spreading to Galicia and from there across the Pyrenees to Aquitaine; it has 'something of that contagion characteristic of a revival Awakening', and 'its effect came to be passionately divisive'. But at the council of Saragossa in 380 and at Priscillian's trial in 386 at Trier, though Patripassianism was added to the other charges against him, the main charge was that of Manicheism, which he disavowed with great vehemence, adjudged by Chadwick to have been 'passionate and surely sincere'.[25] But neither passion nor sincerity proved to be of any help to him, and a combination of ecclesiastical pressure and political connivance succeeded in engineering his

[20] J. McW. Dewart, 1982, 1221, 1227 sums up the position in 412; but in 1231ff. she goes on to describe Augustine's later attacks on the soteriology of Pelagius and his associates.
[21] H. Chadwick, 1976, 146; for references see n. 2.
[22] *Letters* 22, 13; *Against Jovinian* i. 3 (PL 22, 402) (CSEL 54, 161) (PL 23, 212f.)
[23] *C* V, x. 19 (PL 32, 715) (CSEL 33, 106).
[24] H. Chadwick, 1976, 8.
[25] Ibid., 97.

conviction on a primary charge of sorcery and his execution by order of the Emperor Maximus soon afterwards. And 'it was the taint of Manichean heresy that made the graver charge easy to believe.'[26]

This judicial murder is of great significance for anyone who tries to recreate the ecclesiastical climate of the period, highlighting as it does the dangers facing nonconformists of being accused *per saturam* of any heretical beliefs that the establishment could discover even the slightest justification for attributing to them. Like Pelagius, Priscillian had started out with a programme for moral reform of the Church; he ended by being convicted and executed on charges of holding opinions and encouraging practices condemned not only by the Church but also by the civil power. Heresy was now a crime against the State as well as a sin against the Church, and a heretic was now liable to suffer drastic punishment at the hands of the secular authorities, if his case were brought to their attention. We are witnessing the unforeseen consequences of the alliance between Constantine and the Church in the early fourth century, foreshadowing the Caesaropapism of the East and the secular authority of the papacy in the West. By the close of the fourth century, reinforced by imperial edicts against Arians, Manichees, Photinians, Eunomians and Apollinarians, the Church had won for itself such an unassailable position that it could refuse to tolerate any form of Christianity not sanctioned by itself. It might dare to challenge and modify the wishes of the imperial house, as Ambrose succeeded in doing on more than one occasion; but it could also demand its support when such a strategy seemed to be the only one likely to achieve its purposes. All it had to do was to throw the book at its opponents.

At the same time, and through the efforts of Augustine more than anyone else, the Western Church was becoming increasingly conscious of its new rôle as an integrated body outside the boundaries of which there was no hope of salvation – *extra ecclesiam nulla salus*[27] – and within which there was a necessity for united action to eliminate emerging heresy. It was to mobilise such action that Orosius sought the help of Augustine in Africa and Jerome in Palestine in 415, and Augustine's comparative ignorance of Priscillianism at that stage did not inhibit him from writing his treatise against it and Origenism in the same year. Jerome too had displayed little interest in the Spanish heresy and, for him, showed himself 'remarkably neutral';[28] his main interest, when alerted to the danger by Orosius – and that thirty years after the execution of the heresiarch –, was in its connections with Manicheism and so, in his view, with Pelagianism, and he recognised the need to close ranks in defence of the Church. Of Pelagianism, however, he had already made his own diagnosis: had he not already sized up Pelagius and the kind of delinquents with whom he was associated – men like Jovinian, Rufinus of Aquileia and John of Jerusalem? Origenism, Manicheism, Priscillianism, Pelagianism – what did it

---

[26] Ibid., 143f.
[27] *B* IV, xvii. 24 (PL 43, 170) (CSEL 51, 250); the actual order of the words as quoted from Cyprian is *salus extra ecclesiam non est*.
[28] H. Chadwick, 1976, 152.

matter how one classified them, when all were but symptoms of the same malignant disease threatening the body of Mother Church? What did matter was firmness of purpose enabling one to seize the knife and cut the cancer out before its poison could spread any further. His response to Pelagianism was like that of the Spanish bishops to Priscillianism; it was founded on the need for immediate and positive action without bothering too much about theological niceties.

Augustine was more clinical in his approach; it was his practice to examine the symptoms of theological error with the utmost care and to try to coax them away before resorting to radical surgery. But once his patient was on the operating table, he could be as bold as the next man in his incisions. As he saw the situation, the activities of Pelagius could have been left to Rome to deal with, so long as their effects were limited to that area; but once they had spread to Spain, which Priscillianism had shown to be vulnerable to schism and heresy, quite possibly to Sicily, and thence to Africa and Palestine, the very heart of Christianity, it was time not merely to scotch the snake but to kill it. Unlike Jerome, whose primary interest was in biblical exegesis, Augustine had both the knowledge and the experience to perceive that Pelagianism raised issues so profound that, to use Schleiermacher's dictum, if their implications were followed out, the result would be the collapse of the traditional faith as he understood it. It was not enough to accuse Pelagius of trying to resurrect old heresies: the real quarrel with him was over new issues much more fundamental and urgent, namely, his reductionist interpretations of original sin and divine grace resulting from an excessive emphasis on the freedom of the human will.

Now, however closely Augustine's doctrine of original sin might be bound up with that of grace, there was as yet no agreed view of it which could command universal support, as Celestius had astutely pointed out to the Council of Carthage. In the event, it was Pelagius' neglect of divine grace that led to his condemnation, and it was this which demanded Augustine's immediate attention. Pelagius' doctrine of grace was not only totally inadequate in his eyes, but also threatened the sacrament of baptism by its denial of original sin. It was his bounden duty as a bishop of the Church and its acknowledged leader in Africa to search out and destroy anyone who was rash enough to reveal deviationist tendencies in dealing with such vital matters: 'such a man', he affirmed, 'must be removed from the public ear and anathematised by every mouth.'[29] A threat to baptism was a threat to grace.

'The Christian doctrine of God's grace is a complicated and confusing subject, more so than is always realised', wrote Leonard Hodgson in his characteristically lucid analysis of the problems associated with its traditional formulation.[30] Ambiguities and uncertainties, he went on, increase rapidly when one climbs over the fences surrounding one's own denomination and ventures into the territory next door. He asks three questions about grace:

[29] *PMR* xxi. 44 (PL 44, 318) (CSEL 42, 47).
[30] Hodgson, 1968, II, 138; cf. 1936, 34.

27

'How can the same word mean such different things to different traditions of Christian theology, is it merely a disagreement on the meaning of terminology, or is there a deeper issue at stake?' His conclusion is that there *is* such an issue and that it is the problem of 'reconciling the ethical and personal character of the Christian religion with man's utter dependence on God's free gift of salvation'. This was also the conclusion of a report of a theological committee of the Faith and Order Movement in 1929: the recognition both of divine sovereignty and of human freedom is 'the fundamental conviction of religious life'.[31] But in his introduction to this report William Temple had to admit that, although the committee had been able to demonstrate that, in many instances, the same truth was being asserted in different forms, there were still very real differences remaining.

Indeed there were, and some of them were such as to challenge the very assumptions on which the committee had been established and the procedures which it had followed. Only a year after the report was published, a theologian of the Roman Catholic Church, which had elected not to send a representative to join the committee in its deliberations, published a work criticising in the strongest possible terms not only this attempt but any attempt to reconcile differing views on the subject of divine grace as 'a betrayal of the true faith'.[32] In its final statement the committee itself confessed that 'while from the point of view of philosophy the two points of view are irreconcilable, they represent the only basis on which the religious life can be built up'; 'our religious convictions demand dependence on God, our ethical convictions demand human freedom. The mistake that has been made has been that theologians have aimed at philosophical consistency.'[33] If this is a mistake, then both Augustine and Pelagius were guilty of it, since the problem of reconciling divine sovereignty with human freedom lay at the heart of their controversy, each maintaining that he, and not the other, was correctly interpreting key statements and ideas found in the scriptures and especially the Pauline Epistles, as well as in the writings of the early fathers. This was to be their bone of contention, at which they were to tug relentlessly from either end.

By the first century A.D. the Greek word *charis* already bore several senses. In classical and Hellenistic Greek it was used in three main ways: objectively, subjectively and concretely. Objectively, it could mean 'outward grace, charm, beauty', as it does as early as Homer and Hesiod; subjectively, 'grace

[31] Whitley, ed., 20.

[32] Hodgson, 1936, 2; the book referred to there and discussed in detail in 35ff. – A. Nygren, *Agape and Eros* – appeared in English as translated by A. G. Hebert in 1932 but had been written two years before; it cannot therefore be regarded as a reply to the committee of the Faith and Order Movement.

[33] Whitley, ed., 20. H. Chadwick, writing of the 'orthodoxy' of Origen, uses even stronger terms: 'Orthodoxy is a word that suggests clear-cut and absolute lines of division. It begins to look different if we ask whether some theologians may be more orthodox than others, whether there are degrees of understanding, whether, if we all see through a glass darkly, some may be more able to see a little clearly than others . . . absolute confidence is possible only for two classes of people, saints and idiots' (1966, 122f.).

or favour felt by the doer or receiver of a kindness', both being found in Aeschylus and Sophocles; concretely, 'a favour or boon granted or returned', a sense extended in early papyri and inscriptions, for example, as 'a grant from the Emperor'. In view of the steady growth of the imperial cult in the first century A.D. it is not surprising to find examples of a subjective sense of 'imperial favour' in inscriptions from that period. In fact, the sense which we find in them is not far removed from the generalised sense of 'divine grace' in Paul: Nero refers to his conferment of freedom on the Greeks as a gift of his *charis*, Gaius Caligula speaks of the 'abundance of the grace which is immortal' and of promotion 'by the grace of Gaius Caesar'. T. W. Manson may well have been right in seeing such a sense as 'supplying the linguistic starting-point' for its Christian use, especially when its use in the Septuagint appears to be normally confined to rendering the Hebrew word meaning 'favourable inclination or regard', the mercy and loving kindness of God being expressed by the Greek word *eleos* meaning 'mercy'. In the Psalms the word *charis* occurs only twice, both times in the objective sense of 'outward grace', as it does on three occasions when it is used in Proverbs; in Zechariah it occurs twice as the 'spirit of grace', and in Isaiah and Jeremiah not at all. Philo too limits his use of *charis*, normally in the plural, to the natural gifts of God, and in other Jewish religious writers 'the word plays no distinctive part'.[34]

In the New Testament *charis* is to be found on numerous occasions but not in Matthew or Mark and only eight times in Luke and three in John, and none of the occurrences in Luke or John, the latter all in the first chapter, point to the emergence of a new, specifically Christian sense. As Manson put it, 'While therefore Jesus in his own person is the source of the grace of which the New Testament speaks, he is not the source of the language used for describing it. This source was most probably Paul.'[35] It was his intense experience accompanying and following his conversion that impelled Paul to abandon the Jewish system of law and merit in which he had previously placed his whole trust. He determined to build his new life on the secure basis of God's grace and, to describe it, he employed the Greek word which he found ready to hand and already currently in use to denote the gracious favour of the Roman Emperor. This grace, unlike the Jewish idea of mercy, which was no more than an aid to righteousness, offered the possibility of salvation to all by giving them the chance to create a new life and acquire a new status. It was 'a quality manifested in operation', calling and 'justifying', that is, accounting righteous, those whom God had foreknown and selected from the beginning.[36] It was both premundane and temporal, a grace of election and justification but not of sanctification. And, with occasional differences in language and emphasis, the same generalised concept of grace is found in the other New Testament writings.

---

[34] Manson, in Whitley, ed., 33ff.
[35] Ibid., 42.
[36] N. P. Williams, 1930, 11.

29

The early Christians were so deeply convinced of their absolute dependence on God's grace and of the validity of their day-to-day experience of its operation that they saw no reason to differentiate between its manifold aspects or the means by which it was bestowed upon them – beyond, that is, the redemption won for them by Jesus through his crucifixion. The early Greek Fathers give 'only particular descriptions of grace and do not offer formal definitions, for which indeed no necessity arose in the Christian East'.[37] Creation, providence and redemption all fell within the province of 'original' grace, and man shared in these according to his capacity to do so; ·for his eternal salvation he also needed the 'specific' grace conferred only by baptism, which was a prerequisite for spiritual growth. The early Latin Fathers, living as they did in an age of romantic heroism, shared his belief in the saving grace of baptism and were strengthened in it by the bitter exigencies of persecution. Grace, now rendered by the Latin word *gratia*, was offered unconditionally and universally but could be appropriated only through baptism in faith. Thereafter, the Christian would be confirmed by God in the power to do good by his obedience (Tertullian) or his loyalty (Cyprian), which would be properly rewarded by the ability to withstand the trials and temptations of life.[38]

So much for the prehistory of grace, grace before Augustine, who was to be the first to construct a comprehensive doctrine: henceforth, 'the part of God and man in salvation and the harmony between grace and liberty indisputably form the central core of the teaching of the Bishop of Hippo'.[39] By 397, two years after his consecration as bishop, the foundations of his great doctrine of grace had been laid. But it was with his conversion in 386 that his absorbing interest in it may be said to have begun. Like Paul, he underwent a 'cataclysmic experience of instantaneous conversion from sin to God',[40] and, from that moment, his moment of truth, when the veil of uncertainty was torn aside, he was at last able to see the whole of his earlier life as a preliminary to the direct intervention of God. As a young man he had known temptation and

---

[37] Gloubokowsky, in Whitley, ed., 105.
[38] Watson, in Whitley, ed., 106ff.; N. P. Williams, 1930, 16ff.
[39] Portalié, 177.
[40] N. P. Williams, 1930, 19; the 'authenticity' of Augustine's conversion is discussed in Rees, 5ff. But though adhering to his defence of the 'authenticity' of Augustine's conversion experience, the author of this article now readily acknowledges that his interpretation of that experience was simplistic: it fails to give due weight to the fact that Augustine's account of it was written after he had devoted a decade of serious study to Paul's *Epistles* and to the account of Paul's conversion in *Acts* 9 and, as a result, had come to interpret his own experience in the light of his understanding of Paul's. Frederiksen, 1986, has convincingly argued that 'As Augustine's theological opinions changed, so did his views of Paul – and, correspondingly, of himself' (22), and that 'Augustine's account of his conversion in the *Confessions* . . . is a theological reinterpretation of a past event, an attempt to render his past coherent to his present self. It is, in fact, a disguised description of where he stands in the present as much as an ostensible description of what occurred in the past. And he constructs his description from his reading of Acts 9 as well as from his new theological convictions' (24). In general terms, 'the convert thus sees the subsequent events of his life in light of his conversion; but, à *l'inverse*, his description of his conversion should be read in light of these subsequent events' (33). We shall see that, in relation to Augustine's restatement of his doctrine of grace, the crucial turning-point was his reading of the *Epistles* at the time of his replies to his friend Simplicianus in 396–7.

been tortured by doubt, he had searched for a solution to the problem of evil in the philosophers, in the scriptures and in Manicheism, he had listened intently to the sermons of Ambrose, and still he had waited in vain for some light that would guide his feet with certainty, still he remained in 'a state of wavering uncertainty'. His intensive reading of Paul had brought him to the point where he could exclaim in an agony of self-realisation: 'What shall wretched man do? Who shall deliver him from the body of this death but your grace through our Lord Jesus Christ? All this sank down into the heart of my being by some wonderful means, when I read "the least of your Apostles".'[41]

Yet he was still unready to take the leap of faith: his will was still divided, his mind knew at last what it ought to will but was unable to will it, because his will resisted his efforts, and, in despair, he cried out with Paul, 'The good that I would I do not, the evil I would not that I do.' And then, at the right moment of psychological crisis, came the words of a child heard in a garden,[42] 'Take up and read, take up and read!', and they set his will free. The verse which he read gave him an unequivocal answer to the dilemma which he had thought to be intractable. Begging God to give him chastity, he had added 'But not yet!' Now at last he realised that his intellect and his unaided will could take him no further, that he *must* respond to the moral imperative specifically addressed to him. What he had failed all along to do by the exercise of his own will he could only do by surrendering that will to the will of God, revealed to him by an act of grace. 'By grace', he repeated, 'by grace are we saved through faith.' From that moment he was never again to doubt that the evil with which he had been plagued came from within himself and the only cure for it was the divine grace. 'Late', he cries out, 'late have I learned to love you. You were within me, and I was outside in the world; and it was there that I was searching for you. You were with me but I was not with you. Yet it was you who called to me and cried to me and broke down the barrier of my deafness. Now there can be no hope for me except in your great mercy. Give me the grace to do what you command and command me to do what you will.'[43] The verse which he had read spoke to his own condition, pointing to the very sins of which he was most conscious: 'I had no wish to read any further nor any need to do so. For immediately, at the end of this sentence, as if by the illumination of certainty poured into my heart, all the shadows of doubt were dispersed.'

But he did read further – in that same Epistle which he had been commanded to take up and read. And there he was to find most of the raw ingredients for his doctrine of grace and his theory of original sin. Hitherto these two ideas had developed quite independently, insofar as they could be said to have developed at all; now he was to elaborate and combine them in one great intellectual system, identifying the origin and true nature of sin and indicating the only remedy for it, that *amplior medicina*, that grace which was

---

[41] *C* VII, xxi. 27 (PL 32, 748) (CSEL 33, 167f.).
[42] Ibid., VIII, xii. 29 (PL 32, 762) (CSEL 33, 194).
[43] Ibid., X, xxvii. 38, xxix. 40 (PL 32, 795f.) (CSEL 33, 255f.).

infinitely more potent than the evil with which man had been infected. His doctrine of grace would be 'solemnly adopted' by the Church, and the second Council of Orange would borrow its canons 'word for word from his writings'.[44] True, some aspects of it would later be rejected because of misinterpretation and misuse, and others, like original sin and predestination, would be hotly debated over the centuries. But 'it is Augustine who must be reckoned as the real artificer of the ecclesiastical concept of grace in the sense of divine power, as of the companion concept of original sin.'[45] Together they formed the 'reality of faith' with which Pelagius was held to be in conflict, the 'good theology' with which Augustine now attempted to correct the bad.

On a first reading of Pelagius' book *On Nature* it had seemed to Augustine that the writer might be innocent of the charge of denying the grace of God; but, as he read on, his worst suspicions were confirmed, since the grace described there turned out to be quite different from the true doctrine of the Church: Pelagius had too much to say about free will enabling man to choose good but nothing about the grace which is able to prevent the wrong use of free will leading man to sin; indeed, he seemed to be replacing grace by free will as the means of salvation. Thus Augustine had diagnosed what he saw to be the root cause of the Pelagian disease: 'the opinion hitherto kept in concealment is now out in the open, that the possibility of not sinning is attributed to the grace of God because God is the author of that human nature in which it is inseparably implanted'.[46] So, Pelagius *is* denying that God's help must be sought whenever we have to resist temptation and that this help is made available to us in Jesus, 'the medicine of the mediator',[47] which alone has the power to heal our corrupt nature inherited from Adam. The grace which Pelagius teaches turns out in the end to be no more than nature created with free will, 'a poisonous perversion endangering salvation',[48] and his clumsy attempt at Diospolis to combine this 'natural grace' with the help given by God to man in the moral law and the teaching of Jesus may have succeeded in pulling the wool over the eyes of his judges but will never succeed in convincing Augustine that he is not reducing the grace of God to the inferior status of a mere adjunct to the will of man. In his *Letter to Demetrias* Pelagius may speak of men as 'deserving the grace of God and, by the help of the Holy Spirit, more easily resisting the evil spirit', and in his treatise *On Free Will* he may suggest that 'men may more easily accomplish by grace that which they are commanded to do by free will'. 'But why', asks Augustine,

---

[44] Portalié, 177; of the nine canons only three are concerned with the question of grace – 4–6, discussed in Wermelinger, 197ff. and 194. Elsewhere too (224) Portalié claims that 'propositions taken verbatim from Augustine . . . were sanctioned by the Council of Orange'; but, as Küng, 1964, 168 has warned, 'the dogmatic value of II Orange is disputed', and it would be unwise to assume, as Portalié appears to have done, that the second Council of Orange set the seal on 'Augustinian' orthodoxy, since there is some doubt as to whether all the canons, and if all or only the first eight, were approved by Pope Boniface II.
[45] N. P. Williams, 1930, 19.
[46] *NG*, li. 59 (PL 44, 275) (CSEL 60, 276).
[47] Ibid., lxvii. 80 (PL 44, 286) (CSEL 60, 293f.).
[48] *PP* xxiii. 47 (PL 44, 347) (CSEL 42, 101).

'why does he insert the phrase "more easily"? Expunge it, and you leave not only a full but also a sound sense.'[49]

Pelagius gives every indication that he understands the burden of the charge made against him but without on any occasion accepting its validity. 'Very ignorant persons', he complains, no doubt including Augustine among them without mentioning him, 'consider that in this respect we are doing an injury to the divine grace, because we say that it in no way perfects our sanctity without the exercise of our own free will – as if God would have imposed any command on his grace without also supplying its help to those whom he has commanded.'[50] He goes on to add: 'This grace we do not, as you suppose, allow to consist only in the law but also in the help of God. God helps us through his teaching and revelation by opening the eyes of our heart, by pointing out to us the future so that we may not be preoccupied with the present, by uncovering the snares of the devil, by enlightening us with the manifold and ineffable gift of heavenly grace. Does the man who says all this appear to you to be denying grace? Is he not admitting both the free will of man and the grace of God?' 'No', replies Augustine, 'most certainly, no, he does not, because he is making the grace of God consist in the law and teaching.'

This charge is repeated again and again in Augustine's anti-Pelagian treatises: Pelagius is restricting divine grace to the response of the human will to the law as set out in the scriptures and to the teaching of Jesus. He may do his best to conceal this by affirming that 'God works in us to will what is good, to will what is holy, when he rouses us from our devotion to earthly desires and our love of the present only after the manner of dumb animals, by the magnitude of our future glory and the promise of its rewards, when, by revealing wisdom to us, he awakens our sluggish will to longing for him, when he urges upon us all that is good.' 'He means by grace,' Augustine repeats, 'nothing else but law and teaching.'[51] And, 'although he makes that grace of God whereby Christ came into the world to save sinners to consist simply in remission of sins, he can still accommodate his words to this meaning by alleging that the necessity of such grace for every hour, moment and action of our lives comes to this, that while we recollect and keep in mind the forgiveness of past sins, we sin no more, aided not by any supply of power but by the strength of our own free will as it recalls to our minds in our every action the advantage conferred on us by remission of sins'.[52] Thus his theology of grace continues to be built around the very opinion which he condemned at Diospolis, namely, that 'God's grace and assistance are not given for single acts but consist in free will or law and teaching'.[53] 'Let them therefore read and understand, observe and acknowledge that it is not by the voice of law and teaching resounding outside but by a secret, wonderful and

[49] *GC* xxvii. 28, xxix. 30 (PL 44, 374f.) (CSEL 42, 148f.).
[50] Ibid., vii. 8 (PL 44, 364) (CSEL 42, 130f.).
[51] Ibid., x. 11 (PL 44, 365f.) (CSEL 42, 133ff.).
[52] Ibid., ii. 2 (PL 44, 361) (CSEL 42, 125f.).
[53] Ibid., iii. 3 (PL 44, 361) (CSEL 42, 126f.); *PP* xiv. 30 (PL 44, 337) (CSEL 42, 84).

ineffable power from within that God works in men's hearts to produce not only revelations of the truth but also good dispositions of the will'.[54]

Pelagius was thus impaled on the horns of a dilemma of his own making. When he maintained that divine grace had been bestowed on man at his creation by the gift of free will, he laid himself open to a charge of neglecting the possibility of 'any supply of power' thereafter by an infusion of divine grace enabling man to answer God's call. As R. F. Evans, by no means unsympathetic to Pelagius, rightly emphasises: 'It would be unfaithful to the man himself to save his "orthodoxy" by reading in some doctrine of infused grace which is not there.'[55] On the other hand, when Pelagius tried to counter this by anathematising those who denied that God's grace was needed for every action and by affirming that it was made available as a form of assistance to the baptised in the recollection of remission of sins, reinforced by law and teaching and by the example of Jesus, he found himself accused of having no doctrine of *internal* grace, because he could not bring himself to make an unambiguous declaration of the way in which it operated. Even when he attempted to safeguard his position by adding that God helps man by 'the manifold and ineffable gift of heavenly grace', he seemed to his opponents to be thinking in terms of intellectual enlightenment rather than spiritual assistance. His whole teaching of grace was constructed around the central premise of the absolute freedom of man's will when faced with a choice between good and evil, a freedom given to man by God but, once given, not subject to God's interference.

Again and again in the course of the controversy Augustine found it necessary to correct this wrong emphasis on the freedom of the human will and to assert the absolute sovereignty of divine grace and the omnipotence of God. He returned to the subject in one of his last treatises, *On Rebuke and Grace*, in which he replied to the queries of Valentinus and his monks at Hadrumetum in 426/7 and included a brief but definitive summary of the Catholic teaching on relationship between God and man and between divine grace and human conduct: 'It is impossible', he writes, 'to doubt that the wills of men are incapable of resisting the will of God and preventing him from doing what he himself wishes', 'He has the wills of men under his control more than they themselves have', and 'To will or not to will is in the power of one who wills or does not will but only to such an extent that he cannot impede the divine will or overcome its power.' For 'God, without doubt, has most absolute power to incline men's hearts in whatever direction he pleases'.[56]

Augustine and Pelagius were as far apart as the average employer and trade union in a modern industrial dispute – and just about as likely to reach agreement on a mutually satisfactory compromise by what are known as 'conciliation processes'. They had a common interest, namely, the welfare and preservation of the institution to which they both belonged, but they

---

[54] *GC* xxiv. 25 (PL 44, 373) (CSEL 42, 145).
[55] R. F. Evans, 1968(a), 111.
[56] *RG* xiv. 43, 45 (PL 44, 942ff.).

started out from opposite extremes: Augustine began with God, Pelagius with man. His view of man was not of one created perfect only to be corrupted by the sin of Adam passed on from generation to generation but of one who began to sin from that moment when he became consciously able as a child to imitate the sins of others, not because his own flawed nature forced him to do so but because he was ignorant of its true essence and potential. His will had been corrupted not by the sin of Adam but by bad example and habit, and it was this 'long habit of doing wrong'[57] which had been incorrectly identified with, and located in, human nature by those who adhered to the doctrine of original sin. To enable man to correct his faults, God had first provided 'the file of the law';[58] but, in the event, not even this aid could enable man to overcome the overwhelming force of bad habit, though it remained strong enough to enable him to recognise the error of his ways and to become conscious of his sins. Man was still in possession of the capacity to live without sin but was prevented from doing so by his inability to draw upon 'the treasure within his soul',[59] that free will with which God had endowed him at his creation. In order to make full use of this gift, he must develop a right understanding of his nature.

Pelagius begins his *Letter to Demetrias* with an analysis of the human will. 'Whenever', he writes, 'I have to speak about moral instruction and the way to live a blameless life, it is my practice first to demonstrate the power and nature of the human will and to show what it is able to achieve. By a more careful examination of the human will it becomes possible to see that the status of man is better and higher for that very reason for which it is thought to be inferior: it is on the choice of which of two paths to follow, on this freedom to choose either alternative, that the dignity of the rational mind is based . . . and it is from this finally that all the best men win praise, from this their reward; nor would there be any virtue at all in the good of one who perseveres if he had not been able to cross over to the path of evil.'[60]

To enable man to make the right choices, he has been endowed with three faculties or capacities – *posse, velle* and *esse*, 'natural ability or potential', 'will' and 'action'.[61] The first of these is the capacity to be righteous and not to sin, which is part of man's nature, given to him at his creation; the second is the capacity to make his own free choice of right action; the third is the capacity to translate that choice into right action and to live according to the nature given to him by God, that is, without sin. The first cannot be taken away from him, and he never loses the ability to do good; but if he is to exercise it properly, he must employ the second and third, which are both under his control. But what has actually happened is that the first capacity, though

---

[57] *Letter to Demetrias* 8 (PL 30, 23; 33, 1104); cf. 17 and 24 (PL 30, 31f., 38f.; 33, 1111, 1115), and Augustine, *GC* xxxix. 43 (PL 44, 380) (CSEL 42, 156f.) and *OS* xxvi. 30 (PL 44, 400) (CSEL 42, 190).
[58] *Letter to Demetrias*, loc. cit.; cf. *OS* xxvi. 30 (PL 44, 400) (CSEL 42, 190).
[59] *Letter to Demetrias* 6 (PL 30, 22; 33, 1103f.)
[60] Ibid., 2, 3 (PL 30, 16f.; 33, 1100).
[61] *GC* iii. 4, iv. 5 (PL 44. 361ff.) (CSEL 42, 127f.).

reinforced by the law as embodied in the scriptures, has atrophied because of man's failure to make the right use of the second, and in order to bring it into play again, he has been offered the opportunity of redemption by the saving death of Jesus, who forgives his sins, restores his will and sustains it by his own teaching and example.

So Pelagius would argue that he has not neglected grace, since his doctrine provides for a grace of creation, a grace of revelation and a grace of redemption. But he would be anxious to stress the rôle of God not only in these but also in the operation of the will: 'For certainly it is of God alone that man is able to do and carry through a good action, and this capacity can exist alone without the other two but they cannot exist without it.'[62] And, elsewhere, 'How can that possibly be understood to be without the grace of God which is considered to belong specially to him?'[63] Yet, insist though he may again and again that it is God who, in the first place, has given man the possibility of doing good as his original endowment of grace and has confirmed and strengthened it by revelation and by redemption through Jesus, his dialectic compels him to balance this insistence with another, even stronger, that 'when we really do a good thing or speak a good word or think a good thought, it proceeds from ourselves'.[64]

Pelagius' God has been compared to Paley's watchmaker: he built the machine and put its parts in sound working order, stood back to admire his work and, when it proved to be operating inefficiently, intervened dramatically to correct its faults and enable it to function more efficiently in the future. But he stopped short of replacing the part which had been most responsible for the technical breakdown, and he remained outside all the time. For Augustine, on the other hand, the religious life was centred around the realisation that God lives within the human soul while remaining distinct from it, immanent and yet transcendent. 'Soul, self-knowledge and knowledge of God became interdependent: to know oneself properly involves an awareness of the indwelling presence of God, and this awareness can grow only by the power of grace and its consequent redirected love, from dim sensation to surer awareness to eventual vision.'[65] Thus God worked from within, had been there from the beginning and could exercise his power whenever he saw that the right moment to do so had arrived. God is nearer to us, claimed Augustine, than we are to ourselves; he is no remote mechanic, no absentee landlord, but an ever-present force working in us to correct the will which has made the wrong choices and to guide it gently back to the way of salvation.

In one of his anthologies which became so popular in the fifties and sixties Victor Gollancz quoted a definition of grace from the Oxford Dictionary as 'the divine influence which operates in men to regenerate and sanctify, and to impart strength to endure trial and resist temptation'. 'The definition', he

---

[62] Ibid., iv. 5 (PL 44, 362) (CSEL 42, 128).
[63] *NG* xlv. 53 (PL 44, 272) (CSEL 60, 271f.); cf. xliv. 52, li. 59 (PL 44, 272, 275) (CSEL 60, 271, 276).
[64] *GC* xvi. 17 (PL 44, 369) (CSEL 42, 139).
[65] I have been unable to trace the source of this quotation.

comments, 'is as good as any: but no one who has not experienced Grace can really understand it. Most people do experience it sooner or later.'[66] Augustine knew that he had experienced it himself; but he was also convinced that the teaching of Pelagius was not true to his own experience. Pelagius was making the same mistake that he had once made himself, and he must be taught the truth. But he found him to be a most reluctant pupil, one who could never resist the temptation to try to teach his grandmother to suck eggs!

[66] *The New Year of Grace*, ed. V. Gollancz, London 1961, 104.

III

THIS VEXED MATTER

'But that which God's foreknowledge can foresee
Must needs occur, as certain men of learning
Have said. Ask any scholar of discerning;
He'll say the Schools are filled with altercation
On this vexed matter of predestination
Long bandied by a hundred thousand men.'

GEOFFREY CHAUCER[1]

Augustine, as the 'true' spokesman, cannot be faulted for not doing his utmost to 'correct bad theology with good' in his efforts to convince Pelagius that his own interpretation of the grace which he had experienced was the only correct and legitimate one, a task to which he applied all the zeal of a convert and the dedication of a 'twice-born' Christian. But it was all of no avail, for Pelagius refused to abandon his own conviction of the validity of free will and continued to argue his case for giving it a countervailing rôle in the drama of man's salvation. It is true that, when pressed, he yielded to the extent of modifying his view by admitting that human will needed divine assistance, only to be dismissed as a time-server and sophist for his pains. Both men were so engrossed in their debate that they would have turned a deaf ear to the pragmatic advice of a modern novelist, delivered presumably without benefit of theology, that 'freewill has to be experienced, not debated, like colour or the taste of potatoes.'[2] Both instead, like 'the hundred thousand men' of Chaucer's Schools, preferred the verbal gymnastics of a *cause célébre* which was to reverberate down the centuries. And, without doubt, it was Augustine who proved to be holding the stronger brief of the two, by his adroit handling of it satisfying the judges of his day that Pelagius' 'grace of creation' was far from being, as he claimed, an inner force, implanted in man by God to enable him to avoid sin and win salvation. It was no more than a capacity, always present and available perhaps but not always in employment and, even when employed, inadequate by itself. It worked in man only when he willed the

---

[1] *Canterbury Tales: the Nun's Priest's Tale*, ed. N. Coghill, Harmondsworth 1951, 294.

[2] W. Golding, *Free Fall*, London 1959, 5. Hodgson, 1936, 177f., notes that 'the question whether the distinction between those who do and those who do not respond to the redeeming activity of God is to be ascribed to divine predestination or human free will' was 'judged by Temple (*Nature, Man and God*, London 1934, 400ff.) to be insoluble on the knowledge at our disposal', and he adds that 'mysteries remain which we cannot solve but must accept in faith our own ignorance, not trying to make dogmatic assertions about them which are regarded as *articuli stantis aut cadentis ecclesiae*' – 'articles on which the Church stands or falls'.

good but not when he exercised his notional freedom *in alteram partem*, that is, to choose evil. But how, in that case, does God help the will when it chooses good? In the absence of any clear and firm statement to the contrary from Pelagius, it must be concluded that God does so, as Augustine maintains, only through the moral law and the teaching and example of Jesus. With Pelagius it was the human will that prevailed.

Augustine's belief in the inner working of God's grace triumphed over 'the strongly ethical and non-mystical type of religion favoured by Pelagius'.[3] For Augustine, grace was primarily an internal force, an ever-present, ever-available invitation to accept God's help through the exercise of a more profound kind of freedom which modified and directed the operation of the will, and only those who had been given the inner strength to respond to that call could hope to be saved. 'No one prior to Augustine had really asserted anything like this need for an inner working of God within human freedom',[4] and his conviction of this need sprang from his reflection on his own experience of conversion, prompting the only significant amendment of his earlier views on grace as expressed in his treatise *On Free Will*, written between 388 and 395 to defend the freedom of the will against Manichean determinism. Then he had maintained that man's progress depended on his response to a divine call freely made by God and freely accepted by man in faith. But, by 397, when he replied to the questions put to him by his friend Simplicianus, a change of emphasis had taken place, since the definitive solution had been revealed to him. 'Previously', he wrote later, 'I had tried to solve the question by upholding the freedom of the will; but it was the grace of God that prevailed.'[5] By then he had reached the conclusion, which he was to reinforce and defend resolutely and inflexibly ever after, that election to grace must precede any mere human decision to accept it.

The sticking-point for Pelagius was precisely this insistence on the part of Augustine that man receives from God 'both the act of willing and the power to do what is willed',[6] a doctrine of grace which, in his view, undermined the freedom of the human will. But, of course, Augustine did not agree. 'There are some who suppose', he complains towards the end of his life, 'that the freedom of the will is denied whenever God's grace is maintained.'[7] But that is only because they fail to comprehend the true nature of will, which is not a faculty – 'he had no faculty psychology'[8] – but the human psyche in its rôle as moral agent; it is not the will that wills but the man who uses it, the *whole* man employing his will as one of the functions of his soul. Nor is it possible for a man to be forced to will, since every man must be able to decide for himself in accordance with the workings of his own nature. A firm distinction must

[3] N. P. Williams, 1927, 333.
[4] Haight, 36.
[5] *R* II, 1 (PL 32, 629) (CSEL 36, 132), ed. Bogan, II, 27. Like Winston Smith in Orwell's *1984* 'he had won the victory over himself. He loved Big Brother.'
[6] *GC* xxv. 26 (PL 44, 373) (CSEL 42, 146).
[7] *R* II, 66 (PL 32, 656) (CSEL 36, 203), ed. Bogan, II, 92.
[8] Bourke, ed., 68.

therefore be drawn between *voluntas* as 'the man willing' and *liberum arbitrium* as 'freedom of choice'.

When we make our 'free' choice of action, Augustine tells us, we do so by using our *liberum arbitrium* but this, by itself, is not sufficient to enable us to choose good without the aid of the Good which is all powerful; 'it suffices (only) for evil', and so we often fail to put into effect the good choices we have 'freely' made.[9] All good acts require divine aid – *adiutorium Dei* – and it is this divine aid which alone gives us true *libertas*, because it sets us free to do good. This is true freedom of will, infinitely superior to a purely human freedom of choice such as Adam possessed before his Fall. At that time Adam was able *not* to sin but we, his descendants, if we are in a state of grace and if we persevere to the end, are *unable* to sin; *non posse peccare*, 'to be unable to sin' – that is the essence of our true freedom, which we can only realise by God's grace. It is only by God's grace that we are 'set free from sin', whereas those who are not given that grace remain in enslavement to sin through their exercise of *liberum arbitrium* unaided. In order to become truly free, man must become 'a servant of God', in whose service is the only perfect freedom.

It is generally agreed that Augustine's explanation of free will is both more sophisticated than that of Pelagius and truer to Christian experience. But it does raise problems by introducing a theory of predestination which is, to say the least, controversial. 'The totality of mankind' as seen by Augustine has been compared, for instance,[10] to a figure consisting of three concentric circles: the outermost contains 'the vessels of wrath', whose place in the 'damnèd mass' is irredeemable because their subjection to original sin leaves them beyond the reach of God's mercy; the next circle contains those whom the grace of 'justification' – a term used by Augustine not in the Pauline sense of 'accounting righteous' but to mean 'making righteous' – temporarily rescues from the mass but only for them to sink back again into it through lack of the grace of 'perseverance'; the innermost circle is reserved for 'the vessels of mercy', elected from the beginning to salvation, justified by grace and endowed with grace to persevere to the end.

Of the three groups only the last is predestined in the absolute sense, being 'the few chosen' as against 'the many called' but not 'prepared' to answer the call, who differ from the elect in not having 'efficacious' grace as well as the 'sufficient' grace given to all – 'sufficient', it would seem, to be in their case insufficient! The elect have *adiutorium quo*, 'the aid by which they are enabled to be saved', in addition to *adiutorium sine quo non*, 'the aid without which it would be theoretically impossible to be saved'.[11] Thus, while God's grace is in

[9] *RG* xi. 31 (PL 44, 935), reading *parum*, 'insufficient for', not *nihil* 'of no avail'; cf. *GFC* xv. 31 (PL 44, 899f.), *E* xxx–xxxii, 9 (PL 40, 246ff.).

[10] N. P. Williams, 1930, 24f.

[11] Ibid., 36; for the distinction between *adiutorium quo* and *adiutorium sine quo non* see especially *RG* xii. 34 (PL 44, 936f.); for the distinction between *posse non peccare* and *non posse peccare RG* xii. 33 (PL 44, 936). There are several passages in Augustine's works which indicate that, while he is not prepared to deny that *non posse peccare*, 'not to be able to sin', is a theoretical possibility, his own experience and his knowledge of human frailty lead him to conclude that no man is able not to sin *in this world* except by the grace of perseverance, the *adiutorium sine quo non*, nor can any man be sure that he has been given that grace.

theory available to all, in practice only those who have been 'prepared' will accept it when it is offered to them. The non-elect have not been so 'prepared', and we are left with the harsh but seemingly inescapable conclusion that they are not recipients of God's mercy and so are condemned to eternal damnation for a sin which they did not themselves commit but of which, nevertheless, they are held to be guilty, a conclusion which Augustine's remorseless logic does not permit him to mitigate even for children dying unbaptised; their fate can only be referred to the 'occult justice' of God, whose judgements are inscrutable – an echo of the Pauline plea, *O altitudo*: 'O the depth of the riches both of the wisdom and knowledge of God! How unsearchable are his judgements, and his ways past finding out!'[12] All men stand condemned by God's justice because of the sin of Adam, and it is to his mercy alone that the elect owe their remission of sentence; the first we must accept, for the second we must be duly thankful.

This depressing cameo of human destiny would have been classified by Aristotle as a plot with a 'double' ending, leading to a happy outcome for the one set of participants and quite the opposite for the other.[13] To the elected minority it offers a hope of eternal salvation through the intervention of divine benevolence; for the great majority, shut out for ever from the *numerus clausus neque augendus neque minuendus* or 'fixed quota' imposed by divine providence, it means a sentence of condemnation without prospect of remission. In attempting to explain how faith can be man's own act and yet be called forth by God, Augustine for the first time advances a doctrine which was later to be termed 'effective calling' by Calvinists and 'efficacious grace' by Roman Catholicism. It is this *effective* calling, this *efficacious* grace which produces the right response from 'the few chosen', because it is 'congruous' with their condition: their response is held by Augustine to be in perfect harmony with their call, which is made in such a way and at such a time that they, as God alone foreknows, will be unable to reject it.

But if 'that which God's foreknowledge can foresee must needs occur', what place is there for man's exercise of his free will? The paradox had been presented to Origen by his friend and 'taskmaster' two centuries before: 'If God knows the future beforehand and it must come to pass', wrote Ambrose of Alexandria, 'prayer is vain.'[14] More than that, not only prayer but all human action is vain, for what is the point of playing the game, if the dice are loaded? Augustine was to insist in his treatise *On the Predestination of the Saints*, written in 428/9, that predestination and foreknowledge were not the same: 'Predestination cannot exist without foreknowledge, but foreknowledge may exist without predestination.'[15] 'There are things which God foresees, but

[12] Romans 11, 33.

[13] *Poetics*, c. 13, 1453a 30–3.

[14] Origen, *De Oratione* V, 6 – a reference I owe to Lucas, 1970, 71. Origen's reply (VI, 3) was: 'The foreknowledge of God is not the cause of all future events and of the actions which will be performed by us of our own impulse'. Cf. Boethius, *De Consolatione Philosophiae* V, iv, ·13ff.: 'reason, which because it does not consider foreknowledge to be the necessary cause of future events thinks that the freedom of the will is in no way hindered by foreknowledge.'

[15] *PS* x. 19 (PL 44, 975).

which he himself does not intend to bring about' is how he puts it. But for Pelagius, like 'any scholar of discerning', the theory of election outlined above involved a form of predestination which he could not endorse, because it contained implications of what appeared to him to be theological determinism. Was Augustine's doctrine of election really a form of predestination which abolished the freedom of the human will, and ruled out all possibility of reconciling it with divine grace? If so, had there been a change of emphasis, as we have suggested, in Augustine's understanding of the *modus operandi* of election around 396 or 397, when he answered the questions of Simplicianus? And did this in turn, reinforced by his reading of contemporary theologians and his battle with the Donatists, lead around 406 to his adoption of a theory of original sin which marked 'a decisive change in his career as a theologian'?[16]

These are the sort of questions around which the battle-lines of the future were to be drawn up. 'At all times', wrote Eugène Portalié, 'adversaries of freedom of will – predestinarians, Wycliffites, Calvinists, and Jansenists – have availed themselves of the authority of Augustine. Catholic theologians, it is true, have generally recognised that Augustine safeguarded the rights of freedom of will, but they are strangely divided concerning the nature of this freedom and the explanation of the divine action in Augustine's writings.'[17] After citing three weighty dissentients among the Catholic ranks and noting that contemporary Protestants, including even the most sincere admirers of Augustine, are unmerciful in their criticism of him on this score, he goes on to insist that 'Augustine never retracted his principal ideas on freedom of choice; he never modified his thoughts on the factor which is its essential condition, that is its complete power of choosing or determining itself.'[18] He then proceeds to construct the strongest possible defence of Augustine's position, proving at least to his own satisfaction that it enabled him to reconcile divine grace with human freedom. Such a defence, coming from one so highly regarded as an Augustinian scholar, deserves to be treated with the utmost respect, even if to many other scholars it has seemed to be less than objective.

Portalié's case may be summarised under three headings. First, the will, in making any decision, is influenced by certain motives and, in deciding which, if any, of these to follow, it is free to choose for itself: 'nothing attracts the will to action unless it is seen; what each one decides to take or leave is in his power.'[19] *But* it is God who, by virtue of his omnipotence, is able to choose those motives which he will present to man. Secondly, 'man is not the master of his first thoughts': no one has power over what chances to come into his mind but to give consent or withold it is in the power of his own will.'[20] *But* it is God, not chance, who determines what these first thoughts will be. Thirdly, God, by virtue of his omniscience, knows what answer man will give to each of the motives and thoughts presented to him: 'A man does not sin because

[16] TeSelle, 1970, 266.
[17] Portalié, 177f.
[18] Ibid., 197.
[19] *FC* III, xxv. 74 (PL 32, 1307) (CSEL 74, 151).
[20] *SL* xxxiv. 60 (PL 44, 240) (CSEL 60, 220).

42

God, whose knowledge is infallible, foreknew that fortune or fate or something else would sin but that man himself would sin, who, if he wills not, sins not. *But* if he wills to sin, that God also foreknew.'[21] The grace of God thus works not by compulsion but 'by way of infallible attraction', gently guiding and persuading his elect to make their own right choices by presenting them with those thoughts and motives which he foreknows to be congruous with their needs and circumstances, and these, of course, will vary from one man to another.

'The chief theological argument for determinism', comments John Lucas in his discussion of free will,[22] 'is the argument from omniscience, although other arguments from omnipotence and grace are also invoked.' Portalié employs all of these arguments but denies that the result is 'theological determinism'. Furthermore, he does not doubt 'first, that Augustine has formed a true and perfectly logical system without contradictions, the basis of which did not vary since the time he became a bishop if we are to judge by his later works; second, that in this system human liberty was affirmed until the day of his death so accurately that no trace of an irresistible and necessitating impulsion ever appears in it.'[23] A similar conclusion has been reached by another Roman Catholic theologian of a later generation, Mother Mary Clark, in her exhaustive examination of Augustine's teaching on free will, and another Roman Catholic, the philosopher A. H. Armstrong, accepts her conclusion 'that Augustine really tried to maintain in his anti-Pelagian period his admirable earlier teaching on human free will and was to a great extent successful in reconciling it with his belief in predestination'.[24] But he then goes on to amplify his rider 'to a great extent' by explaining that one of the reasons for Pelagian opposition to Augustine – apart, that is, from their conviction of the reality of free will – was 'that the Augustinian account of God's dealings with mankind makes God so intolerably unfair': 'he seems to have lost sight of, or at any rate, to have failed to maintain, that simple belief in God's universal and equitable goodness which is the foundation of the faith of pagan Platonists and Pelagians, and very many orthodox Christians.'[25] In other words, 'the examiner not only knows how many are to pass but has already determined *who* is to pass. All the same, if people fail, it is entirely their own fault. Not everybody finds this reasoning satisfactory.'[26]

Ay, there's the rub! Many, like Pelagius, would see the operation of divine grace on the human will as described by Augustine and defended by Portalié as 'an irresistible cogency of grace', among them the Protestant von Harnack and the great Lutheran Augustinian scholar Loofs.[27] And N. P. Williams

[21] *CG* V, 10 (PL 41, 152f.) (CSEL 40, i. 230).
[22] Lucas, 1970, 71.
[23] Portalié, 179.
[24] A. H. Armstrong, 1972, 22.
[25] Ibid., 23.
[26] Passmore, 99n., paraphrasing 'in the language of John Barth's novel *Giles Goat-Boy*' 'the orthodox Roman Catholic view that although the number of the elect is predetermined, no man is predestined to be damned'.
[27] Portalié, 178f.

43

agrees with the last two at least on this subject: 'There is no struggling against a force which represents all the might of omnipotence, directed by all the intellectual resources of omniscience.' 'God', he continues, 'is in the position of a chess-player, gifted with telepathic and hypnotic power of an infinitely high degree, who not only foresees all the other player's moves, but actually makes them, acting through the other's mind and brain, and consequently has won the game before it has even begun.'[28]

Among the faulty weapons in Augustine's armoury are two of his favourite proof-texts. The first is Proverbs 8, 35, which he quotes more than fifty times – *voluntas praeparatur a Deo*, 'the will (of man) is prepared by God'.[29] But this is not how the text appears in the Vulgate, which reads *hauriet salutem a Deo*, 'he shall obtain favour of the Lord' (AV and RV). Augustine is using a pre-Vulgate, possibly an African Old Latin version, itself a literal rendering of the Greek Septuagint; this gives him 'wish', which he renders by the more positive Latin word for 'will', *voluntas*, instead of the original Hebrew word translated as 'favour', and 'is prepared', *praeparatur*, instead of 'shall obtain'. The first proof-text, 'a consecrated formula to which he returns tirelessly',[30] is thus too insecure to bear the weight which he puts upon it. Even if we were to accept it in the form in which Augustine uses it, what, we would be bound to ask, does *praeparatur* mean in his vocabulary? The question has been hotly debated; for example, 'does *praeparatur* imply that God enables us to will, or that he so arranges that we should in fact will (freely)?',[31] that is, in accordance with his will and through his grace?

If the second, then it could be and has often been argued that all man's powers of self-determination are in that case ruled out, and Augustine is advancing a form of moral determinism. Another of his proof-texts turns out to be just as unsatisfactory: 'For God wishes that all men should be saved . . . not, however, so as to take from them their free will, by the good or bad use of which they will be most righteously judged.'[32] When Augustine goes on to add that 'unbelievers indeed act contrary to the will of God when they do not believe . . . Thus God's will is for ever invincible', he shows that he has again misinterpreted his proof-text, having been misled into a non-universalist perversion of the true meaning of 1 Timothy 2, 4, so that 'who will have all men to be saved' (AV and RV) and 'whose will it is that all men should find salvation' (NEB) become 'all men who are saved are saved by God's will'; in other words, salvation follows of necessity if God so wills, *'quia necesse est fieri si voluerit'*.[33] Elsewhere he seeks to evade the issue – or appears to – by

---

[28] N. P. Williams, 1930, 28; cf. 30, where he adds: 'The human chess-player . . . invariably does what the Divine player wishes him to do: but he does it of his own accord.'

[29] Sage, 1964, 19f., collects the references to Augustine's fifty-three quotations of this verse.

[30] Portalié, 203; Sage, 1964, 1, describes it as acting as a *'fil d'Ariane'* through the undergrowth of the controversy on Augustine's doctrine of grace, and quotes La Bonnardière as emphasising it as 'the *leitmotiv* of the anti-Pelagian polemic' in her article in *REA* IX, 1963, 78.

[31] Rist, 235f.

[32] *SL* xxxiii. 58 (PL 44, 238) (CSEL 60, 216).

[33] *E* ciii. 27 (PL 40, 280).

suggesting that 'all men' is the same as 'all the elect' or 'men of every kind'.[34] Methinks the good saint doth protest too much!

Is Augustine's grace then 'irresistible to those to whom it is offered'?[35] The Abbé Portalié, Mother Mary Clark and many others continue to affirm that at least Augustine did not think so and that he was justified. But Pelagius and many other ministers of grace over the centuries would not agree. Despite Augustine's denials to the contrary, which began as early as 412, when he wrote in his treatise *On the Spirit and the Letter*, 'Do we then by grace nullify free will? God forbid! No, rather we establish free will, since it is grace that cures the will whereby righteousness is freely loved',[36] and for all his ingenuity in attempting to distinguish between 'will' and 'free choice', he has laid himself open to a charge of ambiguity of the kind he himself brought against Pelagius' defence of free will. N. P. Williams has summed up the matter with his usual clarity and objectivity: 'If Christianity had accepted Pelagius' account of human nature as its presupposition, it would have ceased to be a "religion" in any intelligible sense of the term.'[37] But he proceeds to describe Augustine's conception of freedom as 'very abstruse and difficult' and concludes that 'it is clear that Augustine, whether consciously or not, is really trying to run with the hare and hunt with the hounds'.[38] And Leonard Hodgson is no less critical of Pelagianism: for instance, 'there is no form of Christianity which cannot be perverted and debased if Pelagianism is not checked', and 'Pelagianism is bad philosophy as well as bad religion.'[39] But, while detecting a reflection of the Augustinian distinction between 'free choice' and 'freedom' in his own differentiation of two types of freedom, the one imperfect because human and the other perfect because divine, he is fully aware of the danger of preaching determinism, even 'double determinism', to which both he and Augustine could be exposed, and of linking his second type of freedom with a quasi-scientific theory of causation which, in Augustine's case, makes insufficient allowance for the workings of the love of God.[40]

Williams's book on grace was written in the thirties, and Hodgson's Gifford Lectures were delivered in the sixties; both were theologians of high standing in their day, and there is no reason to suspect the soundness of their judgement on an issue which they both considered to be of the greatest importance. But what of the present generation of Protestant theologians writing in English? It could be argued that any selection which we make is bound to be unsatisfactory and that the views expressed will reveal more of the cast of thought of those selected, as well as the predilections of the present writer, than of the merits and demerits of Augustine's theory of predestination.

[34] *RG* xv. 44 (PL 44, 943); *CG* XXII, i. 2 (PL 41, 751f.) (CSEL 40, 2, 582f.); *J* IV, viii. 44 (PL 44, 760). But Thonnard, 1963, 284, 1964, 122, insists that in their context these refinements fit harmoniously into the pattern of Augustine's explanation of predestination.
[35] Rist, 228.
[36] *SL* xxx. 52 (PL 44, 233) (CSEL 60, 208).
[37] N. P. Williams, 1927, 357.
[38] Ibid., 369f.
[39] Hodgson, 1936, 29, 142.
[40] Hodgson, 1968, II, 142.

Still, it should not be too difficult to take a small sample representing different points along the broad spectrum of contemporary theology. Maurice Wiles, for example, in discussing 'the work of the Holy Spirit at the level of personal experience', writes that 'the fundamental problem is that of doing justice both to the integrity of personal being and to the all-pervasive nature of that grace which we are trying to describe.'[41] And, when he turns to the controversy between Pelagius and Augustine as the classic expression of 'the clash of contrasting approaches' to this topic, he agrees with Williams and Hodgson that Augustine won the approval not only of the contemporary Church but also of the majority of later historians of doctrine because of 'his far more profound apprehension of the issues involved', including the nature of human sin. But he concludes that 'it is when he attempts to turn this descriptive insight into a causal account of the origin and transmission of man's sin that the trouble begins', since 'there is no escape, as Augustine himself unwittingly demonstrates, from a doctrine of predestination which strikes at the roots of morality, of true humanity and of belief in a loving God.'[42]

In the course of a discussion of the incarnational theology of some contemporary scholars, including Wiles, R. P. Hanson criticises their view that the doctrine of the incarnation held by the Fathers of the Church 'stands or falls' by their belief in the historicity of the Creation and the Fall, citing the case of Augustine's doctrine of grace against Wiles in particular. 'The historicity of the story of Adam and Eve', he argues, 'was precisely not an integral part of Augustine's doctrine of grace. On the contrary, it was by insisting upon tying his acute and penetrating observations about the human will and the human personality to this story, taken as a scientific account of the origin of the human race, that Augustine ruined his doctrine of grace.'[43] Thus, setting aside the problematical question whether or not Augustine did believe in that Fall as a historical event, we find that Wiles and Hanson, though disagreeing on certain fundamental aspects of the Christian faith, have nevertheless arrived at a not very different position on the Augustinian theory of predestination. Hanson would presumably have accepted Wiles's statement that the results of this attempt to combine a doctrine of grace with a causal, quasi-scientific account of the origin and transmission of sin have been 'disastrous'.

There is then a consensus of opinion among all four Protestant theologians so far quoted that Augustine was at least misguided in persisting in his efforts to protect his doctrine of grace by grappling it with hoops of steel to the myth of Adam and Eve and their Fall as if it were a fact of history, when he had no real need to do so, and that, by so doing, he weakened, rather than strengthened, his own case. What is more, he has left us with an impression of God which makes the Creator appear to be less loving than his creatures are commanded to be. Other contemporary theologians have seized upon this

[41] Wiles, 1974, 94.
[42] Ibid., 95; cf. Wiles, 1982, 129.
[43] Hanson, 1976, 89.

point and have commented upon the paradox that Augustine, surely one of the most loving of men and well-loved by others, should have become so obsessed with the idea of God's power that he left little room for his love, the love of 'a God whose power lives only and wholly in his love'.[44] He thus fell a victim to his own logic when faced with 'the ancient conundrum of a God who is both all-powerful and all-loving'[45] which even today often leaves orthodox Christians at a loss for an answer.

Yet 'most of us today', comments another modern theologian, 'have travelled far enough from Augustine and Calvin to believe that the heavenly Father of Jesus' teaching *wants* to save all men. We can no longer accept the dark doctrine of double predestination with its negation of the central Christian message of the love of God.'[46] Of course, John Hick is not referring specifically here to the Pelagian controversy but is making his comment in the context of a summary of evidence supporting universalism. Nevertheless, his comment is still valid, as is the particular reference to Augustine. Norman Pittenger too, remarking on the failure of early theologians properly to understand the movement of Hebrew religion away from 'primitive Yahwism' to a vision of God as 'the power that makes for righteousness' and its consequent stress on the divine *chesed* or 'faithful loving-mercy', describes the conventional model of God (with Whitehead) as 'ruthless moralism'.[47] He notes also how often some of the greatest theologians in the history of the Church seem to have a dual personality – the one side of it revealing deep faith in God and insistence on his loving care and gracious concern for creation, the other a totally different theological aspect insisting on 'absoluteness, unrelatedness, unchangeableness, and impassibility or inability to share in the world's anguish'. 'Of course', he adds, 'the assertion of God's love is never denied, but it is given a secondary (or adjectival) place.' And his prime example of this dichotomy is none other than Augustine, 'the doctor of the divine love'.[48]

There are also modern philosophers writing about theology who are just as suspicious of the (mainly Catholic) view that Augustine's theory of predestination was never in danger of abolishing the freedom of the human will. In his discussion of theological determinism John Lucas notes that 'theologians are insufficiently reluctant to contradict themselves, and have often taken unwholesome delight in invoking human freedom to explain away evil, and denying it in order to attribute all good to God.'[49] After describing Augustine as 'the most theocentric of all the fathers', he contrasts his explicit statement that man does have free will, for example, in his treatise *On Free Will*, with his later attitude in his controversy with Pelagius, when 'he came to

[44] Pittenger, 15f.
[45] Toynbee, 79. As L. Dewart, 191, comments: 'An omnipotent God would differ from Zeus only in that his bolts had an infinite voltage.'
[46] Hick, 1976, 250.
[47] Pittenger, 13f.
[48] Ibid., 15.
[49] Lucas, 1970, 76.

hold a position in which human freedom has no part to play', because 'the whole tendency of his mind was to attribute everything to God'. Elsewhere he approves of Augustine's insistence that 'not unto him should be ascribed the glory, but unto God' but also of Pelagius' protest that the language used by Augustine, 'if taken literally, denied the manhood of God's children and, in allowing them no mind of their own, put them on a par with sticks and stones'.[50] In other words, 'in forcing man into his kingdom God would have turned the human thou into an it.'[51]

Perhaps the hypothetical objection to quoting from a selection of contemporary students of theology which was made earlier may appear to have been sustained and justified, now that the citations have been paraded for inspection, and we may be reminded of Wittgenstein's advice: 'Whereof one cannot speak thereof one must be silent.'[52] However, our last witness, also a contemporary philosopher, John Rist, cannot possibly be accused of having approached this problem without the necessary degree of objectivity. His contribution to a collection of critical essays on Augustine's philosophy immediately follows a logical analysis by William L. Rowe of Augustine's answer to the character given the name Evodius in the treatise *On Free Will*: 'Since God knew that man would sin, that which God foreknew must necessarily come to pass. How then is the will free when there is apparently this unavoidable necessity?'[53] We are thus brought back by the circling wheel to the question which worried Chaucer, and Rowe formulates it as follows: 'how it is possible both that we voluntarily (freely) will to perform certain actions and that God foreknows that we shall will to perform these actions.'[54] By a process of logic Rowe concludes that Augustine did not succeed in solving the problem of how God's foreknowledge is compatible with free will, the problem, that is to say, which Augustine has made Evodius pose. The subject to which Rist addresses himself is related to this and he attacks it not by means of logic alone but through an exhaustive examination of Augustine's statements on predestination and its relation to free will. He stresses at the outset the danger of pulling contrary opinions out of such a large corpus of writings and of hiding behind the ambiguity of a word like 'freedom', 'now almost a meaningless term' – though not meaningless for Augustine even if 'it did not carry the same emotional overtones as those with which we are familiar'.[55]

No brief summary can do justice to the incisiveness of Rist's argument but we can at least try to indicate the main lines which it takes. After explaining Augustine's doctrine of the nature of the human will upon which his theory of free choice is based, Rist reaches the crucial question whether Augustine's

[50] Lucas, 1976, 1.

[51] Hick, 1976, 243.

[52] Or, in another, less poetic version: 'What can be said at all can be said clearly, and what we cannot talk about we must pass over in silence' (*Tractatus Logico-Philosophicus* 2, Pref., translated by D. F. Pears and B. F. McGuinness, London 1971).

[53] *FC* III, ii. 4 (PL 32, 1272) (CSEL 74, 92f.).

[54] Rowe, 209f.

[55] Rist, 219f.

predestination is twofold, some being predestined to salvation, others to damnation. He quotes the definition of predestination given in the treatise *On the Gift of Perseverance* as a foreknowledge and 'preparation' by God of those acts of kindness by which those who are to be saved are saved, which suggests that, though all those who are saved are saved by God's acts of kindness, it does not follow that all those who are offered such acts of kindness are in fact saved: 'the distinction between positively willing something and being willing to let something happen' is thus one of which Augustine is conscious. But there are passages in which this formal definition 'does not seem to cover his position',[56] since elsewhere he refers to 'predestination to death',[57] 'the hardening of men's hearts' so that they are able to commit sin,[58] and 'predestination to punishment'.[59] Such references do not by themselves provide proof positive that double determination is intended, only perhaps that God *may* allow sin and damnation to take place. Even the notorious sentence taken up by the Jansenists as their trump card against Molinism is open to different interpretations: when Augustine writes that 'assistance is given to the weakness of the human will so that by divine grace it might be *unchangeably and invincibly* influenced in its action',[60] he would appear to be indicating that such grace cannot be resisted. But it has been argued – for example, by Mother Mary Clark – that the true meaning is that it is the will which, through grace, is irresistible, and she, like Rist, points out that Augustine never uses the adjective *irresistibilis* or *insuperabilis* to describe grace itself – does he use these adjectives at all?[61] Nevertheless, Rist concludes that 'such an interpretation is almost certainly incorrect': in this passage as in all of Augustine's works written after 396/7 'man is not even able to accept or reject whatever graces may or may not be offered to him'.[62] Although Augustine could have used material which was to hand so as to develop a theory establishing the priority of grace and the 'preparation' of man's will without denying him the ability to use that will to accept or reject the divine call, he deliberately chose not to do so; 'all men are thus "free", the elect from serious sins, the damned from virtue.'[63]

At this point we might well sympathise with Pelagius and be willing to forgive him if, from his place in heaven or hell or limbo or chained for all eternity to a rock in the Caucasus like that earlier 'heretic' Prometheus, he were to throw back at his old adversary the gibe that the latter once hurled at him: 'Either I do not understand what he means or he does not himself.'[64] We might also go farther and, with some justification, claim that the responsibility for the length and bitterness of the Pelagian controversy can be attributed as

[56] Ibid., 227.
[57] *SO* IV, xi. 16 (PL 44, 533) (CSEL 60, 395f.).
[58] *GFC* xxiii. 45 (PL 44, 910f.).
[59] *E* xxvi. 100 (PL 40, 244f.).
[60] *RG* xii. 38 (PL 44, 940).
[61] Clark, 108ff.
[62] Rist, 239.
[63] Ibid., 241.
[64] *NG* xlvi. 55 (PL 44, 273) (CSEL 60, 273).

much to Augustine's change of front in his understanding of predestination and election as to Pelagius' obduracy in pressing his case for the human will. Having decided that it was not enough to maintain that man could win salvation by freely accepting God's freely given grace, Augustine proceeded to evolve a theory of predestination which ultimately depended on a causal connection between man's sin and Adam's fall – between 'man's first disobedience' and 'the fruit'. As early as the Second Council of Orange the Church found it necessary to tone down his more extreme view of pre-destination, even while accepting the general principle of original sin. And that principle, in turn, was to be re-examined and considerably modified, if not altered out of all recognition, in the Middle Ages.

It has been suggested that if Augustine had been able to jettison his views on infant damnation and if he had not misinterpreted the biblical text that 'God wishes all men to be saved', he might have found it possible to 'develop an understanding of grace and predestination quite different from that usually associated with him'; he would then have been doing 'what many Christian thinkers of all persuasions have done in recent times'.[65] But his theology was a seamless robe, woven closely together in the course of a long life of reflection and controversy, and to suppose that this piece or that could be removed from the whole without damage to the remainder would be to misunderstand the nature of the man himself and of his involvement in the Church of his day. No less than Pelagius, he was a child of his own times, and it was his historical rôle to take ideas which had already been aired and were still being debated by others and to mould them into a comprehensive system acceptable to the African Church as he knew it and to the Christian Church as he wanted it to be, making them 'correlative members of a vast intellectual scheme' and thus adding 'a whole area to the domain of systematic theology'.[66] Within this system his concept of original sin was a close companion of his doctrine of grace, and both were, in his firmly held view, inseparable from his theory of predestination. But such a system, as even one of his most sympathetic interpreters among contemporary Augustinian scholars admits, 'is too legalistic and lacking in charity to reconcile with the continual emphasis laid by Augustine himself on the supernatural virtue of charity, from which the God of his predestinarian writings seems to be wonderfully immune'.[67] And the same scholar goes on to point out that 'Augustinian

[65] TeSelle, 1970, 330.
[66] N. P. Williams, 1930, 19.
[67] Bonner, 1963, 390. But, notwithstanding his reservations as to Augustine's views on predestination, Bonner, 1986(a), 385, in his conclusion to a discussion of Augustine's conception of deification has rightly reminded us that 'predestination is, however, too fundamental to Augustine's mature theology, and too much a part of the heritage of Western Christian theology, to be ignored in serious ecumenical debate. If East and West are to come to a common theological mind, as opposed to publishing agreed statements of doctrine, the issues raised by the doctrines of deification and predestination have alike to be faced, and are not lightly to be dismissed as being, in the one case, unchristian, and in the other as being the rationalisation of the mystery of human freedom and divine grace.' See also his n. 64 on the danger involved in attempting to rationalise the differences between Pelagius and Augustine, which 'fails to do justice to Pelagius, still less to Augustine'.

predestination is not the doctrine of the Church but only the opinion of a distinguished Catholic theologian'.[68] But let us allow N. P. Williams the last word on the subject: 'The conception of Grace as Power, with its logically necessary context of an apparently arbitrary predestinarianism, seems to dissolve away the moral character of God and sublimates Him into a non-moral Absolute, to Whom, or Which, it is useless to cry for mercy or help.'[69] As it turned out, Augustine's obsession with predestination was just as open to criticism as Pelagius' obduracy in defending the freedom of the will, and Pelagius had every justification for resisting it.

[68] Ibid., 392. As Wermelinger, 196, points out, none of the canons of the Council of Carthage in 418 goes into the matter of Augustine's doctrine of predestination, and we shall observe in c. 6 the disturbing effect which its extreme expression in his letter to Sixtus, written in the same year (*L* 194) (PL 33, 874–91) (CSEL 57, 176–214), had upon the monks of Hadrumetum and the objections raised by the Semi-Pelagians when they too found that this novel doctrine threatened to depreciate the proper exercise of free will. By the time he came to formulate his charges against the Pelagians for the last time in 428 in his treatise *On the Heresies* addressed to Quodvultdeus his formulation employs the same material as earlier versions but the perspective has entirely altered: in *H* 88 (PL 33, 47–50) predestination as the logical basis for the absolute gratuity of grace directs his entire presentation of Pelagian ideas. Wermelinger, 282, rightly describes this abbreviated version of the Pelagian heresy as unhistorical and capable of being correctly grasped only if we compare it with earlier abbreviated versions in *TLP* IV, vii. 19 (PL 44, 622f.) (CSEL 60, 542), in *J* III, i. 2 (PL 44, 702f.) and in *GP* ii. 4 (PL 45, 996). Augustine's last word on predestination as an item in his indictment of the Pelagians is to be found in his letter to Vitalis, Bishop of Carthage, written around 427 (PL 33, 984f.) (CSEL 57, 414–16), 'an excellent resumé of his struggle against the Semi-Pelagians' (Portalié, 191), in which he once again emphasises that grace is not given to all but to those to whom God wills to give it, that is, the elect. His opponents might well have reacted by quoting, if they had been able to do so, Spurgeon's perhaps somewhat irreverent 'prayer': 'Lord, hasten to bring in thine elect and then elect some more'!

[69] N. P. Williams, 1930, 6.

51

IV

PECULIAR GRACE

'It was through one man that sin entered the world, and through sin death, and thus death pervaded the whole human race, inasmuch as all men have sinned.'
Romans 5, 12[1]

'God bless us all, this was peculiar grace.'
EDMUND BLUNDEN[2]

In his frank and deeply moving autobiography Harry Williams recounts a nightmare which, though he did not grasp its significance at the time, turned out to be of 'fundamental importance' and pointed the way to his understanding of the spiritual problem which tormented him and to his entry into the Community of the Resurrection at the age of fifty. He dreamt that he was watching a play in a theatre when something prompted him to turn round and look behind him towards the back of the auditorium; there he saw a human monster, unseen by the players and the rest of the audience, engaged in hypnotising the players so that their every word and action resulted from his dictation and they 'were in fact no more than the servile creatures of the monstrous all-powerful hypnotist'.[3] Regardless of their doom, the little victims played!

The monster was human, and Williams does not suggest that his nightmare is an allegory applicable to the general situation of humanity. But one is immediately reminded in the present context of Passmore's examiner, who sets the papers and 'not only knows how many are to pass but has already determined *who* is to pass' and yet punishes the rest for their failure, and of N. P. Williams's telepathic chess-player, 'who not merely foresees all the other player's moves, but actually himself makes them . . . and consequently has won the game before it has even begun'.[4] Is one not reminded too of the God of Augustine's theory of predestination? No, its defenders will reply: Augustine's God is no malevolent hypnotist, no Svengali, but the playwright himself in disguise, employing a benign and appropriate form of therapy which gently induces his actors to play the rôles assigned to them as they

---

[1] *NEB*, Harmondsworth 1964, *The New Testament*, 251f.

[2] *Poems 1914–30*, London 1930, 'Report on Experience', 284.

[3] H. A. Williams, 1984, 147. An earlier version of this story appeared in his contribution to a series of lectures delivered in the University of Cambridge in 1963 and edited by A. R. Vidler (H. A. Williams, 1963, 52ff.). But there the man who had the dream is described as 'a person of some academic intelligence . . . a devout and rather high Anglican', and the monster as 'the god he was really worshipping', which makes the citation even more relevant to the present context.

[4] See c. III, 44, n. 28.

should be played and so not to ruin a performance which would be perfect if it were not for their blunders, while at the same time enabling them fully to realise their own potential. But what if they fail to come up to scratch? Well, that is their fault, not the playwright's, and they should be grateful to him for having given them the chance to show what they can do. Unfair to Augustine? Possibly, but was he 'fair' to Pelagius, and was his God 'fair' to his creatures?

In this connection it may be of use to recall the judgement which Jung once passed on Freud: 'He was a great man and, what is more, a man in the grip of his daimon.'[5] Augustine too could be said to have been in the grip of his daimon, a daimon residing in his lifelong preoccupation with evil as revealed in human sinfulness, and it survived him to cast its shadow over the subsequent history of the Christian Church in the West through the immense influence of his writings. To quote Harry Williams's recollection of the view of Christian thinkers held by a much-loved colleague: 'St Augustine took the worst of St Paul, and Calvin the worst of St Augustine.'[6] It was Paul's teaching on grace that provided Augustine with the foundation of his own much more comprehensive and sophisticated doctrine; but he carried his interpretation of that teaching to limits which left him with a theory of predestination unacceptable to the majority of later theologians – though not to Calvin, who proceeded to carry it even farther. Augustine must bear a major part of the blame for the kind of absurd situations in which Christians get involved when they try to reconcile the goodness of God with the evil of his creation, leaving us often with a picture of 'a God who is half Genghiz Khan and half St Francis'.[7] For example, in the wake of the disaster to York Minster a leader in *The Times* bore the heading 'Act of God', while on another page the Archbishop of Canterbury was reported to have repeated the words of a fire officer, 'The Lord was on our side as we battled against the flames'![8] Evidence of a split personality? Not at all: just a classic illustration of the Augustinian God's practice of tempering justice with mercy.

Yet readers of Jung will know that his judgement of Freud was not intended to be wholly adverse,[9] and our judgement of Augustine would be totally lacking in balance if we were to concentrate solely on his unhappy theory of predestination, neglecting the positive, countervailing merits of his doctrine of grace. The great strength of this doctrine lay in his realisation through personal experience and subsequent reflection of the power of God's love working in us for good; its great weakness resulted from his determination to objectify, even hypostatise, that power and to direct it towards the quasi-juridical correction and vicarious punishment of mankind for a mythical

---

[5] Jung, 176.

[6] H. A. Williams, 1984, 156.

[7] Toynbee, 79.

[8] 11 July 1984; needless to say, the leader and report provoked a long and revealing correspondence in later issues and were to be linked later with 'theological' discussions of the famine in Ethiopia.

[9] Elsewhere (389) he describes himself as also 'in the grip of a daimon', and this is apparently a characteristic of 'a creative person . . . captive and driven by his daimon'.

crime of which it was innocent, thus making man responsible for the fallibility of God's world. Whether or not we are prepared to accept such a damaging criticism of one of the greatest of the Christian Fathers will depend to a great extent on our own theological stance. Some will remain so convinced of the validity of his definition of true freedom, his *libertas* or *libertas maior*, 'the glorious liberty of the sons of God', that they will be prepared to overlook, even justify, the patent defects of his theory of predestination and their consequences for his doctrine of grace; others will find his theory of predestination so flawed that they begin to suspect his doctrine of grace, indeed his entire theodicy, as well. But one thing is certain: the relationship of human freedom to divine grace was the crucial issue on which Augustine and Pelagius differed. Never in the history of philosophical and theological controversy can two protagonists have argued with greater sincerity and conviction about an issue of such fundamental importance not only to the theoretical discussions of philosophers and theologians but also to the religious life of the mass of ordinary men and women. Yet Augustine claimed all along to be as passionate a defender of human freedom as Pelagius, refusing to admit that the debate was between freedom and determinism. Pelagius, on the other hand, was just as adamant in insisting that it was.

If we were able to employ a time-machine to transport them to the late twentieth century, where would Pelagius and Augustine take up their stand in the perennial debate between free will and determinism? Given time to familiarise themselves with the nuances of contemporary terminology, they might well be inclined to apply to each other respectively the labels of 'existentialist' and 'theological determinist'. Pelagius might well add to his eclectic repertoire of citations from his authorities one from John Macquarrie summarising Sartre's view that 'if God has already laid down what humanity is to become, then freedom is an illusion'.[10] Augustine, for his part, might well rejoin by adapting a sentence from the same paragraph to support his claim that human freedom, as defined by Pelagius, was incompatible with the existence of God, because it made insufficient allowance for the operation of his grace. And Pelagius would not be slow to counter the label of 'existentialist' pinned upon him by his adversary with another quotation from the same author: 'But it is with St Augustine that we come to the most powerfully existentialist presentation of Christianity since St Paul, and one that has been of such enduring significance that even today existentialists, Christian and non-Christians alike, acknowledge an affinity with the great North African scholar.'[11]

But if they were to continue to play Augustine's game of answering every quotation made by Pelagius with one of his own, the former would certainly come out best in finding support for his basic tenet that all human exercise of free will is subject to restrictions. Even in Macquarrie, whose reference to his

---

[10] Macquarrie, 1982, 15.
[11] Macquarrie, 1973, 47.

alleged influence on existentialists he would regard as less than complimentary, he could turn up the statement that 'Even if we accept that there is a genuine human freedom, this freedom occurs within a setting that is already determined',[12] and following his normal practice of extending the range of his authorities to those whom he might consider to be more 'orthodox', he might supplement this by a quotation from Pannenberg: 'The principle of individual freedom is not a self-evident fact of human nature.'[13] And, finally and with a gesture of triumph, he would pounce upon another pronouncement by the same theologian in a different work: 'Man's freedom requires a religious basis. Freedom only grows from participation in absolute truth, from the human being's bond with the divine mystery of his life.'[14]

Fortunately for them perhaps, Augustine and Pelagius were not in a position to foresee that their main bone of contention would be gnawed at by their epigoni for centuries to come and from angles and directions so numerous that it would be in danger of being obscured altogether. It would be kinder at this point to reverse the action of our time-machine and return our combatants, not a little bewildered at the way in which the term 'freedom' has been turned into an indispensable weasel-word of the twentieth century, to the age to which they belonged and a theological milieu which they understood. Augustine's theory of predestination, however important and however relevant to his interpretation of human freedom, is only one of a package of related issues during the course of the Pelagian controversy. We must now turn to two others, which he considered to be of equal importance in his controversy with Pelagius – original sin and baptism, both of them issues over which there had already been no lack of disagreement among the Fathers of the Church and between East and West, both of them essential ingredients of the Augustinian doctrine of grace and of the teaching of the Church on salvation and redemption.

When Augustine set about the task of constructing his theory of original sin, there was a substantial store of materials to hand. For scriptural foundation he turned, as ever, to Paul and, in particular, to Romans 5, 12–21. But Paul did not work in a theological vacuum; from popular Jewish thought he would have inherited two different accounts of the Fall of Man in Genesis 3 and 6. The first of these was not the historical source of the doctrine of the Fall, which had emerged in the post-exilic thought of the Jews as they reflected on the actual sin which they experienced within and around them and, seeking to find an explanation of its existence in a world originally created good, fastened upon the narrative contained in Genesis 6. This account had been ousted in time by the alternative version in Genesis 3 with its hint of a link between sin and sexual awareness, 'the first emergence of a *motif* which runs through much of Christian Fall-speculation'.[15] The story of

[12] Macquarrie, 1982, 18.
[13] Pannenberg, 1977(b), 18.
[14] Pannenberg, 1977(a), 47, summarising Hegel's conception of freedom.
[15] N. P. Williams, 1927, xii; cf. 34, 45, 58.

Adam and Eve in Genesis 3, however, does not contain a reference to original sin as such nor does it depict them as 'originally righteous' in the sense in which this has come to be understood. Both of these ideas may well have germinated and developed in the popular religious thought of the pre-Christian period and, combined with Genesis 3, could have produced, in the view of Williams, a doctrine of the Fall showing Adam's fall as resulting not only in human mortality but also in an inherited tendency to do evil (original sin) and an imputed responsibility for it (original guilt). Paul might have seen this possibility, and he may also have known of the idea found in Rabbinical teaching and variously described as 'the evil impulse, inclination, disposition or imagination'.[16] If so, then he chose to use the idea in such a way as to alter its original meaning by making it the effect, and not the cause, of Adam's sin and locating it not in the 'heart' but in the 'flesh' as unreservedly evil.

In fact, however, it is the story in Genesis 3 which forms the main basis of Paul's teaching on original sin, and he has nothing to say about original guilt or original righteousness. In 1 Corinthians 15, 21 and 22 he is concerned solely with the origin of physical death in Adam's sin and does not discuss the question of hereditary sinfulness. But in Romans 5, 12–21 he sees Adam's sin not only as the origin of physical death but also as the origin of sin, and Adam's descendants as infected with sinfulness by some mysterious means which he does not attempt to explain. This crucial passage is notoriously difficult to follow, let alone to interpret, but its main concern is surely not to elucidate the origin of human death and sin in Adam – Paul takes these as axiomatic – but to emphasise that the law has proved to be counter-productive as an antidote to them and that the only remedy is the redemption of man through baptism and membership of Christ. 'Here, at last, we have in fully developed shape, albeit stated without scholastic preciseness of definition, that momentous doctrine of the Fall and the Redemption as correlative conceptions, as twin pillars bearing up the fabric of Christian soteriology.'[17]

Thus Paul identifies the source of death and sin as the Fall of Adam and insists that the inbred disease in man which resulted resided in his 'flesh' or 'members' as an impulse to evil curable only by the grace offered to man by the redemptive act of Jesus. But, of course, he left many questions unanswered, since he was not engaged in writing theological monographs but in addressing letters of rebuke, advice or encouragement to different congregations as the need arose. And so the early Fathers did not inherit from him an unambiguous doctrine of original sin, and the evidence shows that they did not give it serious consideration: according to one authority, 'In all the writings of the Apostolic Fathers the name of Adam occurs but once, and the Earthly Paradise and the fatal tree are not mentioned at all.'[18] Nor did the Greek

[16] Cohen, 496ff., discusses a medieval attempt to identify the 'evil inclination' with original sin in the Thomist sense, and K. Armstrong, 61, comments: 'In Judaism sin is a regrettable fact of life, but not a matter for desperation. Everybody sins but God will forgive.' She also reminds us that the 'evil impulse' is a source of much that is good and creative.

[17] N. P. Williams, 1927, 131.

[18] G. Boas, *Essays on Primitivism and Related Ideas in the Middle Ages*, Baltimore 1948, 15 – a reference I owe to Passmore, 87 and 341, n. 43.

Fathers give it a high priority in their debate and speculations, though generally accepting Pauline teaching on the subject in a vague manner and without closer re-examination. Indeed, neither the Fall nor original sin appears to be mentioned in local baptismal creeds or even in the Nicene creed; for a genuinely Catholic doctrine of both we must apparently go back to the New Testament and Paul.[19]

It was Irenaeus in the second century who first produced a systematic explanation of these subjects in the course of his counter-attack on Gnosticism but his theodicy, far from being a deliberate attempt to develop Paul's teaching, encouraged a much more optimistic view of man. For him, man's rôle is not that of one created perfect only to fall into sin but of one brought into being with all the imperfections endemic in human nature but with the prospect of development as a part of God's creative plan into the divine 'likeness' revealed to him in Jesus. The emphasis here is not on a Fall in the past but upon a growth in the future, and the Irenaean theodicy was later to find many supporters from Nemesius of Emesa and Theodore of Mopsuestia in the fourth and early fifth centuries to Schleiermacher in the eighteenth and nineteenth. There are many echoes of it in modern theology too but, *vis-à-vis* Augustinianism, it was never more than 'a minority report'.[20]

In his massive Bampton Lectures N. P. Williams distinguishes between the two classical versions of the Fall-doctrine which appear in the first four centuries of the Church by categorising them as the 'Hellenic, once-born or minimising' and the 'African, twice-born or maximising', and he traces the first clear sign of a bifurcation to Origen and Tertullian, when they reacted in different ways to the Gnostic threat in the late second and early third centuries. In his first, more optimistic interpretation, which he specifically declares to be no more than speculation and certainly not intended as dogmatic, Origen dismisses the story of Adam and Eve as 'a pictorial façade'[21] and the Fall-doctrine as an inference from Christian reflection on the phenomenon of evil. But in his later writings he tends to juxtapose with this another, more sombre version after being introduced to the practice of infant baptism at Caesarea, rightly perceiving, as many others signally failed to do after him, that the rite preceded the doctrine at least in fact, if not in thought: children were not baptised because of original sin, rather original sin explained why infant baptism was so important. And, in his later view, 'the conception

---

[19] Kelly, 1978, 351, however, finds that there was in the Greek Fathers 'the outline of a real theory of original sin', though it fell short of Augustinianism. 'The Fathers', he goes on, 'might well have filled it in and given it greater sharpness of definition had the subject been directly canvassed in their day.'

[20] Hick, 1983, 97. Beatrice, 1978, 206f., 306 (summary), links Melito with Irenaeus as a supporter of this 'more moderate opinion'. But de Simone, 209, recalls the statement of Daniélou, 1973, II, 404f., that Irenaeus does retain the idea of original sin as the cause of the bondage in which men find themselves as a result of Adam's first sin but presents the latter as 'in the highest degree excusable'; in technical terms, this is the distinction between *peccatum originale originatum*, on the one hand, and *peccatum originale originans*, on the other.

[21] N. P. Williams, 1927, 215.

of original guilt creeps in by the side of original sin'.[22] From being regarded as a weakness, not a disease, or, in more technical terms, as a *privatio*, not a *depravatio*, original sin becomes a more positive kind of pollution having physical consequences with guilt attached to them. But, while emphasising the importance of infant baptism, Origen still sees it as only one step in the process of salvation and assigns a higher priority to the baptism of the Spirit.

N. P. Williams maintains that it was Tertullian who first laid the foundation of an African doctrine of original sin as a form of positive corruption, derived from Adam and transmitted thereafter from parent to child, a hereditary handicap for which he coined the phrase *originis vitium*:[23] he was thus the founder of the theory of traducianism through the physical act of procreation, based on his materialistic view of the soul and on the idea of 'seminal identity'; but he did not go so far as to evolve an explicit doctrine of original guilt, and he held firmly to the view that infant baptism was an unnecessary, possibly even an objectionable, practice in view of the danger of post-baptismal sin. Cyprian, the second of the great African Fathers, took the doctrine a stage further by combining the hereditary infection by sin with redemption from that sin through baptism and therefore stressed the utmost importance of baptism as early as possible, suggesting that original sin might be linked with original guilt. But, fifty years after the appearance of Williams's Bampton Lectures, we have learned to be wary of being tempted to follow him too far in his search for an 'African' origin of the definitive Augustinian statement of the doctrine of original sin and hereditary guilt. It is true that, in appealing to tradition for support in his defence of the essential orthodoxy of his own views on the subject in his treatise *On the Merits and Forgiveness of Sins and Infant Baptism* in 412, Augustine cites Cyprian as his main authority; but he also relies heavily on Jerome and the scriptures in pressing his point that Pelagius is wrong in arguing that original sin is not an article of the true Christian faith.

Had he chosen to do so, he could also have found support in the Greek Fathers for at least some of his tenets: there were brave men before Agamemnon, and there were defenders of original sin before Augustine, Jerome and even Cyprian. In his book *Tradux Peccati* the Italian theologian Beatrice traces the source of the doctrine to territories unexplored by Augustine or, for that matter, N. P. Williams – 'Encratite circles, which were widespread in Egypt in the second half of the second century, and of which Julius Cassianus was an authoritative exponent'. He claims that the doctrine then spread to African and Latin Christianity and that Tertullian, Cyprian,

---

[22] Ibid., 220ff. More recently, J. W. Trigg, 111, describes Origen's theodicy as 'a vision of extraordinary moral grandeur and perhaps as satisfactory a solution, from the perspective of faith, to the problem of theodicy as has ever been suggested'. In 272, n. 31, he finds it 'curious that Hick, 1966, does not deal with Origen, who exemplifies far better than Irenaeus himself the "Irenaean" theodicy'.

[23] *On the Soul*, 41 (PL I, 2, 764). Augustine does not use the phrase *originale peccatum* in his earlier anti-Pelagian works, e.g. *MFS* and *SL*; there he prefers *delictum*. But by the second Council of Carthage *originale peccatum* has become firmly established in Africa and appears in its second canon.

Hilarius, Ambrosiaster and Ambrose all tried to reconcile it with the need to safeguard traditional teachings on creation, marriage and free will. Their successors were left with 'an unresolved antinomy', which Augustine and Pelagius set about trying to resolve in their different ways with the result that both sides in the controversy were forced to adopt extreme positions and 'it was only by dint of extremely refined conceptual acrobatics, with very fine distinctions, did Augustine succeed in proclaiming his allegiance to orthodoxy'.

The present writer lacks the qualifications to assess the evidence presented by Beatrice with the thoroughness which it merits, and Beatrice himself admits that he advances his novel theory with caution in view of the fragmentary nature of the texts employed, which are frequently difficult to decipher. But, notwithstanding this frank admission and the severe drubbing to which Beatrice has been subjected by some scholars, notably R. J. De Simone, if he were right, then the seeds of the doctrine of original sin would have been sown in the East as early as the end of the second century and transplanted from there to Africa and the West by the early third.

For the next development we must look to the writer whose commentary on the Pauline Epistles – omitting Hebrews, still regarded as non-Pauline by the West – is 'generally acknowledged to be the most impressive literary and historical study of those writings prior to the Renaissance'.[24] His precise identity remains uncertain: the name by which we know him, 'Ambrosiaster', was coined by Erasmus and reminds us that his works were long ascribed to Ambrose; but Augustine, who was greatly influenced by his reading of them, referred to him as 'sanctus Hilarius',[25] and many today prefer to describe him as 'Hilarius', though Augustine almost certainly confused this 'Hilarius' with Hilary of Poitiers. In his commentary on the Epistles Augustine found, *inter alia*, a convenient mistranslation of Romans 5, 12 which gave him a scriptural proof-text for 'original guilt': the Greek text meaning 'for that all men sinned' (AV and RV) or 'inasmuch as all men have sinned' (NEB) was incorrectly rendered as 'in whom, i.e. Adam, all men sinned'.[26] 'The fatal legacy was received only too gladly'[27] but it is doubtful if 'Ambrosiaster' had the slightest intention of using his mistranslation in this way, since he, like the Greek Fathers, took it to mean that, while Adam's sin brought physical death to men, it was their own sins that condemned them to a second 'death' in Hell. This is clearly not a doctrine of original guilt or even of original sin, but by his error in translation 'Ambrosiaster' made a significant, if unwitting, contribu-

[24] TeSelle, 1970, 157.

[25] *TLP* IV, iv. 7 (PL 44, 614) (CSEL 60, 528); on Augustine and Ambrosiaster see Beatrice, 159–73.

[26] The Vulgate also gives us *in quo omnes peccaverunt*, a literal rendering of the Septuagint leading to the erroneous interpretation in the first place; but the relative *quo* is too far from its supposed antecedent *unum hominem* to justify such an interpretation – except in the eyes of one who was searching for support in the scriptures for a theory of original sin, as Augustine was. At first, he had taken *quo* as referring to Adam or to sin but then realised that the Greek word for 'sin' was feminine: thus his alternative explanation in *MFS* I, x. 11 (PL 44, 115f.) came to be superseded by his definitive version in *TLP* IV, iv. 7 (PL 44, 614).

[27] N. P. Williams, 1927, 309.

CAMROSE LUTHERAN COLLEGE LIBRARY

tion to the ongoing debate. Ambrose was the first of the Latin Fathers to give unequivocal expression to a doctrine of original righteousness, and at the same time as Gregory of Nyssa, an admirer both of Plotinus and of Origen and 'the first Christian philosopher',[28] was propagating it in the East. For Ambrose, however, this original righteousness did not entirely disappear with the fall of Adam; rather it weakened with each succeeding generation until it died out altogether. Yet, notwithstanding his opposition to traducianism, which he shared with 'Ambrosiaster', he holds the view that the human race *was* identified with Adam, and he makes several references to original sin as an inherited bias to evil and, at least once, to original guilt; but for him, like 'Ambrosiaster', our punishment is the result of our own sins, for which the only remedy is baptism.

All these ideas were in circulation and under discussion at the time when Augustine set himself to produce his own blueprint for a doctrine of original sin. He had already been 'moving steadily away from the metaphysical aspects of the problem of evil, and the academic questions they raised, towards a preoccupation with practical and pastoral aspects which became far more important for him in the last decades of his life'.[29] He was now satisfied that evil was not a substance, a negative force engaged in perennial conflict with the power of positive good, but the privation of that good, to which all the evil in the world was attributable. At the human level sin, suffering and unhappiness were all products of the privation of good in the soul, a malfunction of the personality manifested in the failure of the human will as revealed in Adam's first sin. But the will was non-corporeal, and so Adam's sin must have been transmitted not through the body but the soul; any attempt to argue that 'original sin, lodged by inheritance in the body, moves, as it were, sideways, from the body into the soul' when the latter is created, would remove sin from the province of the will.[30] Such ideas were both erroneous and dangerous; but so was the Pelagian idea that man could avoid sin by the proper exercise of his own free will. There was an urgent need to correct this error by restating the catastrophic effect of Adam's fall on human nature. In the course of this restatement Augustine found it necessary to clarify and refine some of his own earlier ideas on original sin in the light of the intensive study which he had devoted to the story of Adam's fall in his *Literal Commentary on Genesis* during the years 401 to 414.

So, like Paul and many others after him, he returned to the Adam story in Genesis. Adam, he maintained, had sinned through pride, which led him to love himself more than his creator and, as a result, to misuse the free will which God had given him by allowing Eve to tempt him to disobey the divine command not to eat of the tree of the knowledge of good and evil despite a clear and unequivocal warning of the dire consequences. He then again succumbed to pride when he tried to place the whole blame on Eve instead of

[28] Sheldon-Williams, 456.
[29] G. R. Evans, 118f.
[30] Ibid., 125; Augustine is here refuting the errors of Vincentius Victor in *SO* I, vi. 6 (PL 44, 477f.) (CSEL 60, 307).

admitting his own guilt and begging for God's mercy. For his sin he was condemned to banishment from Eden, physical death and eternal punishment and his descendants to suffer the same punishment ever after by inheriting both the fatal flaw resulting from his sin and the guilt attached to it. This flaw, *vitium originis* or the sin of origin, was *concupiscentia carnis*, the sexual desire leading to intercourse, which by his sin he had lost the power to control through exercise of his will. Adam's sin thus brought disaster not only upon Adam himself but upon the whole human race, since the deterioration in his nature resulting from his fall was to be passed on to his descendants, who passed it on in their turn to theirs, so that all children are 'born in sin', except Jesus alone, who, not having been begotten and conceived 'after the flesh', was free from sin.[31] Furthermore, although baptism frees Christians from the guilt, *reatus*, attached to the original sin, even they continue to produce children infected with concupiscence by the act of procreation at the moment of conception:[32] the *reatus*, the guilt is counteracted by baptism but not the *actus* of that concupiscence, which remains inherent in human nature. Thus all men and women are born with a double inheritance, the concupiscence inherited from Adam's sin and the guilt which is remitted in baptism but which returns when the act is again committed.[33] By this clever distinction between the act and the guilt of sin Augustine was able to parry the Pelagians' claim that a baptised man freed from original sin by baptism ought to be able to beget children also free from original sin and so not in need of baptism to free them from it.[34]

Any brief summary of the Augustinian doctrine of original sin is bound to appear over-simplified and to run the risk of misleading the reader, and anyone who makes so bold as to essay such a summary is entitled to point out some of the difficulties involved in his self-imposed task. One of these is that he has to deal with a doctrine which, like many other Augustinian doctrines, was subjected to constant revision under pressure from critics demanding clarification of aspects of it which they seemed incapable of understanding. Another is that Augustine unfortunately left us no explicit definition of original sin: as he himself admits as early as 388 in a treatise written against the Manichees, 'nothing is more a matter of common knowledge as a subject to preach upon, nothing of a mystery to comprehend, than that old sin, *antiquum peccatum*[35] – and in all the years of controversy which followed and during which he struggled to unravel the mystery he found it either unnecessary or impossible to make good that deficiency. But enough has been said so far to enable us to identify the two components which are fundamental: they are concupiscence and seminal identity.

In Augustinian thought generally concupiscence is the human tendency to

---

[31] *J* V, xv. 52 (PL 44, 813). Thus for Augustine 'the only cure [for *concupiscentia*] is through Jesus', because he was born and lived without sin (Bonner, 1962, 310, citing *E* xli. 13) (PL 40, 252f.).

[32] *MC* I, xviii. 20, xix. 21 (PL 44, 425f.) (CSEL 42, 232f.).

[33] Ibid., I, xxvi. 29 (PL 44, 430) (CSEL 42, 241f.).

[34] *MFS* II, ix. 11, xxv. 39 (PL 44, 158, 175) (CSEL 60, 82f.).

[35] *MBC* I, xxii. 40 (PL 32, 1328).

turn away from the supreme good to the lesser goods of creation; it was the first sin, of which Adam was guilty by his disobedience, but it also contained within it the seeds of many other sins. Augustine lists the sins of concupiscence as pride, sacrilege, homicide, spiritual fornication, avarice and theft[36] but, in this connection, its chief manifestation is sexual desire, fed and watered by man's instinct to reproduce his species, in itself necessary, of course, but nevertheless of all forms of concupiscence 'the most violent and the least amenable to the commands of reason and of God'.[37] Adam's first sin was a sin of pride, attributable to concupiscence in its broadest sense of self-love or self-centredness; but it was to the concupiscence which resulted, *concupiscentia carnis* or sexual concupiscence, that his descendants were to be in thrall ever after: they formed the *massa damnati*, 'the lump of sin', and were condemned to remain there by God's judgement, unless they were released by his mercy. Concupiscence as sexual desire is both the original sin, the *peccatum* to which all are heirs, and the reciprocal penalty which it incurs, the *poena peccati*.[38]

Of these two Augustinian notions the first is easier to assimilate today, when we are accustomed to the idea of inherited defects in the human personality and may well be willing to accept that the defect inherent in original sin might qualify as one of them, since it is not an acquired characteristic or adaptive change in the Lamarckian, physical sense. But if, in these times of so-called enlightenment, we are no longer prepared to believe that a person named Adam ever existed, it would follow that there was no fall of Adam and that any defect of personality to which humanity may be prone is therefore the result not of a sin committed by 'the first man' but, along with other human tendencies, capacities and propensities, of our genetic inheritance: the story of the fall is 'not about Adam but about Man'.[39] As for the second notion – that all men are by inheritance liable to reciprocal punishment as a result of Adam's fall – this too is *a priori* untenable on grounds already given for rejecting the first. But, in fairness to Augustine, we are obliged to examine his reasons for holding this notion and not to dismiss it out of hand on grounds which he can hardly be blamed for not anticipating.

We find that his main justification was the mistranslated verse Romans 5, 12, supported by the reference to Levi in Hebrews 7, 9–10. From these two proof-texts he deduced that all men are 'in their fathers' loins' before conception and that all who have ever lived or will live in the future are 'infinitesimally minute portions of the Adam who sinned',[40] and so they participate prenatally in the primeval sin. He is thus able to find them guilty on two counts – of having 'sinned in Adam' and of possessing concupiscence as a result by seminal identity with Adam, an idea which he found, for example, in Ambrose but which had been hinted at earlier by Irenaeus, Origen and Tertullian. He also appeals to other scriptural passages, but we

[36] *E* xiii. 45 (PL 40, 254).
[37] N. P. Williams, 1927, 366.
[38] *MFS* II, xxii. 36 (PL 44, 173) (CSEL 60, 107f.).
[39] Lucas, 1976, 42.
[40] N. P. Williams, 1927, 372.

find that three of these are also mistranslations;[41] to tradition, but his triumphant demonstration of it to Julian somehow manages to omit reference to those of the Fathers who held views contrary to his own;[42] to established practices which featured in the rite of baptism and would be inexplicable if there were no original sin, such as insufflation, exorcism and renunciation of the devil, but this we can dismiss as a blatant *petitio principii*; and, finally, to the actual state of the contemporary world, which we might well prefer to explain in other ways more acceptable to the twentieth century.

Much has been written in recent years on the subject of Augustine's theory of sexuality and, in particular, the radical change which it underwent as he laboured to defend himself against the criticisms of the Pelagians and especially of Julian of Eclanum. Brown, for example, has drawn our attention to an important addition to the evidence for such a change contained in a letter, recently discovered and published by Divjak and written by Augustine around 420–1.[43] This letter is a part of his campaign to protect himself against the claim made by Julian and his supporters that he had condemned the urge to marry, *concupiscentia nuptiarum*, and to prove that his critics were themselves guilty of failing to make the vital distinction between this urge to marry and the urge of the flesh, *concupiscentia carnis*. The urge to marry had been blessed by God and was a human response to the need for social cohesion as supplied by the legitimate union of man and woman for the purpose of begetting children; *concupiscentia carnis*, on the other hand, the sexuality which all men had inherited in consequence of Adam's first sin, was asocial, and not even the Christian institution of marriage could entirely eradicate it. The institution of marriage was thus linked to the creation, the present nature of sexuality to the fall of Adam. The letter to Atticus reveals Augustine's anxiety to establish once and for all that his critics had misunderstood his teaching on sexuality and were totally mistaken in attributing to him a suggestion that it had originated with Adam's fall or had been inspired by the devil.

Adam's first sin was not a result of his sexuality: it was a capacity with which God had endowed him but which, as a result of his sin, he lost the power to control by use of his free will. Adam and Eve had not been created as asexual beings in an 'angelic' state only to slip from it into a more 'material' condition. Such an explanation of the fall of man had satisfied Christians for many generations and, at the time of his conversion, had seemed to Augustine too to be entirely acceptable; in 386 it had appealed to him, as it had to Ambrose and others, as a satisfactory model for the ascetic way of life. How

[41] His favourite texts are: Psalms 51, 5; Job 14, 4, 5 (Septuagint version); John 3, 5; Ephesians 2, 3; and, of course, Romans 5, 12.

[42] *J* I, vii. 30 (PL 44, 661): 'You are convicted of error from all sides; the great testimonies of the Saints are clearer than the light of day.' In I, vii. 34 (PL 44, 665) he appeals to the authority of Jerome, whose extensive knowledge of the scriptures and the Fathers he acknowledges, and in *MC* II, xii. 25 (PL 44, 450f.) he insists that 'it was not I who invented the theory of original sin, which the catholic faith has believed from ancient times'.

[43] No. 6 in Divjak's collection; see also H. Chadwick, 1983, 429. In trying to summarise the effect of this change on Augustine's theory of sexuality I have been greatly helped by Brown, 1983(a) and (b), and by Bonner, 1986(b), a very recent article of which he sent me an offprint with his customary kindness.

then had he come to reject it thirty years later on the grounds that it was an inadequate, even mistaken, explanation of human sexuality? The answer is to be found in the thorough re-examination to which he had subjected the evidence for Adam's fall in the course of writing the twelve books of his *Literal Commentary on Genesis*: this is the watershed in the history of his intellectual progress towards a definitive view of sexuality and its relation to marriage. His intensive study of the earlier chapters of Genesis led him to change his understanding of God's command to Adam and Eve to increase and multiply and replenish the earth, which he now interpreted literally, not allegorically as hitherto, and to advance a fresh view of Adam's sexuality in paradise. This new interpretation, adumbrated in his commentary on Genesis, was later to be expounded in full in the fourteenth book of his *City of God* as his considered view of the human condition and to be maintained and repeated until his death. Augustine had come to see human sexuality, *concupiscentia carnis*, no longer as a sin *tout court* but as a symptom of the malaise resulting from Adam's sin which had infected the human condition thereafter, rendering the whole of humanity subject to a reciprocal punishment from which it could gain remission only through the mercy and by the grace of God. Adam's sin was thus a paradigm of the sinfulness of mankind and its estrangement from the will of God, and human sexuality, *concupiscentia carnis*, the most revealing, though not the only, manifestation of its fallen state.

In constructing his doctrine of original sin over a period of years Augustine, as we have seen, did not begin with a *tabula rasa*: Cyprian, Ambrose and 'Ambrosiaster' can all be said to have at least suggested the idea of original guilt, the idea of concupiscence is found in Tertullian and that of seminal identity in Ambrose and others – and it may well be that the source of the doctrine is to be located in second-century Egypt. Augustine did not pluck his doctrine out of the air nor did he proceed to force a doctrine of his own invention on the African Church. His colleagues there had certainly by this time come to regard him as *'le grand porte-parole de la théologie africaine'*[44] but there was nothing to prevent them from opposing his views if they considered them to be extreme or even 'unorthodox'; instead, they gave him their unqualified support throughout the Pelagian controversy. As Bonner has pointed out, not only was Aurelius, Bishop of Carthage, enunciating an Augustinian doctrine of original sin as early as 411 at the Council of Carthage which condemned Celestius but more than two hundred African bishops reaffirmed it in the canons of the Council held in 418, the first two of which are *'un sommaire satisfiant des quatres premières thèses de 411'*.[45] There is thus an

[44] Bonner, 1967, 99.
[45] Ibid., 103. In his detailed analysis of the canons of 418 Wermelinger, 168, notes that the emphasis of the theological discussion underlying them has shifted since 411, only the first three now treating the connection between Adam's sin and inherited guilt. He also maintains (174) that the canons of 418 do not *sanction* the Augustinian theory of inherited sin as such (my emphasis) but, rather, provide no more than an answer to objections made to it by its opponents, omitting any reference to essential features of Augustine's thought on the subject such as the idea of 'corporative personality' and the connection between sin and *concupiscentia* and giving only a hint of Augustinian *reatus* or guilt (175).

element of continuity in their decisions which gives the lie to anyone trying to suggest that there had been a sudden change of front on the subject of original sin brought about by Augustine. Even if, as it has been argued,[46] Pope Zosimus in his *Epistola Tractoria* of 418 did see fit to water down the second canon of Carthage referring to the original guilt of unbaptised children, there is good reason to believe that the question of the damnation of infants dying unbaptised was a *theologoumenon*, a topic for theological discussion, not only in Africa but also in Italy and, possibly, in Gaul and Spain also before the Pelagian controversy had begun.[47]

The voices which gave assent to the nine canons of the Council of Carthage in 418 were those of the African bishops but the spirit which informed them was that of Augustine, and it is inconceivable that he would not have played a major rôle in formulating them or at least the last seven,[48] so closely do they correspond to the views which he had been expressing over and over again in the course of his debate with Pelagius. Nor is this surprising if we recall that the major points in his doctrine of original sin had already been aired as long ago as 396/7 in his reply to questions on the faith addressed to him by his old friend and adviser Simplicianus. It was to this treatise that he was to refer frequently in later years to support his contention that his teaching on grace and related topics had remained substantially consistent ever since the beginning of his episcopate. There we find his first use of the terms *originale peccatum*, *originalis reatus* and, taken from 'Ambrosiaster', *massa peccati*;[49] there too the ideas of concupiscence and original righteousness are adumbrated. Of course he will refine or elaborate upon the meaning of all these terms in the intervening years before the start of the Pelagian controversy. In those years he will go on to grapple afresh with his conception of the nature of man, to work out in detail his theory of predestination and to integrate them and weave them into the fabric of his definitive doctrine of grace.

In his analysis of Augustine's line of thought at this time, TeSelle takes up Sage's point that the term *originale peccatum* as used in the treatise *To Simplicianus* does not yet bear the full sense of '*péché originel*' as 'original sin' but signifies no more than '*péché d'origine*' or 'sin from the beginning', that is, of each individual life.[50] And he accepts that 'there is not yet a doctrine of

---

[46] Floëri, 1954, 755ff. Wermelinger's book *Rom und Pelagius* is essentially an attempt to answer the question raised by Floëri: to what extent does Zosimus in his *Tractoria* identify himself with the African doctrine of *tradux peccati*? His final conclusion (283ff.) is that there is no absolute certainty as to how far he (Zosimus) has moved towards it but considerable doubt as to whether he has accepted it in its full sense. In other words, his stance on the subject was, possibly deliberately, ambiguous; and on the subject of infant baptism the fragments of his *Tractoria* which have been preserved (PL 20, 693f.) leave open the question whether the sin which must be expiated in baptism is inherited. It goes without saying that, in the circumstances, his position was differently interpreted by the opposing sides in the subsequent debate about the correctness of the decision taken by Carthage and by Honorius, though it must be observed that neither ever appealed to Zosimus as an authority when recalling the decisive factors leading to the condemnation of Pelagius and Celestius.

[47] Refoulé, 1963(a), 49.

[48] Bonner, 1967, 103.

[49] *VQS* I, q. 1, 10; q. 2, 16, 20 (PL 40, 106, 121, 125).

[50] Sage, 1967, 212.

original sin' at least in the sense given to it in Augustine's later and final formulation, since the meaning of *originalis reatus* in the reply to the second question posed by Simplicianus has been misinterpreted. 'But now', he goes on, 'Augustine begins to think of man as captured by his first sin and becoming increasingly accustomed and addicted to them.'[51] Various shifts of emphasis are detected in this period and attributed to such factors as the influence of the Donatist controversy and, possibly, of the *Book of Rules* of the Donatist theologian Tyconius,[52] his extensive study of the works of Cyprian and the ever-present reminder of the teachings of his hero Ambrose provided by Paulinus of Milan, who had come to Carthage about 405 to write his biography of Ambrose and remained there to lead the attack on Celestius in 411. TeSelle even goes so far as to suggest that the 'decisive change' leading to Augustine's formulation of his definitive doctrine of original sin may be located in or around the year 406 not long after Paulinus' arrival in Africa.[53]

Niceties of this kind can safely be left to the professional theologians to discuss, even if it is unlikely that they will ever be resolved to everyone's satisfaction. But the general question of the credibility of the Augustinian doctrine of original sin is far too important to be entrusted to professionals alone, since many of them, while rejecting Augustine's mistaken attempt to base his arguments on the historicity of the myth of the Fall and Adam's first sin, still tend to defend the ultimate validity of the theory which resulted as a true description of the human condition and show great anxiety to save the baby when disposing of the bath-water. Hence, they still do their best to uncover the universal truth which they believe to be enshrined in it, its 'symbolic' meaning, its 'religious significance', its 'essential' as opposed to its 'accidental' element,[54] the wine in the bottle which is worth preserving even if the label may be out-of-date. For example, N. P. Williams concludes that 'Augustine's picture of a "Golden Age" and of an earthly Paradise tenanted by a saintly couple belongs to the realm of mythology'. Yet, when he comes to evaluate Augustine's doctrine of original sin, his resolution fails him, and he tails off into the face-saving statement that 'in the sense of the *vitium* or inbred disease of human nature, it would seem to be marked by psychological acuteness and truth'.[55]

What then is this symbolic meaning, so valuable that it must be preserved at all costs? That man has a radical propensity to evil?[56] But may he not also

[51] TeSelle, 1970, 180.

[52] On the possible influence of Tyconius see TeSelle, 1970, 180ff., where he discusses Pincherle's case, and for a possible similarity to the views of Tyconius Babcock, 1982, 1212ff.

[53] TeSelle, 1970, 266.

[54] Webb, 75.

[55] N. P. Williams, 382. Bonner, 1962, 311ff., finds Augustine's 'theological doctrine of the Fall' 'scientifically untenable' but his teaching on *concupiscentia* 'surprisingly modern' and suggests that Augustine is 'nowhere more relevant than in the field of psychology'.

[56] Webb, 116ff., suggests that Kant, though rejecting the doctrine of grace, reveals in his own teaching of a radical evil in the will a doctrine very close to that of original sin or, as he terms it, *peccatum originarium*, eschewing the German word for it, *Erbsünde*, because he does not accept that it was a hereditary disease.

have a radical propensity to good, being capable, as Pelagius argued, of turning *in utramque partem*, 'in either direction'? 'Is there, in human nature, as theology has often taught and as the not unpopular neo-Calvinism appears to teach, an ingrained bias to evil?'[57] If so, how are we to reconcile it with evolutionary theory and the DNA code of modern genetics? Knowing, as we have done since the discoveries of Mendel, that our genes, passed on from one generation to another in the germ cells, 'from time to time undergo sudden, spontaneous and apparently random changes in their form, technically termed mutations',[58] are we to see original sin as a product of one such mutation, 'some morally lethal gene, which arose as a result of a single mutation at a past moment of time'?[59] Do we then go on to attribute it not to a combination of random chance and iron necessity, as the molecular biologist Jacques Monod has done,[60] but as a part of God's programming of his eternal design for man?[61] Or try another tack and explain the fallen state of man as a residual effect of his 'animal past'? But such an interpretation would be 'profoundly unfair to animals'.[62]

Many prefer to resist the temptation to indulge in such exercises in mental acrobatics in order to explain *obscurum per obscurius* and to concentrate on extracting the 'essential' element in original sin as the key to its symbolic meaning, and the majority nowadays see pride as the front runner. 'Pride', we are told, 'is the movement whereby a creature . . . tried to set up on its own, to exist for itself',[63] 'that unwanted but unavoidable self-centredness, that sense of alienation and tension and moral failure which we experience and observe within ourselves and others as an empirically encountered phenomenon';[64] it is 'perhaps the oldest of human temptations. . . . Many theologians, from Augustine to Niebuhr, have believed that pride is the ultimate sin'.[65] And Geoffrey Lampe, in a posthumous paper in which he accepted as 'still meaningful' the interpretation of salvation as deliverance from sin itself, understood as 'alienation from God through the choice of self-centredness', went on to refer to 'Augustine's disastrous notion that sexual desire and activity is a primary expression of irrational and ungodly selfishness (*concupiscentia*)'.[66] All this, of course, is true in relation to human experience, and we have had occasion to note that pride or self-centredness was included in Augustine's list of sins inherent in Adam's first sin. But it is essential for the

[57] Bezzant, 97.
[58] Hardy, 1975, 30.
[59] Lucas, 1976, 42.
[60] Bartholomew, 16ff., provides a comprehensive review of Monod's case and of responses to it by theologians, scientists and philosophers.
[61] See, for example, Thorpe and, more recently, Montefiore.
[62] Badham, 57 and 136, n. 33.
[63] C. S. Lewis, as quoted in Joad, 338.
[64] Hanson, 1976, 42.
[65] Macquarrie, 1982, 240; before Augustine Ambrose did the same, and Augustine regarded him as his most weighty authority in the controversy over grace, though as Wermelinger, 273, rightly points out, in his register of witnesses against the Pelagians in *TLP* IV, viii. 20 – xii. 32 (PL 44, 623ff.) he gives far greater space to Cyprian.
[66] Lampe, 1981, 20.

sake of clarity to distinguish between that first sin of Adam and original sin as the flaw to which Augustine was to attribute all subsequent sins. The 'ultimate sin' may well be pride but the original sin resulting from it, the flaw, was in Augustine's view concupiscence in the sense of 'carnal desire'. If it were not so, it would seem very strange that Augustine should have written a whole treatise devoted to an examination of the relationship between marriage and concupiscence, in which he explicitly defines concupiscence as 'carnal desire', at once the cause of the first act of procreation and the stigma attached to it and to all such acts thereafter, the very root of man's propensity to evil.

It was precisely this propensity that the Fall-doctrine was pressed into service to explain in the first place, and, on an evolutionary view of man's origin and development, that doctrine, along with Adam and Eve and the Serpent and the Garden and all its other paraphernalia, simply disappears from history and reverts to its proper place in the creation-myths of other religions. If the Adam-story were to continue to fulfil its traditional Augustinian rôle as a form of theodicy, it would need 'to be understood in a historical and not merely symbolic way':[67] it would be seen in parallel with the historical event of the death of Jesus, as Paul unquestionably was the first to see it. His teaching on the Fall and original sin was solidly based on the historicity of both events; but what happens if the historicity of the second event succeeds, as it has done, in surviving the intensive criticism to which the biblical evidence has been subjected since the beginning of the nineteenth century, whereas the first has long lost any claim to be deemed historical? The blunt answer is that the first 'event' is an event no longer and has been deprived *ipso facto* of its traditional *raison d'être*, which was to buttress a theory of sub-stitutionary atonement.

But even when this *raison d'être* still escaped without challenge, the Augustinian doctrine of original sin never fully satisfied the Vincentian triad of criteria for acceptance as a dogma of the Christian Church – that is, of having been believed *ubique, semper et ab omnibus*, 'in all places, at all times and by all Christians'. After the Council of Ephesus in 431, when the 'opinions of Celestius' were formally condemned but in the vaguest and most general of terms by the East, down to the 'Great Schism' of 1054, only a modified Augustinian doctrine survived in the West and the East showed practically no interest in the subject. In the late twentieth century its survival is as tenuous as the fading smile on the face of the Cheshire Cat, and it could be argued that all that is left behind of the symbolic truth which it once contained is the self-evident statement that there are in our personalities certain inherited, as distinct from environmental, features which lead us to want to put Number One first and, not infrequently, to harm other people in doing so.

Against the backcloth of modern biology, physiology and psychology perhaps it would be more honest to stop paying lip-service to this morbid

[67] Wiles, 1974, 67f.

doctrine of 'sin . . . accumulating at compound interest'[68] and to consign it to that region of limbo which is reserved for such failed theories as alchemy and phrenology, phlogiston and Piltdown man. This suggestion is not as frivolous as it might appear to be nor is it prompted only by the naïve attitude of those who 'reject the doctrine of original sin because the law-abiding citizen will rightly refuse to be held responsible for the crimes committed by his ancestors'.[69] Rather it springs from a strongly held conviction that it is a doctrine which has done the Christian Church far more harm than good. By preaching the absolute necessity to purge man of his inherited sin in order to save his soul, it has provided countless 'well-meaning' individuals with a ready-made pretext for pursuing their diligent campaign for souls without any thought for the mere lives of their victims – witness the heresy trials of the Middle Ages, the ruthlessness of the Crusades, the sadistic horrors of the Inquisition and so on *ad nauseam*. It has also fostered that obsessive antipathy to the sexual act which marred the thought of the Church from Paul onwards until it was elevated into doctrine by Augustine's stigma on the act of procreation. Even the Mariological doctrines of the Virgin Birth and the 'immaculate conception' often confused with it, though both derive most of their authority from a scatter of dubious texts, 'have something to do with the negative valuation of the sexual act on the part of the Fathers of the Church', as Hans Küng has put it with his usual frankness.[70] Both of them, and especially the second, he continues, 'have become largely pointless as a result of increasing criticism of the Augustinian view'. From this standpoint Augustine has a lot to answer for. What, if anything, can we find to say in his favour in the light of modern theology and science?

When he makes his final assessment of the value of Augustine's doctrine of the Fall and original sin, N. P. Williams comes to the conclusion that two of his 'great conceptions', those of original righteousness and original guilt, 'in their strict Augustinian form, are worthless from the point of view of modern thought'; as for the third, original sin itself, 'the common underlying element' in Christian teaching over the centuries goes back to Paul, the authority 'unquestionably claimed by all who have handled the subject from Justin Martyr to Baius and Quesnel'. He summarises this common underlying element as 'the inherent infirmity' in human nature, consisting in the discord between 'flesh' and 'spirit', 'which may be described in modern terms as weakness of will-power, defective control over the emotional impulses, or imperfect power of inhibiting the spontaneous flow of psychic energy along the channels of the primary instincts'. This, he maintains, is the only conception of the inherent infirmity misnamed 'original sin' which can be said to be truly 'Catholic' in the Vincentian sense, and it is already present in the Pauline idea of 'inherent weakness of will': 'tradition and dogmatic development, broadly interpreted, have added absolutely nothing to the language of Scripture'. As for the Fall, he maintains that 'Catholic Christianity as such is

---

[68] Hanson, 1976, 41.
[69] Webb, 75; cf. 72.
[70] Küng, 1977, 454.

committed to no more than the bare assertion that there *was* a Fall, a primal rebellion of a created will', 'a pre-cosmic vitiation of the whole Life-Force at the very beginning of cosmic evolution', resulting in an 'inbred disease of human nature'.[71]

Such an evaluation contains many echoes of the intellectual milieu or *episteme*[72] of the period in which Williams wrote and published his Bampton Lectures and of its limitations. But, over sixty years later, in his exciting clarification of biblical faith in the light of current evolutionary theory Gerd Theissen also returns to Paul and, in particular, to the contrast which he draws in Galatians 5, 19ff., between the fruits of the 'spirit' and the works of the flesh, forms of behaviour with a biological orientation and involving sexuality, aggression and greed. 'The biological conditioning of sins in the sphere of sexuality and the consumption of food is obvious. In the major group of aggressive forms of behaviour – enmity, dispute, jealousy, anger, intrigues, discord, partisan behaviour and envy – it is probable.' Paul, he continues, 'goes directly against the modern approach which by contrast sees the origin of anti-social behaviour in the "suppression" of biological needs', and he 'rather than our all-too-superficial modern awareness is right in seeing an antagonism in principle between flesh and Spirit, i.e. between tendencies towards behaviour with a biological foundation, on the one hand, and human culture, *even if Spirit is more than human culture* (my emphasis), on the other'. Tendencies in the opposite direction, that is, towards altruism – 'original goodness' – derive their strongest support from a religious faith capable of offering symbols of fellowship and community, brotherhood and sisterhood that discourage genetic rivalry and enable human beings 'to take that small (*sic*) step beyond previous evolution which allows them to have inklings of a freedom from the power of genetic and social egoism'. In support of this view he quotes Dawkins' book *The Selfish Gene* with 'its impressive confession of the human capacity to transcend natural and social "egoism"': 'we alone can rebel', affirms Dawkins, 'against the tyranny of the selfish replicators.'[73]

Theissen's main argument is drawn in part from two papers by the psychologist and evolutionary scientist D. T. Campbell, written as a plea for 'effective social curbs on human selfishness in the society of the future' and a protest against the hostility of 'present-day psychology and psychiatry in all their major forms to the inhibitory messages of traditional religious moralising'.[74] And his conclusion is in line with these two statements of Campbell: 'the truth could be what liberal theologians love to deny, that we have preprogrammed tendencies of behaviour which are held in check by strong cultural control in the opposite direction and that when the cultural systems of restraints collapse they unleash a terrifying "proneness to degeneration

[71] N. P. Williams, 1927, 380, 459f.

[72] I first came across this Greek word used in the sense of 'the system of thought characteristic of a particular historical epoch' in Cupitt, 1985, 4; Cupitt tells us that it was introduced by Foucault in his book *Les Mots et les Choses*.

[73] Theissen, 134ff., 140ff., 188, n. 14; Dawkins, 1976, 215.

[74] Campbell, 1975, 253; 1976, 167.

among human beings". We experience the tension within us between biological and cultural evolution as "guilt". We are aware that we need not automatically follow predisposed tendencies to behave. We can direct them. But all too often we are defeated by them. We are predisposed to sin.' In the conflict between this biological disposition to sin and the social and cultural demands for altruism our only help comes from the operations of the Holy Spirit.[75] Campbell, writing from a scientific and non-religious standpoint, expresses the same opinion differently: 'human urban social complexity is a product of social evolution and has had to counter with inhibitory moral terms the biological selfishness which genetic competition selects continually.'[76]

What would Augustine have to say about all this? We can imagine him grunting at this point, 'He means nothing more than the law and teaching.' True, he might find in Campbell's papers some support for his own view of 'seminal identity'; but he would obviously deplore the disappearance from the scene of divine grace and the absence of any mention of the Fall, as well as the fact that the actual term 'original sin' appears only in the title of the first paper. What of Theissen? He too makes no mention of the Fall and, as Augustine would be quick to perceive, describes 'original sin' at one point as 'certainly not a very good term'. But while the scientist defines altruism in purely genetic terms, the theologian does at least acknowledge a 'proneness to degeneration in human beings' and, what is more, identifies the Holy Spirit as the sole cure for the disease. Thus Augustine might be able to hear faint echoes of his *concupiscentia* and his *medicina* for it in Theissen: after all, he has at least advanced one step beyond Pelagius by discounting the possibility that mankind can raise itself by its own bootstraps,[77] even if his statement that 'the central reality offers its unconditional support to their imperfect trial and error' might send off a dangerous whiff of Pelagianism. It is in this respect that the theologian takes a leap of faith over the boundaries of the scientist's definition of culture in purely human terms, and he is able to do so because he believes that God the creator has not entirely abandoned men to their own feeble resources and that they still retain 'the possibility of experiencing, now, already – within a transitory and often unsuccessful life – the intrinsic goal of the whole of evolution: harmony with God'.[78]

I am aware that I may be criticised for concentrating on Campbell's thesis, on his own admission heterodox, when there are others much more truly representative of current orthodoxy in the fields of psychology and evolutionary theory. But I have selected it precisely because it seems to me to be more

[75] Theissen, 146ff.

[76] Campbell, 1976, 202; cf. D. Young, 1974(a), 403: '. . . during evolution it may be expected that the genetic programming of the behaviour of the species will tend increasingly to be influenced by the social behaviour of that species'.

[77] This is the 'falsely consoling thought' involved in 'that very English disease, Pelagianism' according to an Anglican clergyman Peter Mullen, attacking the 'psychological or spiritual teachings of Jenkins and Cupitt' (*The Times*, 25 May 1985): 'historically considered', such teachings are 'a recrudescence of Pelagianism'. On reading that they are 'Pelagians', Jenkins and Cupitt may well have felt rather like Monsieur Jourdain in *Le Bourgeois Gentilhomme* when he learnt that he had been using prose all his life without knowing it!

[78] Theissen, 174.

favourable to Augustine than any other variation on the theme of natural selection – be it Darwinist, neo-Darwinist or anti-Darwinist – that I have so far met: by his development of it Theissen is enabled to reconcile it with biblical faith and with the Christian belief in God as the creator and preserver of all mankind. But does modern evolutionary theory permit such a divine rôle within the parameters of genetic research? Has it not been entirely undermined by those who hold that the universe is no more than a product of a combination of 'chance and necessity', to use the title of a book which its author Monod believed to be 'a virtual disproof of almost (*sic*) all that religion stands for', 'biological proof of the absence of a master-plan', establishing once and for all that 'belief in a universe in which man is destined to appear is contrary to modern biology'?[79] Monod's case is founded on the discovery of the DNA code and the unpredictable mutations which occur in the process of molecular replication, and as yet it has not been 'seriously challenged, though it is claimed to be incomplete at a number of points'.[80] But what Monod has actually done is to state a case for the non-existence of God in its most extreme form; he has not succeeded in *proving* the non-existence of God or of a divine plan or that human beings are not an integral part of such a plan. When he asserts that 'our number came up in the Monte Carlo game' and that 'man at last knows he is alone in the unfeeling immensity of the universe, out of which he emerged only by chance', he is making a deduction which owes more to his own attitudes as a self-confessed atheist than to his acknowledged expertise in molecular biology.[81] There are many others who have examined the same kind of evidence as Monod, as well as other kinds of evidence which he did not take into account, and have reached a different conclusion.

For example, a professor of statistics who, like myself, admits to being only an amateur theologian, after a thorough examination of the views of those who have taken up the challenge made by Monod, concludes that 'the reality of chance is not merely compatible with the doctrine of creation but is required by it' and proceeds to formulate 'a doctrine of providence which, while allowing that God is ultimately responsible for everything that happens', does not postulate 'his intimate involvement in all things'. And, in the present context, it is worth taking note of his claim 'that only in a world of real uncertainty can people grow into free responsible children of their heavenly father'.[82] Nor is Bartholomew a voice crying in the wilderness: the Quaker

---

[79] Bartholomew, 2, 16; the second quotation is taken from a BBC interview with Peter Medawar at the time when Monod's book first appeared.

[80] Ibid., 19; the author suggests that 'Monod has set up what might be called a "natural anti-theology"'.

[81] Monod, 137, 167. But Gunton, 526, in his discussion of the theological conclusions emerging from Young's articles in the same number of *Theology*, rightly comments that 'theologians, at least in principle, are not bound to be terrified by discoveries in the biological sciences; yet these discoveries, he adds (528), provide 'an essential backdrop for any contemporary theology of man', quoting from D. Young, 1974(b), 477. Young also emphasises (471) that 'it is particularly easy to overlook the limitations of the biological approach and *to slide from biology into philosophical discussion*' (my emphasis).

[82] Bartholomew, 145.

animal ethologist Thorpe, while agreeing with Monod that 'to attempt to understand the natural world in the way in which science attempts the task is inherently worth doing', maintains that science can also 'yield some understanding, however dim, of the enduring reality underlying the transient natural world'.[83] Neither Bartholomew nor Thorpe denies the rôle of chance in evolution, as the titles of their books – *God of Chance* and *Purpose in a World of Chance* – abundantly show; but both reject the idea that the element of chance rules out the possibility of a divine purpose. And they have the support of the Anglican Bishop of Birmingham in a former book in which he is concerned to explain 'how God could be conceived of as acting purposefully in a world where the driving force appears to be chance – the very antithesis of purpose' and finds the most probable explanation to be that 'matter orders itself in a way that is optimal for life by the personal will of an omniscient and infinite God'.[84] All three, approaching the problem from different angles, are able, like Theissen, to develop a doctrine of the Spirit based on natural religion and to affirm God's immanence without contradicting the findings of modern science. But, it may be argued, just as Monod is an atheist, these three are convinced Christians and every bit as likely to be lacking in objectivity. Was Koestler then also a Christian? It was he who wrote the memorable sentence: 'Man is neither a plaything of the gods nor a marionette suspended on its chromosomes.'[85]

'If the hand of God is to be recognised in this continuous creation, it must be found not in isolated intrusions, not in any gaps, but in the very process itself.'[86] This conclusion broadly summarises the common denominator in the arguments of the statistician, ethologist and theologian from whom we have just quoted. But not one of them, as far as I have been able to discover, finds it necessary to discuss Augustine's doctrine of original sin in the light of contemporary science and philosophy, although presumably all three would agree that we have a 'natural' inclination to do evil, a 'proneness to degeneration'. This apart, what is left of the Augustinian synthesis? The plain truth is that modern evolutionary theory, warts and all, has just about completed the work of demolishing it, begun by the Pelagians and Semi-Pelagians and continued by Aquinas, Duns Scotus, the Franciscans and others in the Middle Ages, as well as the Reformers. Augustine's extrapolation of Paul's insight into the true nature of the human and cosmic struggle with evil was flawed from the outset by his insistence on tying it firmly to the story of the Fall. Whether or not he really believed that the story contained in the early chapters of Genesis was the literal truth is open to debate;[87] but he certainly behaved as if he did, and when as a result he proceeded to base his doctrine of original sin upon it, he was building on sand, and his elegant

[83] Thorpe, 1f.
[84] Montefiore, 171.
[85] Thorpe, 115, cites Koestler's sentence but without giving the reference.
[86] Taylor, 28.
[87] On occasions Augustine suggests that he had at least an inkling of what we now know as evolution, when he is discussing creation and related topics; a brief selection of relevant passages from *CG*, *T* and *LCG* will be found in Bourke, ed., 100ff.

structure now lies shattered like a child's sand-castle in the ebbing tide. It was biology that gave it the final push, and even the Christian myth of original sin makes sense in the late twentieth century only if it is expressed in terms that are not inconsistent with the discoveries of modern biology and is treated as a symbolic description of man's inbuilt tendency to place his own selfish interests before those of his fellow-creatures, be they human or animal, vegetable or mineral.

As for the term 'original sin', it is 'certainly not a good one', especially when it has been stripped of almost all its Augustinian associations and has been reduced, if not to a cliché, at most to serving as a convenient synonym for man's tendency to evil or as a useful antidote to modern notions of perfectibility. If we wish to employ it to express this tendency to evil, we must remember to allow for another, opposing tendency which man has developed in response to the civilising influence of human culture. Man's tendency to do evil is not the result of a sin committed by his first ancestor but of his genetic inheritance, which stretches back to that moment in time when molecules first merged to form DNA and pairs of cells joined and multiplied in the primeval soup. In the course of human evolution this tendency has been to some extent counteracted by a tendency to altruism, stimulated and encouraged by ethical constraints and religious experience; both of these tendencies have reacted and continue to react to man's physical and social environment *in utramque partem*, leaving him as a pig-in-the-middle, caught in the perennial encounter between the forces of good and evil. The Christian's choice between these opposed forces stems not from a divine election made once and for all in the remote past, but from the way in which he or she responds or fails to respond to the message and example of Jesus and to the subconscious pressures of the Spirit, deftly applied.[88]

All this, of course, is anathema to the Roman Catholic Church – not least because of the possible implications for its theology of infant baptism. Writing his *Apologia pro Vita Sua* only five years after the appearance of Darwin's *The Origin of Species*, Newman set the scene: he could see no reason to change his mind on the subject of the doctrine of original sin, maintaining that for him it was 'almost as certain as that the world exists, and as the existence of God'. This is not at all surprising when we take into account his view of dogma as

---

[88] This view of the interaction between genetic selfishness and cultural altruism approximates to that of Theissen; while accepting that 'there is a continuity between biological and cultural evolution' (9), he rejects the idea that the latter is simply the continuation of the former. He also notes (184, n. 38) that Wilson's conclusion in his book *Sociobiology: the New Synthesis* that 'religions develop to the degree that they further the survival and influence of their adherents' is criticised by Austin's article in *Zygon*. The question to what extent, if at all, altruism is able to counteract the 'selfish gene' has been the subject of a sharp, though so far inconclusive, debate. For example, Wilson's book and Dawkins' *The Selfish Gene*, as well as Mackie's article in *Philosophy*, have come under fire from Mary Midgeley, 1979, which provoked replies from Dawkins and Mackie two years later in the same journal. Unrepentant, Midgeley has carried on her attack in her most recent book (1985); Singer and Trigg have also made important contributions to the ongoing debate, as have Lumsden and Wilson, but the latter appears to have modified his earlier, more extreme thesis to some extent. I am indebted to my friend Robin Attfield for his help with the bibliography on which this note is based.

expressed earlier in the same work: 'From the age of fifteen, dogma has been the fundamental principle of my religion; I know no other religion; I cannot enter into the idea of any other sort of religion.'[89] It is hardly more surprising, even if it is not a little daunting, to find Pope Pius XII insisting a hundred years later that the first eleven chapters of Genesis 'do pertain to history in the true sense and must not be considered on a par with myths'.[90] What, in that case, is truth, and what is myth, and what is the distinction between them, we may well ask? Dogma has never really changed; it has only become more complex, and its history reveals no more than a negative struggle to avoid 'the hateful charge of novelty'.[91] As for the Anglican Church, original sin and predestination are still enshrined in its Thirty-Nine Articles, to which its clergy have to give a general assent, and any attempt to remove or even amend them would drive its Anglo-Catholic minority into doctrinal schism.

Further West in recent years we have observed the emergence and grow-ing influence in America of a movement among conservative, evangelical Christians to turn back the clock by arguing that evolution is not a fact but either a philosophical theory or a scientific myth and that the Genesis version of creation and the Garden of Eden demands a literal interpretation.[92] Certainly we have no right to assume that biology has spoken its last word on the subject of evolution nor must we fall into the trap of allowing it to usurp the functions of sociology and ethics. But this does not entitle the 'creationists', or anyone else for that matter, to attempt to expose scientists to ridicule merely because they have the honesty to admit that natural selection can no longer be regarded as the only significant factor in the process of evolution and engage in open debate on the origins of life and of the universe. Theologians too who bravely endeavour to explain contemporary theories of creation and evolution in terms which make sense to ordinary Christians 'in the pew' deserve better treatment than to be pilloried by some of their colleagues and thrown to the wolves lurking in the sensation-seeking media. When will the Church wake up to the fact that it must stop dusting paper flowers and begin cultivating roses?[93] Not so long as it refuses to acknowledge 'the possibility of profiting by encouraging exploration along divergent paths', not so long as it continues to confuse myth with history, not so long as it 'dreams of things that never were'.[94]

Alas, poor Pelagius, where rode he the while? Certainly not on the back of a horse named Original Sin, which he had crossed off his list of potential starters before the race had even begun: *non est dogma* was his dismissive

[89] Newman, 218, 67.

[90] *Humani Generis²*, trans. A. C. Cotter, Weston, Mass., 1952, a reference which I owe to Cupitt, 1979, 77.

[91] The heading of c. 5 in Wilken, taken from a paraphrase of Matthias Flacius, *Catalogus testium veritatis*, Frankfurt 1666, Pref., 1f., cited on p. 109.

[92] The 'creationists' seem to have had the support of no less an authority than the President of the United States of America, who, 'during his campaign for the Presidency, referred to evolution as "only a theory"' (Angela Tilby, *The Times*, 15 August 1981).

[93] Küng, 1977, 121; I am grateful to Marion Eames for giving me the precise reference.

[94] L. Dewart, 150; Wilken, 193.

comment at Diospolis.[95] Out of the package of goodies offered to him under the label of original sin by Augustine all he was prepared to accept was that Adam's sin resulted not only in his own death but also in that of the whole of mankind, and he, like Augustine but with a different interpretation, accepted the current Latin mistranslation of Romans 5, 12 as 'in whom (that is, Adam) all men sinned', since he knew even less Greek than his more distinguished opponent.[96] More than that he defiantly refused to swallow. The main authority for his views he, like Augustine, found in Paul, and he saw no reason to question the statements contained in 1 Corinthians 15, 22 and in Romans 5, 12 to 19. But his interpretation of these was very different from that of Augustine, as he had made abundantly clear in his commentary on the Pauline Epistles written in 405–9, where he had explained Romans 5, 12, 15 and 19 as referring to man's sin as the result not of an inheritance from Adam but of imitation of his *example*.[97] As we have noted, it was such a denial of original sin which first attracted the adverse attention of Augustine to the Pelagians in 411, although it was Rufinus of Syria and Celestius who were then his main targets. This denial had implied a thoughtless but none the less dangerous threat to the rite of infant baptism, and his subsequent reading of Pelagius' commentary and of his works *On Nature* and *On Free Will* confirmed his suspicions that Pelagius was just as culpable in this respect as his associates, indeed largely responsible for the wrong views that they held.

On baptism Augustine and Pelagius were separated from each other by an apparently impassable gulf, covered with 'thick-ribbèd ice'. For Augustine baptism made available to man a means of grace by which he could be set free from the penalty attached to original sin as well as the sins which he had actually committed. It did not, however, take away the urge to sin, which required the constant application of grace to resist it and reinforce the right exercise of 'free' choice, nor did it make man perfect: 'it merely cleans the

---

[95] 'I anathematise them as fools but not as heretics, for there is no dogma' – referring to those who held the opinions attributed to him under the sixth item in the charge-sheet.

[96] Scholars have differed on the question whether Pelagius knew Greek. For example, R. F. Evans, 1964, 21, n. 5, states that 'he cannot understand the assertion of Hedde and Amann, 392, that Pelagius made his replies to the council [of Diospolis] in Greek' and quotes *PP* i. 2 in support of this statement. But he has misunderstood the passage quoted, which refers not to a verbal response made by Pelagius but to a reading in Latin from one of his works, which, like the charges against him, was translated by an interpreter. *Contra*, Wermelinger, 58, n. 81, claims that Pelagius spoke Greek at Diospolis on the authority of Augustus' statement in *PP* ii. 4; but he too has misread his text: all that it tells us is that Pelagius' response to one of the questions put to him by his judges was *Graeco eloquio prolatum*, that is, *'expressed* in Greek' – again by the official interpreter. What we do know is that Pelagius read the works of Origen and the *Sentences of Sextus* in Rufinus' Latin translation of them (R. F. Evans, 1968(a), 47, 65; H. Chadwick, 1959, 120). If he knew any Greek at all, it would not have been, as Hugh Williams, 1912, mistakenly believed, because he was 'one of many Latin Christians of the West to begin to visit sacred sites in the East c. 380', but simply because some of the Greek of his *amanuensis*, Annianus of Celeda, may have rubbed off onto him through their constant association. Pelagius interpreted Romans 5, 12 as meaning that all men sin by following the *example* of Adam and not through inheriting his sin by transmission (PLS 1, 1136; Souter, 1922/31, 41).

[97] PLS 1, 1136ff.; Beatrice, 41–63, has a good summary of the Pelagian criticisms of the doctrine of original sin.

slate for him.'[98] What of Pelagius' teaching? His commentary on Paul contains many references to the sacrament of baptism as applied to adults: briefly, it is 'the sacrament of justification by faith *alone*'[99] – and this addition of the word 'alone' encouraged the great Augustinian scholar Loofs to comment that the *sola fide* had no more energetic defender before Luther than Pelagius! Those who seek baptism, said Pelagius, show that they possess 'trust from the whole heart', 'faith in the promises of God',[100] and by baptism they are cleansed of their sins, that is, those which they have committed, and made righteous by the grace of God. Thereafter, freed from their previous sins by the 'word' speaking to them in baptism, they need the help of that word again in the form of *doctrina*, 'teaching', in order to remain righteous by obeying the law of God. Baptism is thus needed to cancel actual sins committed, and no more. And Pelagius, following 'Ambrosiaster', identifies predestination with foreknowledge:[101] God foreknows those who will accept faith and seek to be baptised but he does not compel them to accept baptism nor does he compel them to persevere in their search for righteousness. Rather, he provides them in Jesus with the teaching which will enable them to do so.[102] We are again reminded of Augustine's wry and oft-repeated comment: 'he means nothing but the law and teaching.'

And what of the baptism of infants as opposed to that of adults? Here Pelagius was presented with a problem with which he never succeeded in coming to terms. 'Nowhere', comments R. F. Evans in summing up Pelagius' theology of baptism, 'does Pelagius show that he was able to refine his theological language in such a way as to offer an intelligible rationalisation for speaking of redemption and the remission of sins as applied to infants.'[103] Thus we arrive at a question which is of vital importance for anyone trying to understand Pelagius' attitude to the charge of heresy which was brought against him and, to use a modern phrase, made to stick. Why was he not as explicit on the subject of infant baptism in his *Liber de Fide* as Celestius was in his? Both statements of belief were presented to the Pope at the same time and were couched in language which is almost verbally identical, except that Celestius added certain phrases and sentences to his version which are not present in that of Pelagius, among them an amplification of his views on baptism.[104] Although we have no evidence that the two men sat down together to work out their affirmations in close collaboration, thus presenting

[98] G. R. Evans, 131.
[99] R. F. Evans, 1968(a), 113; for examples of Pelagius' use of the phrase *sola fide* see his expository notes on Romans 3, 28; 4, 5,; 5, 1; Galatians 3, 11 and 26; Ephesians 2.8; 3.11; (PLS I, 1129, 1131, 1133f., 1149, 1277, 1279, 1293, 1296).
[100] On 1 Timothy 6, 10 (PLS I, 1357); on Galatians 3, 11 (PLS 1, 1277); *On the Divine Law*, 2 (PL 30, 107).
[101] On Romans 8, 29, 30 (PLS I, 1149f.).
[102] On Galatians 3, 24 (PLS I, 1279).
[103] R. F. Evans, 1968(a), 118f.; on the relation between infant baptism and original sin see Beatrice, 105–19.
[104] Garnier printed the two confessions of faith side by side for easier comparison in his fifth dissertation on the first part of Marius Mercator's works (PL 48, 498ff.).

a united front to their accusers, it is difficult to explain such a degree of unanimity if they did not do so. If they did, it is understandable that Celestius, as a trained lawyer, would insist on qualifying the terms employed in the statement so as to make their precise meaning more precise. But it is just as possible that Pelagius deliberately chose not to be as explicit as his friend on some subjects. He, unlike Celestius, confined himself to affirming that 'we' – and he is here speaking for himself – 'hold likewise one baptism, which we maintain ought to be administered with the same sacramental formula to infants as to adults.'[105]

Augustine had no difficulty in showing up the blatant inconsistency of this statement and describing it as simply 'a heresy struggling to conceal itself under ambiguous words',[106] and it is hard to believe that Pelagius himself was unaware of this basic inconsistency.[107] He must have known that only Tertullian of the Latin Fathers had opposed the practice of infant baptism and that Cyprian, on the other hand, had affirmed that it was needed for remission not only of sins but of original sin as well. He must also have realised that, though theories of original sin and original guilt were being used to safeguard and justify infant baptism – or so it must have seemed to him –, in fact they were historically preceded by it as a traditional institution of the Church, and he never questioned the scriptural evidence on which it was originally based. Either he did not understand what was involved in his denial of original sin or he was trying to protect himself against a charge which had proved to be successful when brought against Celestius. The second of these possibilities, the one which Jerome and Augustine strenuously maintained, is the only tenable answer but it calls for some qualification. Plinval suggested that 'anything touching on the rites and practices of the Church was very much more serious than that which affected controversial and still not defined points of pure theory: search for the precise nature of Adam's sin and evaluation of its subsequent repercussions could offer only a speculative interest, but considerable importance was at once attached to what directly affected the practice and real efficacy of the sacrament.'[108] Bonner too seems to be moving in the same direction when he writes that 'perhaps, indeed, the clue to Pelagius' orthodoxy or unorthodoxy lies not so much in his concept of grace as in that other, vehemently debated topic, the baptism of infants *in remissionem peccatorum*, "for the remission of their sins".'[109] It is always dangerous to attempt to project into the distant past an interpretation which appears convincing many centuries later; but, in this case, Pelagius' seemingly conscious decision to avoid the issue in his *Liber de Fide* would seem to justify us in concluding that he *was* fully aware that to deny the efficacy of baptism for infants would be to forfeit any residual claim to orthodoxy on his part. The picture that others had built up of one whose

[105] PL 48, 502.
[106] *OS* xxi. 23 (PL 44, 396) (CSEL 42, 182).
[107] Augustine exposes it in *MFS* I, xxxiv. 63 (PL 44, 146f.) (CSEL 60, 63f.).
[108] Plinval, 1943, 257.
[109] Bonner, 1966, 358.

orthodoxy was already undermined by his heretical views on grace would be completed if he could also be shown by his own confession to be casting doubt on a practice which was essential to the Christian Church.

But it would not be sufficient or equitable to attribute Pelagius' affirmation of baptism merely to a conscious attempt to deceive: of course he must have realised that, if he wanted, as he certainly did want, to be known as an *integer Christianus*, 'a complete Christian', he *had* to accept baptism as an essential tenet of the faith. Nor is there reason to doubt that he accepted it in all sincerity, for was it not also essential to his own teaching on the need for regeneration? The only significant difference between Augustine and himself was that he wanted to limit its efficacy to the remission of sins already committed, whereas Augustine was determined to maintain its validity as a means to the remission of original sin as well. Thus Pelagius finished up by adopting an ambiguous position, affirming his belief in baptism and his acceptance of the rite by which it was traditionally administered in one article of his confession of faith, while continuing in another to maintain the freedom of the human will to make its own choices, though 'always', he was careful to add, 'with divine assistance'.[110] But one of these choices was presumably to seek and accept baptism, and this infants were unable to do because, as he argued elsewhere, 'they do not yet make use of the rational will'.[111] On his own premises and the conclusions which he had built upon them he was in this way shown to be in favour of admitting infants to a sacrament for which he could offer no theoretical support; as Augustine was quick to point out, he was making a mockery of baptism.[112] His only justification of this paradox was to ask, 'Who is so impious as to forbid the common redemption of the human race to an infant of any age?'[113] 'What redemption does he mean?', asked his opponent scornfully: 'Is it from evil to good, or from good to better?' If the former, from what source could the evil have come other than the original sin of Adam? If the latter, then Pelagius would be falling back on the opinion of Celestius that infants at birth were in the same state as Adam before his fall, an opinion which, along with others attributed to his friend, he had anathematised at Diospolis. He was thus confronted with 'Hobson's choice' or, to use a contemporary metaphor, a 'catch 22 situation': if he renounced infant baptism, he would be declared a heretic; if he affirmed it, his whole theology became a nonsense.

It was left to the last and most acute of Augustine's Pelagian adversaries, Julian of Eclanum, to spell out in full what his predecessors had either adumbrated (Rufinus of Syria and Celestius) or glossed over (Pelagius), that infants, though untainted by Adam's sin were still capable of receiving through baptism 'spiritual illumination, adoption into the sons of God, membership of the heavenly city of Jerusalem, sanctification and transfer into

---

[110] PL 48, 491, 504.
[111] *OS* xv. 16 (PL 44, 393) (CSEL 42, 177f.).
[112] *MFS* I, xxxiv. 63 (PL 44, 146) (CSEL 60, 64); cf. *J* III, v. 11 (PL 44, 708).
[113] *OS* xix. 21 (PL 44, 395) (CSEL 42, 181).

the members of Christ with possession of the kingdom of heaven'.[114] Julian's terminology reminds us of Garnier's observation that the writings of the Pelagians reveal here and there a kind of anticipation of medieval views on sanctifying grace, and de Blic also refers to the statement of Celestius that infants 'because they have no natural strength, must have baptism conferred on them by the generosity of grace' as being of remarkable modernity'.[115] The last phrase tempts us to reflect whether the Church is any further forward today in its search for a solution to the age-old problem of infant baptism than it was in the fifth century. To judge by a recent report commissioned by the World Council of Churches, it is still wrestling with the same problem of reconciling opposing views on the subject, and its difficulties seem even more intractable in the light of the proliferation of its internal divisions since the Reformation. The report submitted by theologians of all shades of opinion and entitled 'Baptism, Eucharist and Ministry' – the order of the words is not without significance – makes it clear that if Church unity is to be visibly achieved, one of the essential prerequisites is a basic agreement on baptism, and denominations are urged to prepare the way for such an agreement by reconsidering their own position on baptism – and, where applicable, confirmation – and re-examining their theology of baptism before turning to their actual practice of it. The question that they must face fairly and squarely is 'whether infant baptism can bear the full weight of the theology of baptism and the consequent nature of the baptismal commitment'. The report does not claim that it has been able to resolve the question of infant baptism vis-à-vis the baptism of believers, but it does conclude that 'while infant baptism may have been practised in the apostolic church, baptism on profession of faith is the most clearly attested pattern'. To be baptised, it maintains, means to be admitted to share in the life, death and resurrection of Jesus after confession of sin and conversion of heart and to undergo an ethical orientation through the Holy Spirit.[116]

Plus ça change, plus c'est la même chose? Pelagius at least might have thought so; he would certainly not have hesitated to accept the substance of the last three sentences, after mastering the terminology in which they are expressed. He would have thoroughly approved of the statement of the meaning of baptism and, in particular, of the query placed against infant baptism, and he would have been delighted with the reference to a fresh 'ethical orientation through the Holy Spirit'. He was unfortunate in being long before his time. Today, with the deck swept almost clean of the last traces of his two pet aversions,

[114] In his letter to Florus, a great part of which Augustine has preserved in his replies to the points raised in it in *IWJ* I, 53 (PL 45, 1076) (CSEL 85/1, 50).

[115] *Dissertation* VII (PL 48, 658). Cf. Brown, 1967, 387, where specific reference is made to Thomas Aquinas, 'whose humane synthesis Julian had anticipated on many points'. I shall say something about different views of Julian in c. VI.

[116] For this summary I am indebted to an article by John Pilkington which appeared under the heading 'Muddle over Christian Initiation' in *The Times*, 9 June 1984. The quotations are from *Baptism, Eucharist and Ministry*, usually referred to as the Lima Document and published by the World Council of Churches, Geneva 1982, Commentary 6, p. 3, and IV, C, 16. See also the Seven Studies with the same title by John Matthews, published by The British Council of Churches, 3ff.

Augustinian predestination and original sin, and the ship's officers under orders to rethink the aims and methods of one of their favourite drills, infant baptism, he might have had to suffer no worse a fate than to face a campaign mounted by them so as to prevent him from gaining promotion to their own ranks – like the bishop who has recently found himself in the centre of an unwelcome controversy but, if he had had the misfortune to serve under the command of the Bishop of Hippo, might have been forced to walk the plank in the steps of John McLeod Campbell, F. D. Maurice, Edward King and Rowland Williams in the nineteenth century and Bishops Barnes and Pike, Teilhard de Chardin and Hans Küng, John Robinson and Don Cupitt and many others in living memory![117] *Autres temps, autres moeurs*: as it turned out, the fate which Pelagius suffered was one which he shared with many other radical teachers of the past, that of not being understood, let alone appreciated, by his contemporaries. And, like Origen and unlike John Chrysostom, who, though little influenced by Origen, fell an unlikely victim to the fourth-century campaign against Origenism and to whom Julian of Eclanum frequently refers as one of his authorities, Pelagius was never to be rehabilitated. To adapt an oft-quoted line of a Latin poet: *Victrix causa deis placuit sed victa Britanno*, 'the gods backed the winning cause, the Briton the one that lost'.[118] Yet, as we have tried to demonstrate, the cause of Augustine in the matter of original sin and infant baptism was far from being well founded, as in that other 'vexed matter' of predestination. Though 'no Christian thinker in his senses will maintain that Augustinianism is a heresy' – except, perhaps, a 'heresy in the truth' – 'a theological opinion may be profoundly erroneous without being either formally or materially heretical'.[119] Augustine, unlike Pelagius, backed a winning cause but, in so doing, he betrayed the fact that his was indeed a 'peculiar grace'.

[117] The least well-known of these, Rowland Williams, Vice-Principal of St David's College, Lampeter from 1850 to 1862, provides us with an interesting case in point. One of the seven Anglican contributors to *Essays and Reviews* (1860), he was suspended from his benefice as Vicar of Broad Chalke for a year by the Dean of Arches as a result, though the judgement was reversed by the Judicial Committee on the Privy Council in 1864. His first book, *Rational Godliness* (1855), had provoked a reviewer in the Welsh theological journal *Yr Haul* to proclaim: 'Parents, it is no longer safe for you to send your sons to Lampeter College while the German principles of *Rational Godliness* are taught there.' His contribution to *Essays and Reviews* was regarded as a fierce challenge, 'as if the author were determined to throw into the orthodox camp a bomb which should not fail to explode'. But his opinions 'seem very unexciting today' (see O. W. Jones, iv–v; Price, 97ff.). In an article in which he considers *Essays and Reviews* in the light of more recent theology Ieuan Ellis comments that 'on the face of it now (and this was already true by the 1890s) it is hard to see what all the controversy was about', and 'it inevitably lost its novel features by the end of the century' (396f.).
[118] Lucan, *The Civil War* I, 128 – reading *Britanno* for *Catoni*, which incidentally does not alter the metrical scansion of the line.
[119] N. P. Williams, 1927, 382. Anyone who has read his Bampton Lectures will recognise the extent to which I am indebted to him for his patient research and illuminating comments on the history of the doctrines of the Fall and Original Sin – though I am not unaware that his considered views on both subjects have not found favour with everyone and that some aspects of them require revision.

V

A DIFFERENT DRUMMER?

'If a man does not keep pace with his companions, perhaps it is because he
hears a different drummer – let him step to the music he hears however
measured or far away.'

H. D. THOREAU[1]

Reflecting on the great storm of controversy which followed the appearance of
the second, revised edition of his commentary on the Pauline Epistles, Karl
Barth is said to have remarked: 'It was like a man climbing inside a church
steeple in the dark: stumbling up the steps, he clutches for support, only to
discover that he has taken hold of the bell-rope – and, before he realises what
is happening, he has caused the bell to ring out with an almighty boom.'[2]
Perhaps Pelagius felt much the same when he became aware of the angry
reactions to his writings among the church leaders of his day. He might fairly
be described as one who had adversarial theology thrust upon him, one who
would have been content if he had been able to go on just writing his letters
and treatises for the benefit of his Roman circle of friends sympathetic to his
campaign for the moral reform of the Church.

Certainly he gives little impression of having realised what a hornets' nest
he was stirring up about his ears when he set up his standard again in
Palestine and began preaching his crusade there. It was a time when the Holy
Land was becoming a place of refuge for 'a new breed of enforced pilgrims'[3] –
'latter-day Lazaruses in flight from the west and packing the holy places', as
Jerome typically described them while struggling to find time to complete his
commentary on Ezekiel.[4] There Pelagius was confronted first by his old
antagonist Jerome, then by Paul Orosius, 'a young man set upon me by my
enemies',[5] and, finally, by the two Gallican bishops, Heros of Arles and
Lazarus of Aix, expelled for supporting Constantine III and excommunicated by the Pope as trouble-makers. The warm support of old associates

---

[1] *Walden*, London 1968, 287.
[2] Berger, 72; Bainton, 1950, 64, applied the same passage to Luther's experience after the
appearance of *Ninety-Five Theses*.
[3] Hunt, 204.
[4] Apart from numerous references to them in the Prefaces to his *Commentary on Ezekiel* he also
complains of the disturbances to 'the peace and quiet which he longed for' in the Prefaces to his
Commentary on Jeremiah (PL 24, 758) (CSEL 59, 221) and to his *Dialogue against the Pelagians* (PL 23,
517). By this time he must have been approaching his eightieth year.
[5] In his letter to Pope Innocent; the surviving fragments come from *GC* and *OS* and were
assembled by Garnier in his *Dissertation* VI (PL 48, 610f.), this reference being to 610B.

from Rome now also in exile and of Bishop John, the arch-enemy of Jerome, and his acquittal at Diospolis lulled him into a false sense of security; up to the very end he seems to have laboured under the misapprehension that, once his theological position had been made perfectly clear to his critics, reason would prevail and he would be left to live out his life in peace. In the event, he was as much to blame as any other member of that 'amazing group of *emigrés*' which had settled in Palestine for turning the Holy Land into 'a theological bear-garden'.[6] His haven of rest became a fiery furnace, through which he passed without ever seeming to grasp just how he had come to be in it in the first place.

It is tempting to allow our sympathy for Pelagius' plight to run away with our capacity for objective judgement and to see him as the innocent victim of the machinations of powerful opponents. Such an impression would not be true to the facts of the case: even the polemic of Jerome, often distasteful and misdirected though it was, did not lack a certain foundation of truth, and Augustine, as we have seen, expended much time and effort which he could ill afford in exposing the errors of Pelagian teaching on free will and grace. Yet even Pelagius' *Liber de Fide*, his final attempt to convince the established Church of his essential orthodoxy, while it contained twenty-six articles of faith, most of them quite impeccable by any standard, was largely irrelevant to the main charges brought against him and only showed him to be as stubborn as ever in his defence of free will and its controlling part in the operation of the divine grace. In the twenty-fifth article he can still affirm his own formula for reconciling free will and grace as if all Augustine's Olympian thunder had fallen on deaf ears: 'We confess the freedom of the will in such a way that we always need the grace of God.'[7] He was indeed marching to the beat of a different drummer, firmly resolved to keep to his own pace regardless of that set by others.

Is it conceivable then that 'he rather missed the point of the attack'?[8] Opinions will always differ on this question but one thing is certain: his own out-and-out refusal to admit that his critics had some basis for their charges itself supplied them with ammunition of which they were happy to take advantage. The two treatises which he wrote in Palestine to explain and defend his case were to be skilfully mined and exploited by his more experienced opponents, using judiciously selected quotations from them in order to set him up as an Aunt Sally for their own missiles. It is true that these quotations are all that remain of the two original works and that we must allow for the risks attendant on a procedure which takes discrete passages from an author's writings out of their context; but nothing we can find in them can fairly be said to have been out of keeping with the opinions expressed in Pelagius' surviving letters and in his commentary on the Pauline

[6] Brown, 1967, 356, where he compares this 'amazing group of Latin *emigrés* settled in Jerusalem' to 'the white Russians in Paris in the 1920s'.

[7] PL 48, 491, 504; the term *Libellus Fidei* is often used as an alternative to *Liber de Fide* in describing such confessions of faith.

[8] Bonner, 1966, 356.

Epistles. His own sheer cussedness contributed as much to his eventual downfall as the superior tactics and ecclesiastical clout of his adversaries. Battles are lost more often than they are won – in the theological arena as on the military front.

There is another temptation to which many have succumbed, and that is to try to transplant to the contemporary scene the Pelagius revealed to us in the course of his controversy with Jerome and Augustine, a lot which he shares with many other, more renowned personalities of antiquity. Some see him as primarily a humanist, striving to fight his way out of the dim shadows of revealed religion into the purer air of rationalistic humanism. But he was no humanist or rationalist, and, as for those whose enlightened twentieth-century liberalism leads them to envisage him as a bluff, rather jolly, Dickensian figure vainly pitting his puny strength in defence of human freedom against obscurantist theories of divine omnipotence – why, they would run miles to get out of his sight if confronted with the real Pelagius in person! Here was a man who would have turned the whole Christian Church into a reform school if he had had his way and, this accomplished to his own satisfaction, would have had not the slightest compunction in consigning to Hell all who remained outside of their own choice: 'In the day of judgement', he solemnly pronounced, 'no forbearance will be shown to the ungodly and the sinners but they will be consumed in eternal fires.'[9] He was a moral perfectionist for whom even the most venial sin brought with it the danger of everlasting punishment, and his personal opposition to Augustine's concept of a *massa damnata* stemmed not so much from humanitarian feelings as from his uncompromising denial of the latter's teaching on original sin and predestination on *a priori* grounds. The identification of Pelagius with the 'once-born' and Augustine with the 'twice-born' Christian, though not without some superficial attraction, is simplistic and seriously distorts our picture of both men.[10]

Another rich source of misunderstanding in connection with Pelagius has been the perennial attempt by scholars to determine the extent to which his theology can be claimed to have been original, playing their favourite game of *Quellensforschung* and combing his extant works for echoes of previous writers. Jerome was the first in the field as soon as he detected Pelagius' indebtedness to the *Sentences of Sextus*, a second-century collection of moral and religous aphorisms attributed to the third-century martyr Pope Xystus or Sixtus II by Rufinus of Aquileia in his preface to his Latin translation. This ascription was accepted by Pelagius without question and, at first, by Augustine too but he

[9] *PP* iii. 9 (PL 44, 325) (CSEL 42, 60).
[10] N. P. Williams, 1927, 331f., and elsewhere overstresses this identification: in some respects Pelagius was more like what we now know as the 'twice-born' or 'born-again' Christians than was Augustine. Little is gained, and perhaps much lost, by trying to categorise the personalities of the past in terms of present ideas. And Pelagius seems to have suffered from misrepresentation at the hands of both his critics and his admirers: I have read of his 'cheerful liberalism' and of his 'theology . . . closely akin to modern humanism', and I have seen him described as 'the herald of Love' and most odd of all, as 'a British cleric who stressed the idea of grace'. But I shall refrain from naming the scholars concerned in order to spare their blushes.

was later to be 'corrected' by Jerome, who held that the true author of the work was none other than 'the heathen philosopher Sextus', identified by him as a Pythagorean.[11] Augustine was naturally very happy to accept this identification, since he, like Jerome, thereby found another way to discredit Pelagius for claiming the support of a greatly venerated Christian for his teaching – and Jerome, of course, was never slow to grasp another cudgel with which to batter the ghost of his old antagonist Rufinus at the same time. But, as Henry Chadwick has demonstrated in his authoritative study of the *Sentences*, Rufinus did no more than state that there was a tradition – *tradunt*[12] – to the effect that Xystus was the author, and this was undoubtedly true in the fourth and early fifth centuries. Since then many attempts have been made to identify the author but all alike have foundered on the reefs of inadequate or misinterpreted evidence: 'All we know', concludes Chadwick, 'is that the author was Sextus, that Origen thought that the book was Christian, that some Christians in the fourth century came to identify him with Xystus II.'[13] Pelagius, though wrong in accepting on the seeming authority of Rufinus of Aquileia that Xystus II was the compiler of the *Sentences*, was right in thinking that it was written by a Christian, 'whose ecclesiastical principles and spiritual ideals determined his choice of material'.[14]

Chadwick is interested not in the question 'Where did he (Sextus) find this?' but in another, much more important and more likely to meet with a satisfactory answer – 'What did he do when he found it?' The same question could be applied to Pelagius' use of Sextus. What he found in him was a summary of teaching on the theme of how to achieve moral and spiritual perfection which was wholly consistent with his own ethical approach to Christianity. As to his use of what he found one example speaks volumes. When he maintained the God-given sovereignty of the human will, he could point to the thirty-sixth *Sentence*: 'God has granted to men the freedom of their own choice with the undoubted end in view that by living purely and without sin they might become like God.' In his treatise *On Nature and Grace* Augustine, at that time under the impression that the quotation came from a work by a Christian bishop and martyr, dismissed it as a misunderstanding of true doctrine, using Romans 5, 4 to support his contention. What would he have said if he had known at the time of writing, as he came to know later, that Xystus was not the author of the *Sentences* and that Pelagius' proof-text was no more reliable than some of his own? R. F. Evans has shown that Rufinus had imported into his Latin version of this *Sentence* views not in the Greek version of Origen, which reads: 'God has given to the believing man a freedom which is divine and therefore pure and without sin.'[15] Reading the *Sentences* in

[11] *Commentary on Ezekiel* VI, 18 (PL 25, 173); *Commentary on Jeremiah* IV, 22, 24ff. (PL 24, 817) (CSEL 59, 267); *Letters* 133, 3 (PL 22, 1152) (CSEL 56, 246); *NG* lxiv. 77 (PL 44, 285) (CSEL 60, 291); *R* II, 42 (PL 32, 647) (CSEL 36, 180) (Bogan, ed., II, 68).
[12] In his Preface to the *Sentences*, 7f.; H. Chadwick, 1959, 9.
[13] Ibid., 135.
[14] Ibid., 137.
[15] R. F. Evans, 1968(a), 64 – the printing errors in the Greek of n. 148 are of no importance as far as the meaning is concerned.

Rufinus' Latin version, Pelagius was 'encouraged to suppose that he had found, in a precise maxim of the bishop Xystus, authority for one of his most cherished teachings' – to which we might add, 'and one that was absolutely fundamental to his whole theology'.[16] The answer to our question, 'What did he do when he found it?', as applied to Pelagius, is that he used it to enhance his own claim to orthodoxy in defending his views on the freedom of the human will as God's gift to man.

But Jerome, like Augustine, was not to know of Pelagius' error in following Rufinus' text, and his charge against him in this connection was therefore misguided when he accused him not of having misused his source but of having relied on Stoic teaching transmitted by Origen in order to propagate and strengthen his own. Here Jerome was on less firm ground: Pelagius was not heavily indebted to Stoicism despite what has been described as his 'Stoic-like severity of judgement',[17] and Jerome's attempt to characterise him as more Stoic than Christian at heart does not stand up to closer examination, being largely based on the great scholar's own incorrect identification of the author of the *Sentences* as a pagan philosopher, coupled with his equation of Pelagius' 'sinlessness' with Stoic *apatheia*. The same initial prejudice led him to go even farther in trying to blacken Pelagius' name by association. In a letter written around 414 to his friend Ctesiphon he names as Pelagius' precursors in the heresy not only Origen, Jovinian and Rufinus of Aquileia but also Evagrius of Pontus, Palladius, Priscillian, the Manichees, the Euchites, a fourth-century Mesopotamian sect otherwise known as 'the Messalians', and other 'heralds of sinlessness' unnamed – for good measure![18] All of these were equally disreputable characters in Jerome's eyes, and he gleefully summoned them up from the past to discredit Pelagius. And another contemporary of Augustine and Pelagius, Marius Mercator, as well-disposed to the former as he was hostile to the latter, addressed two of his works to an attack upon the Pelagians. He saw Rufinus of Syria as the founder of the heresy and the main villain of the piece, using Pelagius and Celestius as his mouthpieces; but he also suggested that its origins were to be found in Theodore of Mopsuestia,[19] and his seventeenth-century editor, the Jesuit Jean Garnier, after an eloquent comparison of heresies with great rivers whose sources can be traced far back to small, remote streams, added Paul of Samosata to Theodore as another of these tributaries.[20]

But if we are to throw away Occam's razor altogether and include in the list of Pelagius' precursors Paul of Samosata, 'a convenient whipping-boy to take the blame for doctrinal aberrations with which he had little connection',[21] and

---

[16] Ibid., 65; H. Chadwick, 1959, 120 also comments that Pelagius certainly found Rufinus' translation 'highly congenial reading'.

[17] Passmore, 95.

[18] *Letters* 133 (PL 22, 1150ff.) (CSEL 56, 241ff.); see Garnier, *Dissertation* I (PL 48, 257).

[19] PL 48, 258ff.

[20] Ibid., 257f., where Theodore is said to have received the 'poison' from Paul and then transmitted it to both Nestorius and the Pelagians.

[21] Wallace-Hadrill, 70.

Theodore of Mopsuestia, who is 'neither a Pelagian nor an Augustinian',[22] why not go even farther and add Nemesius of Emesa as well, since he too 'has been accused (slightly anachronistically) of Pelagianism',[23] though he seems rather to have been a Synergist before his time? Obviously, if we were left only with the 'evidence' relied on by these self-appointed detectives, we might wonder whether Pelagius had a mind of his own at all and, if so, whether there was a single original thought in it. But, fortunately, the researches of the present century have pointed us towards a safer way through the 'wand'ring mazes'. In particular, Torgny Bohlin's exhaustive examination of the sources of Pelagius' theology, based on Souter's monumental edition of his commentary on the Epistles, 'has provided a new point of departure for Pelagian studies'.[24] His conclusion is that no single line of Pelagius' thought can be traced back to an earlier tradition but that his main achievement – his *Meisterstück* – was rather to have built upon what he found in both western and eastern theology and to have drawn together from them a synthesis of two distinct and contrasting emphases, the one on creation and the other on atonement. This new unity he employed as a powerful weapon against the Arians and his *bêtes noires*, the Manichees, quoting chapter and verse from his authorities as he went along. He found the idea of will as a gift from God in Rufinus of Aquileia's version of Origen's commentary on Romans, as he did that of the freedom of the human will; this he developed into a form of grace, blending the western and eastern traditions to produce a grace of creation and a grace of redemption, ideas which he would also have met in his reading of 'Ambrosiaster'. His objection to the idea of the inevitability of sin, as taught by the Manichees, would have been reinforced by his reading of Rufinus the Syrian's *Liber de Fide*, where too he found confirmation of his own views on original sin and infant baptism.

Plinval's comment is, at least to a certain extent, a just one when he refers to Pelagius' 'disposition to assimilate from an author only what agreed with his own ideas'.[25] And Augustine would certainly have supported this judgement: for example, towards the end of his treatise *On Nature and Grace* he gives several illustrations of Pelagius' habit of employing to his own advantage passages which could be understood in a neutral sense, taken from Lactantius, 'the blessed Hilary', Ambrose, John Chrysostom and, the supreme act of lese-majesty, from Augustine's own works written at an earlier date.[26] But that does not necessarily mean that Pelagius was some kind of intellectual magpie, scavenging industriously amongst the débris left by others for items which were to his own taste. If it did, then which one of us could claim to be entirely immune to the same charge? The practice followed by Pelagius is one which is common to all writers who enter into debate with opponents, and

---

[22] Ibid., 163; Norris, 184ff., and Appendix I, 240ff., has surely disposed for the last time of the charge that Theodore was a 'Pelagian'.

[23] F. M. Young, 1983, 168.

[24] Bonner, 1966, 352.

[25] Plinval, 1943, 81.

[26] *NG* lxi. 71–lxvii. 81 (PL 44, 282ff.) (CSEL 60, 286ff.).

that not only in the theological field. Many – possibly too many – quotations have been made in this book by the present writer but what does that tell the reader about him? Only that he has read certain works and used them to support or illuminate his arguments, not necessarily that he has met the ideas expressed in them for the first time; he may, on the contrary, have reached at least some of them under his own steam and then rejoiced to find that others have advanced similar ideas independently and with greater authority and clarity of expression. Pelagius does not always name the sources of his quotations but he is not thereby convicted of plagiarism – or should we coin a word 'Pelagiarism'? The writers of antiquity were never as critical of plagiarism as we are, and, in the period when Pelagius was writing, it was common practice among theologians not to name their authorities, unless they were scriptural, and no disgrace was attached to it.

Bonner is right when he warns us that 'no final judgement upon the personal views of Pelagius seems possible at the present state of our knowledge.'[27] *O si sic omnes!* There would then be some hope of a reduction in the number of misleading judgements which are still being made by contemporary writers. As it is, we are not in a position to slip back into those early years in the fifth century and to discover by that means exactly how Pelagius' mind worked when he wrote his treatises after his arrival in Palestine. But it would not be unreasonable to suggest, however tentatively, that his views on infant baptism, sinlessness, predestination and original sin – all of which his critics claim to have identified as borrowings from others – followed logically from his own *idée fixe* of the freedom of the human will and were used to provide a theological framework within which to defend it. It was this concept which formed the corner-stone of all his teaching and to which he returned with monotonous regularity, refusing to abandon it even when he submitted his confession of faith to the Pope. It was his fear that Augustine, the very man who had so vigorously and successfully defended free will against the Manichees, might now be weakening it by his teaching on grace, which aroused his first protest in Rome in the early years of the century. From it the rest of his theology followed 'as the night the day'; around it centred not only the great controversy which was to plague Augustine to the very end of his days but also the continuing debate which has niggled the established Church from time to time ever since. Nor was Pelagius the only Christian theologian to be concerned in the defence of free will: Origen had insisted on it, John Chrysostom was still preaching it at the time when Pelagius was launching his movement for moral reform at Rome, lesser mortals like Nemesius and Theodore also proclaimed it, Nestorius compounded his difficulties by making man's capacity to make a free response to the divine call an essential part of his doctrine – and, centuries later, Erasmus was to leap to its defence against Luther.

No, it does not inevitably follow from Pelagius' practice of quoting Catholic authorities that he was merely appropriating their ideas for his own use; what

---

[27] Bonner, 1966, 375.

it does indicate is that his main motive was to employ them to protect his own claim to orthodoxy. This was what infuriated Augustine most of all, especially when some of the works cited were his own, written before he had achieved his reputation as 'the Doctor of Grace' and his maturity as a theologian. But the plain truth is that he was no better placed than we are to single out individual items in the teaching of Pelagius and to state categorically, 'This is borrowed from X and that from Y'. In fact, he gives no indication of having tried to do so. At the time it was virtually impossible to make such judgements in the midst of the confusion which had begun to surround the Pelagians from the moment when they first appeared on the theological stage. There is no recognised body of doctrine which can fairly be described *tout court* as 'Pelagianism' in the sense that it can be attributed to Pelagius alone; rather there are opinions of Rufinus the Syrian, of Celestius, of the Sicilian Anonymous, of Julian of Eclanum, and of Pelagius himself, some of which but by no means all they can be said to have held in common, others on which they disagreed, and yet others which are more strongly emphasised in the teaching of each one in turn. But, in the eyes of Jerome and Augustine and their supporters, all were tarred with the same brush: *ab uno disce omnes* was the considered verdict of the early-fifth-century Church.

We are reminded of the ambiguous situation facing Darwin and Wallace in the nineteenth century when the latter 'put forward his views as early as 1864, only five years after Darwin's *Origin of Species* and seven years *before* Darwin's *The Descent of Man*'.[28] Who then was the true founder of Darwinism? A similar question faces us in connection with Pelagius and Pelagianism: it is the most difficult question of all, the sixty-four or, allowing for inflation, sixty-four thousand dollar question – was Pelagius justifiably regarded and designated as the true heresiarch by his contemporaries and so by posterity? Not, surely, if that means that he was the 'only begetter' of the heresy which bears his name. In fact, it does not seem to have needed one: like little Topsy, 'it just growed and growed' in the minds of its opponents. But there can be no doubt that Pelagius was regarded as the leading figure amongst the group around which it was seen to have developed, and the name *Pelagiani* appears for the first time to describe them in 415, when Jerome wrote his treatise against them.[29] In his works directed against them before 415 Augustine had scrupulously avoided naming names partly in order to give an opportunity to these embryonic heretics to amend their ways, as he himself claimed, and partly,

[28] Hardy, 1975, 62; cf. 1965, 64ff. and 1966, 35f.: 'it was a good thing that he [Darwin] let Lyall and Hooker know [of his own theory of natural selection]. Otherwise perhaps we might not be talking of Darwinism today but of Wallacism.'

[29] *Dialogue against the Pelagians* (PL 23, 495–590). Plinval, 1943, 216, n. 3, suggests that the name *Pelagiani* may have originated among Pelagius' friends, quoting Jerome's sardonic remark in *Letters* 133, 12 (PL 22, 1160): 'You laugh and rejoice that some are called by your name, others by that of Christ.' He also claims that Augustine once refers to the Pelagians as *Pelagianistae* in *S* 183, viii. 12 (PL 38, 992) but that word is used in the vocative *singular* in the passage cited. It is also found in Cassian, *On the Incarnation of Christ* I, 3 (PL 50, 23), in Possidius' *Life of Saint of Augustine*, 18 (PL 32, 48) and in Gennadius, *Prolegomena on the Writers of the Church*, 86 (PL 58, 1052); Praedestinatus, *Heresies*, 88 (PL 53, 618) refers to 'Pelagians or Celestians'.

also, in accordance with the convention of the time. Now he adopted the name with the greatest alacrity and, one must in fairness to him add, with every justification. By virtue of his reputation and his writings Pelagius stood out above Rufinus the Syrian and Celestius and the others, and above Celestius by seniority as well. Rufinus had died at the end of the first decade and took no part in the actual controversy, though his *Liber de Fide* left significant marks upon it; Celestius had been condemned in 411, and his excommunication relegated him to the rôle of cheer-leader from the touchline.

But Pelagius remained on the field, Pelagius was continuing to write, Pelagius had gathered a fresh band of supporters in Palestine. What other name could have been given to the heresy, since heresies must have a name – otherwise how can one attack them? Aristophanes the Greek comedian, if he had been alive, might have coined a new, portmanteau word 'Rufino-Celestio-Pelagianism', and even Garnier in the seventeenth century sometimes referred to 'the Celestian heresy', which is not surprising, since he, perhaps more than anyone before the twentieth century, realised and tried to grapple with the complexity of its origins and the issues involved in the controversy. But, at the time, Augustine and his supporters, not to speak of Jerome, were not concerned with such minutiae: for them 'Pelagianism' was the only possible name to give to the heresy. Thus Pelagius became, *faute de mieux*, the eponymous founder of a heresy for which he was both then and for ever after to be held responsible. Once he had written his two treatises *On Free Will* and *On Nature* the die was cast: it was only a matter of time before the mills of the Church would grind him out of existence.

'How Pelagian was Pelagius?' Pelagianism has had a long and varied history in one form or another, in the course of which it has been used as an appropriate whipping-post to which to tie anyone who has been suspected of challenging the Augustinian doctrine of grace, and as a result, many misunderstandings of the original teaching of Pelagius have arisen. But, after the condemnation of Pelagius and Celestius and the entry into the fray of the last of the Pelagians proper, Augustine did his best to set the record straight in his treatise addressed to Pope Boniface in 421 and directed against two letters from Julian and eighteen other bishops who refused to subscribe to Zosimus' *Epistula Tractoria* condemning Pelagius and Celestius. Smarting from their personal attacks upon him as a kind of recidivist Manichee, he conceived the brilliant idea of demonstrating that, far from being neo-Manichean, the Catholic Church, of which he was the spokesman, stood firmly, like an Aristotelian mean, between the extremes of Manicheism and Pelagianism. He summed up the main issues on which the Pelagians were at variance with the teaching of the Church under three headings: denying original sin, denying that God's grace is essential to salvation and preaching that, by the right use of his free will, a baptised Christian is able to remain without sin.[30] Of course, there are subsidiary charges of a minor nature but these three are at the heart

[30] *TLP* III, viii. 24 (PL 44, 606f.) (CSEL 60, 516).

of the matter, and he repeats the same summary of Pelagian errors in *On the Gift of Perseverance*, written in 428–9.[31] This then is what it means to be a Pelagian.

Was Pelagius a Pelagian in the sense that he could fairly be found guilty on all three main counts? Certainly, he would have to plead guilty on the first: like the other Pelagians, he strongly denied the existence of original sin. Augustine quotes him as saying in his book *On Free Will*, 'Evil is not born with us, and we are procreated without fault',[32] a statement frequently reiterated in different words elsewhere in his writings. So much for the first charge. The second is, however, more complex, and the case against the accused less clear-cut than the prosecutor – one is tempted to say 'the inquisitor' – ever succeeded in realising. Like many brilliant and dynamic personalities, Augustine tends sometimes to assume too readily that terminology can bear only the interpretation which he himself put on it and, as with his misguided attempt to establish that Pelagians equated 'the kingdom of God' with 'eternal life',[33] an equation more acceptable to theologians of the twentieth century than to those of the early fifth, that everyone else must have started out from the same premises as himself. Yet, at an early stage in the controversy, even he is forced to admit that he has been encouraged by Pelagius' words to believe that he is not denying the grace of God – only to discover as he reads further, that he is mistaken in this assumption. And, in his defence, the accused is able to refer to passages in his works as cited by the prosecutor in which he insists that man needs God's help to be good and be saved: for example, 'God helps us by his teaching and revelation, opening the eyes of our heart, pointing us to the future so that we may not be absorbed in the present, discovering to us the snares of the devil, enlightening us with the manifold and ineffable gift of heavenly grace.'[34] This very quotation was one which J. B. Mozley used to support his contention that Pelagius includes in his idea of grace 'those divine impulses and spiritual assistance commonly denoted by the word'.[35]

But one swallow does not make a summer, and even this statement of Pelagius can be attacked by the prosecution on the grounds that it is only a little less disingenuous than many others from his works. Why then did he 'never make an unambiguous declaration of true internal assisting grace'?[36] Why did he always couch his description of it in terms which made it appear to his opponents to be no more than a form of divine *assistance* to human free will? Surely because he, like the other Pelagians, was bound to give his loyalty first and foremost to the idea of free will as implanted in man by God, the 'grace of creation', which, along with the 'grace of atonement', that is, of

---

[31] *GP* ii. 4 (PL 45, 996). Wermelinger, 278ff., traces the various changes of emphasis in the formulations of the charges against Pelagius.
[32] *OS* xiii. 14 (PL 44, 392) (CSEL 42, 175f.).
[33] Refoulé, 1963(b), especially 253f.
[34] *GC* vii. 8 (PL 44, 364) (CSEL 42, 131).
[35] Mozley, 1855, 54, 1878, 50; see Bonner, 1966, 351, n. 4.
[36] Bonner, 1966, 356.

forgiveness through baptism, gave him the twin pillars of his doctrine. For example, 'That we are able to do, say, think any good comes from him who has endowed us with this ability and who also *assists* it . . . but that we really do a good thing or speak a good word or think a good thought proceeds from our own selves.'[37] And again, 'The man who hastens to the Lord and desires to be directed by him, that is, who makes his own will depend upon God's . . . does all this by nothing else than by his freedom of will.'[38] A third statement, in his *Letter to Demetrias*, brings Pelagius even closer to the brink when he says: 'It is by doing his will that we may *merit* his divine grace.'[39]

Augustine takes pains to spell this out in his summary of the second main charge against the Pelagians: they refuse to deny the charge of claiming that 'the grace of God whereby we are justified is not given freely but according to our merits'.[40] And so, despite his frequent assertions in his commentary on the Epistles that baptism is the sacrament of justification *by faith alone*, on which we have already remarked, Pelagius seems to understand this faith not as something inspired by God but as something which proceeds naturally from the right use of free will, which is no more than a faculty, albeit God-given, and, still worse, as something which 'merits' the divine gift of grace.[41] How can Pelagius insist that baptism is the sacrament of justification *by faith alone*, while still maintaining that faith 'merits' the grace of God? As R. F. Evans has shown in his admirable account of Pelagius' theology of baptism, it is a matter not so much of inconsistency as of the misleading use of language and particularly, of the words 'faith' and 'merit'.[42] By faith Pelagius means the trust in Jesus with which the convert approaches God when he seeks 'justification' through baptism and by which alone he can be said to 'merit' grace to absolve his past sins and so 'justify' him, that is, make him righteous. He then 'has the same status as one who has fulfilled the whole law';[43] 'water has cleansed his body, the 'word' has cleansed his soul'.[44] Man's faith is thus securely based on the act of Jesus in intervening to redeem man through baptism by his death and to strengthen him thereafter by his teaching and example. Yet man is a sinner who has no merit by virtue of which he may claim this grace of atonement and revelation: 'faith merits grace only in the sense that it is the indispensable and freely chosen condition of the effectual working of grace.'[45] Thus Pelagius could argue that his 'merit by faith' is not to be equated with merit by works, since it is not merit by works which makes the sinner righteous but faith alone, rewarded by forgiveness of sins through baptism: faith alone 'absolves him as to the past,

---

[37] *GC* xvi. 17 (PL 44, 369) (CSEL 42, 139).
[38] Ibid., xxii. 24 (PL 44, 371f.) (CSEL 42, 143).
[39] *Letter to Demetrias* 25 (PL 30, 40; 33, 1117).
[40] *TLP* III, viii. 24 (PL 44, 606) (CSEL 60, 516f.); cf. *GP* ii. 4 (PL 44, 996).
[41] *GC* xxxi. 34 (PL 44, 376) (CSEL 42, 152); cf. *On the Divine Law* 2 (PL 30, 107).
[42] R. F. Evans, 1968(a), 117ff.
[43] On Romans 10, 4 (PLS 1, 1157).
[44] On Ephesians 5, 26 (PLS 1, 1304).
[45] R. F. Evans, 1968(a), 118.

justifies him as to the present and prepares him for future works of faith'.[46] It is vital to observe the precise sequence of events – faith first, then righteousness of faith, then righteousness of works, bringing the whole process to its proper fulfilment.

'Righteousness of works'? This phrase at once revives the old doubt in the minds of the jury, and it is confirmed when they hear the third charge, that of preaching 'sinlessness', which almost overlaps the second and had been brought against Pelagius in the first and sixth items of the case made out by his accusers at the Synod of Diospolis. Under the first item he had been confronted with his statement that 'a man cannot be without sin unless he has acquired a knowledge of the law'.[47] To this he had replied that he had used these words but not in the sense in which they were understood by others: 'I did not say that a man cannot sin if he has acquired a knowledge of the law but that by knowledge of the law he is helped not to sin, as it is written, "He hath given them a law for help"'. This reply had been accepted by the Synod but Augustine attributed that to their inability to understand the contents of Pelagius' book, which was in Latin, and to their being misled by his reply, which was also in Latin and was translated into Greek for their benefit and was understood by them in their own terms. Under the sixth item his accusers had cited another statement from the same book: 'A man can be without sin if he wishes'.[48] Augustine quotes his reply to this in full: 'I did indeed say that a man can be without sin and keep the commandments of God, if he wishes; for this ability has been given to him by God. However, I did not say that any man can be found who has never sinned from his infancy to his old age but that, having been converted from his sins, he can be without sin by his own efforts and God's grace, yet not even by this means is he incapable of change in future.' Again the Synod expressed itself satisfied with his reply, which they took in the sense that 'a man is able to be without sin with God's help and God's grace.' Augustine, on the other hand, pointed to the vagueness of Pelagius' affirmation of grace, which his judges generously interpreted as being consistent with Paul's teaching, not realising that elsewhere in his writings Pelagius had explicitly stated that this 'grace' depended on the capacity of not sinning which man had received from God at creation through the gift of free will. And, again, Augustine maintained that the Synod had wrongly acquitted Pelagius because they misunderstood his statements.

It was Jerome, of course, who had first drawn attention to Pelagius' teaching of 'sinlessness' and accused him of lifting this idea bodily from Rufinus of Aquileia's version of the *Sentences of Sextus*. In a letter written around 414[49] and in his *Dialogue against the Pelagians* he concentrated his attack upon this idea as a reiteration of Origen's teaching that it is possible for a man

---

[46] On Romans 4, 6 (PLS 1, 1131).
[47] *PP* i. 2 (PL 44, 321) (CSEL 42, 52).
[48] Ibid., vi. 16 (PL 44, 329) (CSEL 42, 68f.).
[49] *Letters* 133 (PL 22, 1147ff.) (CSEL 56, 241ff.).

to attain God's perfection – it is a *ramusculus Origenis*, 'a little twig of Origen'[50] – and the Stoic doctrine of *apatheia*. He linked this with Pelagius' insistence that all commandments of God were equally binding on Christians, which he saw as the equivalent of the Stoic teaching of the equality of sins. To this secondary charge Pelagius replied that he did not teach that all sins were equal in gravity but that, once a man has fallen into the habit of committing minor sins, he is in danger of going on to commit major sins as well; God's punishment, however, is graded according to the gravity of the sins committed.[51] To the main charge of preaching 'sinlessness' he replied that he was referring to the standard by which a *man* can be judged to be 'sinless', not that which would be applicable to *God*: God, he maintained, would not ask man to match that divine standard but one appropriate to man's status and condition, nor would he ask man to match even that standard by obeying his commands, if it were impossible for him to do so.[52] But it was not impossible, at least in theory, for a man to attain perfection in this life, though it could not be claimed with any certainty that anyone had, in practice, succeeded in doing so and in remaining sinless to the end.[53] Pelagius' proof-text is from the Sermon on the Mount: 'Be ye therefore perfect, even as your Father which is in heaven is perfect',[54] the very same text which has become a *locus classicus* – one might say *tritus* – in all subsequent debate on the subject of Christian perfectibility, as theologians have striven to reconcile it with the Hellenic concept of God as 'simple, absolute being', on the one hand, and with Augustinian teaching on man's inevitable sinfulness, on the other.[55] The *NEB*, for example, renders it: 'You must therefore be all goodness, just as your heavenly Father is all good.'

However many new facets of the problem have been revealed in later discussion of it, there can be little doubt that the majority of Christians have found Pelagius' teaching on sinlessness to be unacceptable. In the present context and not for the first time, Pelagius found himself driven into a tight

[50] *Dialogue against the Pelagians*, Pref., 1 (PL 23, 495ff.); *Letters* 133, 3 (PL 22, 1152) (CSEL 56, 247). The word *impeccantia* does not occur in classical Latin, though the adjective *impeccabilis*, meaning 'faultless', appears in Aulus Gellius once in the second century A.D. It may well have been a neologism coined by Jerome to express the sense of the Greek *apatheia*; if so, perhaps he should have taken note of Seneca's warning in *Letters* 9, 2 that even the literal translation of *apatheia*, that is, *impatientia*, is inadequate: 'we are bound to fall into ambiguity, if we want to express *apatheia* summarily by a single word and render it by *impatientia*, since this may be understood in the opposite sense to that which we wish it to bear.' The word *impeccantia* is no less ambiguous, and I have been unable to find a single instance of its use in Augustine. In any case, although the charge of preaching 'sinlessness' was brought against Pelagius at the Synod of Diospolis, it was declared to be orthodox as long as it did not involve a renunciation of divine grace, and its importance decreased as Augustine laid more and more stress on his doctrine of grace with its corollaries, original sin and predestination (Wermelinger, 82, 281).
[51] *Liber de Fide* 16 (PL 48, 490, 502); *Letter to Celantia* 6 (PL 22, 1207); *On Virginity* 7 (PL 30, 167ff.).
[52] *Dialogue against the Pelagians* I, 16, 21 (PL 23, 509, 514).
[53] Souter, 1907, 437 (PLS I, 1541f., fr. 2).
[54] Matthew 5, 48.
[55] Passmore, 69, describes the first concept as 'metaphysical' and the second as 'moral or anthropological', that is, relating to man.

corner from which he had his work cut out in trying to extricate himself. Jerome had awakened a suspicion which was to attach itself to Pelagius ever after, so that, whenever Christians have to oppose the idea of human perfectibility, they always see in it 'a latent Pelagianism or "angelism", the idea that man can attain perfection by some heroic endeavour',[56] and when they describe an individual or his doctrine or his prayer as 'Pelagian', it is that idea which is foremost in their minds and not his denial of original sin, or, much less, his defence of free will. He might be prepared to admit that his citation of long list of patriarchs, prophets and others from the scriptures as examples of righteous men and women 'did not necessarily involve him maintaining that any individual had in fact achieved such sinless living',[57] and he could hardly fail to do so when his prosecutor pointed out to him that righteousness and sinlessness were not synonymous terms.[58] But it would have been contrary to his moral theology and his teaching on man if he had been willing to abandon the possibility of sinlessness altogether, and, above all else, it would have been a betrayal of his emphasis on the freedom of the will to choose for itself: free will is necessary to the man who wishes not to sin, and that free will has been given to him by the same God who wishes him to be without sin. For him, free will and sinlessness walked hand in hand.

Such an emphasis on free will was, as we have seen again and again, anathema to Pelagius' chief prosecutor, because it led, in his view, to the neglect of the paramount need for indwelling grace. At first, it was not the idea of sinlessness by itself which attracted Augustine's main criticism, and, in 412, when writing his treatise *On the Spirit and the Letter*, though he draws attention to it as a Pelagian tenet, he does not bother to press home his attack on those who maintain that a sinless life is possible in this world; they are not, he says, 'not a cause for great concern on that account'.[59] It is when they go farther and argue that such sinlessness is made possible by the use of free will, not the grace of God as he understands it, that he takes serious issue with it. It was in vain that Pelagius continued to protest that the will itself was a form of grace given to man at his creation; nor were his accusers able to comprehend his argument that the God who had created man would be an unjust God if he punished him for committing sins which, by his very nature, he was incapable of avoiding. In his *Liber de Fide* he tried for the last time to defend himself against the charge of preaching sinlessness by summarising his true position: 'Those who say with the Manichee that man cannot avoid sin are as much in error as those who assert with Jovinian that a man is unable to sin.'[60] Taken by itself, this statement is unexceptionable, making the point that Pelagius is both anti-Manichee and anti-Jovinian; but he then went on to destroy the effect of it by adding: 'Both of these are wrong because they remove the freedom of the will, whereas we always maintain that a man is always able to

[56] See E. J. Tinsley in Richardson, ed., 255.
[57] *PP* vi. 16 (PL 44, 329f.) (CSEL 42, 69).
[58] *NG* xxxviii. 45 (PL 44, 268f.) (CSEL 60, 267).
[59] *SL* ii. 3 (PL 44, 202) (CSEL 60, 156); the actual words used are *multum molesti*.
[60] *Liber de Fide* 25(PL 48, 491, 504).

sin and not to sin, so that we always confess that we are endowed with free choice.' In this instance his statement is verbally identical with that of Celestius, and, as his prosecutor immediately perceived, it was only another reiteration of his idea of a free will which could work *in utramque partem*, 'in either direction'.

Of the three main charges then it could be fairly said that all three were proven – proven, that is to say, in that Pelagius' denial of original sin, his theology of grace and his perfectionism all conflicted with the teaching of the contemporary Western Church and of Augustine, in particular, which was to mean for centuries much the same thing. Yet the fear that Pelagius expressed that Augustine's teaching on grace in the *Confessions* at first and then in his anti-Pelagian treatises and elsewhere could be interpreted by misguided Christians as an open invitation to forget their own rôle in their own salvation was to re-echo down the centuries. Even Luther, who would have no truck with Pelagius and regarded Augustine, along with Paul, as his most reliable guide to a true Christian faith, was to lament the apathy and abuse arising from misunderstanding of Augustinian doctrine and endemic in his own day. A millennium earlier John Cassian had foreseen this danger and had given voice to his concern that the views of Augustine on grace might, if accepted in their extreme form and without modification, deprive the members of his community of the motivation needed to keep them on the path of righteousness: 'Cassian knew his own monks.'[61] Thus, in the lifetime of Augustine and possibly even before Pelagius was at rest in his grave, a respected Christian described by some as the father of Semi-Pelagianism and by others as the father of Semi-Augustinianism pointed to a *media via* between the two main protagonists in the Pelagian controversy. Semi-Pelagianism would meet with the same fate as Pelagianism and would be condemned along with it at the Council of Orange; but it remained on the agenda, a thorn in the flesh of the establishment for all that, and it would be revived in the sixteenth century by Philip Melanchthon in the form of Synergism, a name which was an invention of his opponents and not himself.

The misgivings of Pelagius were never to be completely stifled: he was destined to become 'a Phoenix too frequent', and perhaps this is the most impressive vindication of the countervailing misgivings of Jerome and Augustine when they foresaw the very real danger to the unity of the Church – 'the wild thickets of this heresy, which we are sorry to see shooting out buds, nay, growing into trees, day by day'.[62] Day by day? No, century by century, and perhaps for as long as the foundations of Christian belief are still debated,

---

[61] Passmore, 98. Elsewhere (114) he quotes Karl Barth as asking in a lecture on 'The Humanity of God', delivered in 1956, 'What if the result of the new hymn to the majesty of God should be a new confirmation of the hopelessness of all human activity?', and (115) refers to Perry Miller's description of how Pelagianism developed in a New England community as it came to find itself incapable of 'disciplining those who sat back and waited for God's grace to fall, or not to fall, upon them': 'if God can, if he chooses, lift a saint from a dunghill, why not be warm and cosy in the dunghill, awaiting his grace?'.

[62] *PP* xxxv. 65 (PL 44, 357) (CSEL 42, 120).

the buds continue to grow into trees and those trees to flourish! There will always be those who, like Leslie Dewart, will find themselves compelled in all honesty and even at the risk of giving offence to conclude: 'It is possible that the maintenance of bare orthodoxy is no criterion of the sufficiency and adequacy of the authoritative (and other) teaching of the Church.'[63] 'Amen to that!' could have been Pelagius' last *cri de coeur*.

[63] L. Dewart, 71f., n. 17; cf. 128, n. 6. As H. Chadwick comments in his discussi n of the orthodoxy of Origen, 'Orthodoxy is a word that suggests clear-cut and absolute lines of division. It begins to look different if we ask whether some theologians may be more orthodox than others, whether there are degrees of understanding, whether, if we all see through a glass darkly, some may be able to see a little more clearly than others'; and 'If he [Origen] remains a perennially enigmatic and embarrassing figure in the history of Christian thought, this is perhaps most due to the fact that we tend to begin the study of Origen by asking whether or not he is orthodox, and find that in the process we are continually driven back to the prior question: what is the essence of orthodoxy?' (1966, 122f.).

VI

MARCHING ON

'John Brown's body lies a mould'ring in the grave,
His soul is marching on.'

CHARLES S. HALL[1]

In 418 Pelagius was condemned by the Pope and excommunicated by the
Church which he had set out to reform; in 431 the 'opinions of Celestius' and
all who were associated with him were again condemned, this time by the
third ecumenical council at Ephesus. But in the years between, the establishment's battle with Pelagianism had continued to rage furiously while Julian of
Eclanum, 'a natural dialectician, with a bent for speculative thought that
Pelagius did not possess',[2] vigorously probed the weaknesses of Augustine's
position, and Augustine responded with 'the cold competence of an old, tired
man, who knew only too well how to set about the harsh business of
ecclesiastical controversy'.[3] Julian, who came of noble stock and whose father
was a bishop, had won for himself a high reputation in the best circles as a
young man for his many talents and for his attachment to the simple life: he
had even sold his estates to relieve the poor at a time of great famine, and
Paulinus of Nola, a friend of his father, had composed a poem in his honour to
celebrate his marriage to the daughter of another bishop.[4] Had it not been for
his enthusiasm in the cause of Pelagius and Celestius he 'might have ended

---

[1] *John Brown's Body*, attributed to Charles Sprague Hall in the edition of the *Oxford Dictionary of
Quotations* which I possess, though it seems to have been removed from the latest edition. Perhaps
this is because it has been attributed also to Thomas Brigham Young and Frank E. Jerome
amongst others, and no one appears to be quite certain who its author was. In some versions 'is'
is found in place of 'lies' in the first line.

[2] G. R. Evans, 143.

[3] Brown, 1967, 384; Burnaby, 1938, 231, writes in a similar vein of the later Augustine: 'a man
whose energy has burned out, whose love has gone cold'. But though he did not complete his last
reply to Julian, *IWJ*, he managed to find enough energy to write six books of it and, in his last
three years, also wrote *PS* and *GP* as well as *H* and two other works.

[4] Gennadius, *On Famous Men*, 45 (PL 58, 1084), in his continuation of Jerome's work with the
same title; Paulinus, *Poems* 25 (PL 61, 633f.). Frend, 1984, 802, refers to Gennadius as a
'Semi-Pelagian' – he was a friend of Faustus of Riez – and notes that he was one of the few
Westerners of his day who knew Greek, and it is interesting to observe that it is he who tells us
that Julian also had a thorough knowledge of Greek (op. cit. 46). Wermelinger, 228, suggests that
his knowledge of eastern theologians may have been overestimated, since he cites only two of
them in his treatise *To Turbantius*, John Chrysostom and Basil of Caesarea, according to
Augustine, *J* I, v. 16–17, vi. 21 (PL 44, 650f., 654f.), and the same two with Theodore of
Mopsuestia added in *To Florus*, III, 111 (PL 45, 1295) (CSEL 85/1, 432). But Augustine is
notoriously selective in his citations of the works of his opponents.

his days as an honoured figure in the Church'.[5] But instead, in 418, along with eighteen other Italian bishops, he was deposed from his see and banished for refusing to subscribe to Zosimus' *Epistula Tractoria*, and in 419 he retired to the Near East, whence he launched a spate of letters and treatises against Augustine and his supporters.[6]

The strength of Augustine's reaction to these criticisms may be gauged by the fact that no fewer than ten of his fifteen anti-Pelagian works date from the period following the condemnation of Pelagius and Celestius in 418, all of them written as rejoinders either to Julian or to those of his own friends and correspondents who raised questions on issues involved in his debate with Pelagius. The first of these, entitled *On the Grace of Christ and Original Sin*, was written soon after 'the conviction and condemnation of the Pelagian heresy along with its authors by the bishops of the Church at Rome – first Innocent and then Zosimus – with the co-operation of letters from African councils',[7] and was addressed to Pinianus, his wife Melania and her mother Albina, who had been befriended by him at Thagaste and were now in Palestine. His intention in writing it was to reassure them by providing them with a definitive summary of his case against the Pelagians and an answer to the defence made by Pelagius in a letter which he had written to them after his condemnation, protesting his orthodoxy and knowing them to have been sympathetic to his cause at the time when they had all been together in Rome.

Not long after this Augustine addressed two books *On Marriage and Concupiscence* to Count Valerius, a long-established supporter of his views who has been described as '*plus catholique que le pape*',[8] the second of them being a reply to criticisms of the first contained in the four books of Julian's treatise *To*

---

[5] Bonner, 1963, 347. His earlier career had been unexceptionable: a *lector* in his father's church at the time of his marriage (Paulinus, *Poems* 25, 143f.) (PL 61, 633f.) and a deacon *c.* 408, when Augustine asked his bishop, Memorius, to pass on to him a copy of the sixth book of his treatise *On Music*, referring to him in the most complimentary and affectionate terms and inviting him to Hippo (*L* 101, 4) (PL 33, 369) (CSEL 34, 543), he was made Bishop of Eclanum by Pope Innocent I *c.* 416, when he was about thirty years old. It is difficult to reconcile the aspersions cast on his morality by Augustine in *J* V, vi. 24 (PL 44, 799) with his high reputation as a young man and the esteem in which Augustine himself professes to hold him in *L* 101; and Mercator's assertion (*Book of Notes on Words of Julian* iv. 5) (PL 48, 132) that he had corrupted one of his sisters after his adoption of them on the death of their parents must be taken to refer to indoctrination and not to immoral behaviour on his part. As for the eighteen bishops who supported him originally by refusing to subscribe to the condemnation of Pelagius and Celestius on the grounds that they had not been given a fair trial, not all of them can be proved to have persisted in their loyalty to him by joining him in exile; for example, Augustine makes much of the defection of Turbantius in *IWJ* I, 1, II, 11, IV, 30 and V, 6 (PL 45, 1051, 1146, 1353, 1436f.) (CSEL 85/1, 5, 170).

[6] A complete list of fragments attributed to Julian as well as other writings on which there is no general agreement as to his authorship of them may be found in PLS 1, 1571; see also *CC* 88, 335–98 and Duval, 1979, 162–70.

[7] *R* II, 50 (PL 32, 650) (CSEL 36, 187) (Bogan, ed. II, 76); the attentive reader will have noticed that Bogan has numbered the entries in *R* continuously from the beginning of Book I to the end of Book II. CCSL 57, 1984, ed. A. Mutzenbecher, is an up-to-date edition and commentary to which I have been unable to refer.

[8] Brown, 1967, 362.

Turbantius, now lost.[9] The revived controversy was continued by Julian's eight books *To Florus*, also lost, and three treatises of Augustine written between 420 and 429.[10] Since Julian's works have not survived, we have to judge him on the many quotations which Augustine made from them, setting them out in dialogue form along with his own replies. It is therefore difficult, if not impossible, to reconstruct a coherent picture of Julian's theology, and it comes as no surprise to find that scholars have differed considerably in their assessment of his personality and his contribution to the ongoing debate. Bonner, for example, detects in Julian's character 'an arrogance of a most unattractive nature' and criticises him both for his lack of respect for Augustine, whom he dismisses on different occasions as the 'Punic Aristotle', a 'Punic philosophiser' and 'defender of the donkeys', and for being 'well nigh obsessed' with the idea of concupiscence.[11] Brown, on the other hand, though he too finds Julian to be 'not a sympathetic person', is a little more kindly disposed towards him and believes that 'we have only begun to appreciate the extent of his learning and originality'.[12] The actual debate between the two protagonists, as it is recorded by Augustine, seems to have done little more than grind out the old, well-worn issues all over again – free will, infant baptism, original sin, predestination and, of course, Augustine's alleged neo-Manicheism, a topic with which he became more and more exasperated under the provocation of his new opponent's bitter and often damaging attacks. Despite Julian's attempts to open up new lines of criticism, the controversy between the two men resembles one of those bare-fisted fights which took place before the Queensberry Rules were introduced to 'civilise' boxing and offers a most unedifying example of the combination of jaw-jaw with war-war. The record of it provided by Augustine reflects small credit on either of the two participants and can hardly be recommended to budding

[9] *MC* (PL 44, 413–74) (CSEL 42, 211–319); *R* II, 53 (PL 32, 651) (CSEL 36, 189f.) (Bogan, ed. II, 79).

[10] *TLP* (PL 44, 549–638) (CSEL 60, 423–570), addressed to Pope Boniface; *J* (PL 44, 641–874); *IWJ* (PL 45, 1049–608) (CSEL 85/1, 3–506).

[11] Bonner, 1963, 347; 1962, 303; see also Brown, 1967, 383. Brown, 1983(a), has more recently demonstrated that Julian's most important contribution to the Pelagian controversy may well have been his success in provoking Augustine to undertake an intensive re-examination of his views on marriage and *concupiscentia* and, as a result, to formulate a theory of sexuality which was in direct conflict with current medical opinion but was to exert a profound influence on the moral and social climate of Latin Christianity. Brown, 63ff., summarises the essential differences between Augustine and Julian on this subject 'by setting Augustine's attitude against the inherited conglomerate of late classical notions with which it tacitly parted company' – and led Julian to describe him, not altogether inaptly, as a *novus iste physicus* (*IWJ* V, 11; PL 45, 1142).

[12] Brown, 1967, 383, 387. Wermelinger, 228, points out that there is no evidence for any direct pupil-teacher relationship between Julian and Pelagius, though they may have met in Rome, and describes the former as an unusually independent thinker: he mentions Pelagius by name only once according to Wermelinger, 228, n. 54, in *IWJ* IV, 112 (PL 45, 1405) but even there the names of Pelagius and Celestius do not seem to occur in a direct quotation. Wermelinger, 264ff., examines the changes which have taken place in the modern evaluation of Julian's thought since Bruckner's study as a result of the work of Refoulé and Bouwman and concludes that the Bishop of Eclanum can no longer be labelled as a 'faithless rationalist', even if Bouwman still maintains that he was a 'radical rationalist' in his polemical works (265, n. 262).

theologians as good bedside reading: in all this 'there's no musick, no harmony, no peace'.

In 423 Julian had sought refuge with Theodore of Mopsuestia, mistakenly supposing that he would find him sympathetic to the Pelagian cause. We have no reason to suppose that he was treated with anything but courtesy and kindness by Theodore but his admiration for the learned bishop was not reciprocated, and Marius Mercator, who had no great love for either, records that, after Julian's departure for Constantinople to try his luck there, the Cilician bishop was persuaded by his colleagues to concur in the decision of a local synod which anathematised Julian and his doctrine.[13] After his condemnation in 431, along with Celestius and other Pelagians, by the Council of Ephesus, Julian made his way back to Italy, where he failed to obtain reinstatement as bishop, and eventually died in Sicily after a life of which almost half had been spent in exile. And so the last of the Pelagians also bit the dust, and a life which had started with promise of great things finished in dishonourable exile, and the man who had made Augustine's last years so uncomfortable that he was described as 'the Cain of our times', passed his own in teaching Latin to the children of a Pelagian family.[14]

By then Augustine had gone to his long rest; but he had done so in the sure knowledge that, although the Vandals were already encamped around the walls of his beloved Hippo, the bastion which he had constructed to defend his own reputation and the teaching on which it was founded had been seen to be impregnable against all the assaults of the Pelagians. Was there not in his library a copy of the imperial rescript of Honorius and Theodosius II which empowered bishops to depose and banish from any part of the Empire all those who might still cling to the last vestiges of Pelagianism, and had not a later edict, issued to the propraetor of Gaul by Theodosius II and Valentinian III and instructing him to summon to a court of enquiry Gallican bishops who were still recalcitrant, demonstrated to the Church that the imperial policy with regard to Pelagianism was being conscientiously pursued by the secular authorities?[15] Yet all was not quiet on the western front or even in that African sector in which Augustine was established as the chief spokesman of the Church. Not all the documents relating to the controversy had penetrated to the monasteries, and not all of the monks had digested those which had. Around 426 a bombshell shattered the peace of the monastery at Hadrumetum on the south-eastern coast of Tunisia, when a monk named Florus, visiting his home at Uzalis near Carthage, came across a copy of Augustine's letter to the Roman presbyter Sixtus, later to become Pope Sixtus III, written about 419 and setting out his doctrine of predestination in its severest form.[16] Florus, who appears to have been an admirer of Augustine, was obviously delighted with his find and made a copy to the dictation of his companion Felix, with

---

[13] PL 48, 297, 360; for the last years of his life see Vignier in PL 45, 1040ff.
[14] PL 48, 297.
[15] PL 45, 1726f.; *L* 201 (PL 33, 927) (CSEL 57, 296ff.); PL 45, 1751.
[16] *L* 194 (PL 33, 874ff.) (CSEL 57, 176ff.); 216, 2, 3 (PL 33, 975; 44, 914) (CSEL 57, 397ff.).

whom he sent it back to Hadrumetum, while he himself stopped off at Carthage on the return journey.

Felix returned in due course to his monastery at Hadrumetum with the copy of the letter to Sixtus and, unbeknown to his abbot Valentinus, circulated it among the brethren. It immediately set the cat among the pigeons; it had been 'a manifesto of unconditional surrender written in the heat of controversy'[17] and at once became the subject of intense disagreement among the monks, some of them favouring a doctrine of grace which denied the freedom of the will, others maintaining that the free will is assisted by grace so as to enable men to know and to do what is right. Augustine was made aware of this disagreement by two of the monks, Cresconius and Felix, when they visited him at Hippo, and he at once wrote to the abbot explaining the true meaning of his letter to Sixtus to the best of his ability in the space available in a letter and, at the same time, asking him to send to him at Hippo the man by whom they said the disturbance had been caused, meaning Florus.[18] Florus did make the journey to Hippo himself but found Augustine prevented by poor health from discussing the matter as fully as he would have liked to do.[19] But meanwhile Augustine kept with him under instruction Cresconius and Felix as well as another Felix, who may well have been the monk who had brought the copy of the letter to Sixtus back to the monastery. Doubtless he set about his self-imposed task of assuaging their fears with 'the serene intransigence of a man who was sure of the heart of his message';[20] but he also sent another letter to Valentinus and his monks as well as a whole treatise addressed to the abbot and his brethren,[21] and, for good measure, a batch of documents relevant to the Pelagian controversy from the authorities of the Church at Rome, at Carthage and in Numidia, including the canons of the Council of Carthage and letters written by himself. This, he thought, would settle the matter once and for all; but, as often happened to him in the course of his many battles for the faith, he overestimated the power of his arguments to dispel the doubts of those who did not fully appreciate their strength and essential reasonableness.

In the event one word only led to another, and, faced with the objection made by the monks that his statements meant that we ought not to rebuke a man for failing to keep God's commandments but only to pray that he be given the grace which would alone enable him to keep them, he found himself constrained to compose yet another treatise, in which he contended that we are justified in rebuking a fellow Christian who sins but that such a rebuke would be effective only if he were one of God's elect.[22] The abbot Valentinus had written in the meantime to explain how the incident at Hadrumetum had arisen and how he had tried to deal with it and to exonerate Florus from any

---

[17] Brown, 1967, 399.
[18] *L* 214 (PL 33, 968ff.) (CSEL 57, 380ff.).
[19] Morin, *RB* 18, 1901, 243; cf. 1896, 481ff.
[20] Brown, 1967, 403.
[21] *L* 215 (PL 33, 971–4; 44, 875–80) (CSEL 57, 387–96); *GFC* (PL 44, 881–912).
[22] *RG* (PL 44, 915–46).

blame attached to his part in it. In his letter he described how he had sought the advice and support of his neighbours, Evodius of Uzalis, an old friend and supporter of Augustine, and a presbyter named Sabinus, as soon as he had learned of the trouble which the letter to Sixtus was causing among his monks, only to find that even their replies had failed to convince the dissidents. What a fascinating picture! Of an abbot sitting on a theological volcano without being aware of its existence, of monks trekking to and fro across north Africa to sit at the feet of Augustine and receive instruction from him, and of the great man himself, whose polemic had restored order in the African Church and whose teaching was to shape the development of Christian theology for centuries, finding the time and the patience to allay the fears of a handful of worried individuals. And this, as Brown reminds us, 'was the vehement opponent of Julian of Eclanum'.[23] It was but the smile on the face of the tiger, and the abbot and his monks could count themselves lucky that Augustine does not seem to have been troubled thereafter by the disturbances at their monastery. It had arisen in the first place because the majority of the monks were simple men, dedicated to the pursuit of the ascetic life and holding uncomplicated Christian beliefs, so that much of the great battle which had been waged in the more subtle atmosphere of the theologians had passed over their heads almost unnoticed. What the Hadrumetum incident gives us is 'an exceptional opportunity of watching the immediate reaction of the humbler religious of St. Augustine's time to some of the more difficult of his writings'.[24]

We may assume therefore that peace returned to Hadrumetum as a result of Augustine's efforts and that he could dismiss the incident as no more than a storm in a teacup. But his treatise *On Rebuke and Grace*, like that *Against Julian*, did not escape the notice of others elsewhere, and a more serious debate was soon to begin in southern Gaul which was to lead to the rise of Semi-Pelagianism and to compete with Augustine's debate with Julian for his attention as a polemicist until the end of his life in 430. In 427/8 an old friend and correspondent, Prosper Tiro of Aquitaine, wrote to him warning him of unrest among the monks at Marseilles: 'many of the servants of Christ who live in the city of Marseilles', he wrote, 'believe that the part of your writings against the Pelagian heretics which argues for the calling of the elect in accordance with divine intervention is contrary to the opinion of the Fathers and to the common feeling of the Church.' In other words, they held that Jesus came into the world to bring salvation to all men alike and rejected the notion that only some are predestined to salvation, the others to damnation. The bone of contention is thus the same as it had been in the case of the monks of Hadrumetum: it was Augustine's extreme doctrine of predestination. The monks, it seems, made a firm distinction between predestination and foreknowledge, and Prosper further warns that they were not without the backing of influential spokesmen, mentioning one in particular who was an

[23] Brown, 1967, 402.
[24] N. K. Chadwick, 1955, 179.

admirer and adherent of Augustine's doctrine in all respects except this one of predestination, Helladius or Euladius, Bishop of Arles, who had long expressed an intention of writing to him for an explanation.[25] A letter couched in similar terms from a distinguished layman Hilary must have reached Hippo about the same time, referring to the same difference of opinion in the region of southern Provence.[26]

Augustine's response to these two warning letters came with the usual promptness and took the form of another dose of prescribed reading in a treatise in two books *On the Predestination of the Saints* and *On the Gift of Perseverance*, the second of which is traditionally published as a separate work; both are dated in 428/9 and neither reveals the slightest hint of compromise.[27] The monks, Augustine maintains, are in error if they suppose that his doctrine of predestination is a novel one and contrary to the teaching of the Church, since it has always been proclaimed and is a logical development of the teaching of Paul. What greater authority can they, or anyone, ask for? If they are concerned about the possible effect of the doctrine on their fellow-monks and their congregations, then the correct tactic is not to disturb them by over-emphasising predestination to damnation but, rather, to adapt their message to the needs and understanding of their hearers, stressing that all who try sincerely to obey the will of God will be given the strength to follow his commandments and the perseverance to maintain their faith to the very end. Haunted as he was by the spectre of advancing barbarism and its threat to the very existence of the Church, he was convinced that perseverance was the only answer for Christians concerned for their own salvation as well as the survival of their religion. But such a message, 'a doctrine for fighting men', 'a hard message for a hard age', 'a doctrine for survival, a fierce insistence that God alone could provide men with an irreducible core', was too strong for Christians for whom the bell had not yet tolled and whose main concern was for the preservation of their own chosen way of life and the quest for their own salvation sustained by the simple belief that 'God wishes all men to be saved' – a text which Augustine continued to misinterpret and even Prosper could dismiss as 'a trite objection'.[28]

The monks of southern Gaul were part of the great monastic movement which had sprung up in Egypt in the third century and had spread to the west in the fourth, and they were by nature and training more attuned to the theology of the eastern Church than to that of the west. They had come to regard themselves as the true custodians of the faith and of its ancient

[25] *L* 225 (PL 33, 1002–7; 44, 947–54) (CSEL 57, 454–68). In para. 9 all but one of the MSS give us *Hilarium* but O. Chadwick, 1945, and 1968, 128, puts forward a convincing argument for accepting that the sole MS which reads *elladium* provides a more intelligible chronology for the Bishops of Arles from 426 to 430 as well as for Augustine's last three years, if we take it to refer to Euladius or, possibly, Helladius. It seems to be generally accepted now that Euladius was the bishop in question.

[26] *L* 226 (PL 33, 1007–12; 44, 954–60) (CSEL 57, 468–81).

[27] *PS* (PL 44, 959–92); *GP* (PL 45, 914–1034).

[28] Brown, 1967, 403ff., 401; Prosper, *Letter to Rufinus* xiii. 14 (PL 51, 85A) – literally, 'an objection made by men of no understanding'.

traditions, and the niceties of recent controversy elsewhere seem to have escaped their notice. Now they realised that their whole way of life was being challenged and the partnership between divine grace and human will which they had always hitherto taken for granted was in danger of being undermined. They found a worthy champion in John Cassian, to whom Prosper and Hilary had not referred by name in their letters but who was to become the central figure in the ensuing debate. A former disciple of John Chrysostom, he had fled to the west in 405, a victim no doubt, like his master, of the Origenist witch-hunt in the east. It was he who had founded the two monasteries, one for men and the other for women, at Marseilles around 415, and his reputation stood high in the western Church, so high that he was invited in 429/30 by Leo, archdeacon and later Pope of Rome, to act as its spokesman against Nestorius. He was certainly no Pelagian; on the contrary, he would connect Pelagianism with Nestorianism as Marius Mercator did and might well have agreed that 'the Nestorian God is the father of the Pelagian man'. He faithfully performed the task imposed upon him by Leo the Great, with whom he had formed a friendship in Rome many years earlier, by composing his treatise *On the Incarnation of Christ* in seven books in 430 or soon after.[29] Thus his credentials as priest, abbot and theologian were impeccable.

Cassian accepted the 'full Augustinian meaning of grace as an interior working of God within the soul'; likewise he rejected the Pelagian idea of 'perfect liberty to choose between right and wrong' as a definition of free will.[30] But his experience of teaching novices, for whom he had already written his *Institutes* setting out the rules for a monastic life,[31] showed him that, within the operation of divine grace, room had to be left for the will to exercise responsibility for a man's choice of action. Again and again in this work he emphasises the imperative need to strive by daily effort and constant prayer to employ the will rightly and to the limits of its capacity, while never forgetting that the grace of God is necessary in order to achieve this end. 'No absurdity is to be seen in the retention of these two propositions within one man', comments Owen Chadwick, but he goes on to add that they 'appear incompatible in Cassian' and that 'Cassian is not the only writer in whom they have looked incompatible'.[32] It was his theological training in the east and his experience of the monastic life that led him to overlook this incompatibility. He came to favour a successive theory of will and grace: 'first the will acts, then the grace is given. The eastern monks had said, "Grace springs from the desire for it." Cassian followed them.'[33] Thus he was not an Augustinian in the strict sense of the word since he could not share Augustine's view of the Fall or of concupiscence. All this he was to explain in his thirteenth *Conference*, which he devoted to a study of grace and in which,

[29] PL 50, 9–376.
[30] O. Chadwick, 1968, 113f.
[31] PL 49, 53–476.
[32] O. Chadwick, 1968, 116.
[33] Ibid., 114.

though reiterating the absolute dependence of man upon God, he advanced an alternative view of predestination in an attempt to rescue the Augustinian doctrine from the charge of fatalism.[34] He was soon to be supported by other leaders of the monks in southern Gaul, Vincent of Lérins, and, a little later, Faustus, abbot of Lérins and later Bishop of Riez, both of whom were more outspoken in their attack on Augustinian predestination.[35]

And so the group described by Prosper in his letter to Augustine as 'the remnants of the Pelagian heresy' and by their contemporaries in Provence as 'the Massilians' came to gain the name of 'Semi-Pelagians' in the seventeenth century, when the relationship between predestination and grace again became one of the principal items on the agenda of theological controversy. This traditional description of the Massilians has often been criticised as misleading on the grounds that they were much closer to Augustine than Pelagius: Harnack, for example, dismissed it as 'a malicious heretical term' and identified Semi-Pelagianism as 'popular Catholicism made more definite and profound by Augustine's doctrine'.[36] Some, like Loofs, preferred the term 'Semi-Augustinians', and others have settled for 'Anti-Augustinians', though this may well be regarded as even more misleading. But it was certainly as opponents of Augustine that Prosper saw them when he leapt to the latter's defence and took on the rôle of custodian of Augustinianism in southern Gaul – 'le chevalier d'une grande cause'.[37]

At first, in his Letter to Rufinus and poem On the Graceless,[38] he limited himself to an indirect attack on Cassian and his supporters in the manner of Augustine in his earliest anti-Pelagian period; but when this provoked others to reply, he appealed to Pope Celestine for a decree against Pelagianism. In 431 he and his friend Hilary journeyed to Rome to put their case in person but Cassian's high reputation protected him, and the papal decree which resulted in 431, entitled Apostolici Verba and addressed to the bishops of Gaul and especially Cassian's bishop, Venerius of Marseilles, failed to express either approval of Augustinianism or open condemnation of the Massilians, so that both sides felt justified in interpreting it in their own favour. Prosper was forced to moderate his attack on Cassian and change his ground to a criticism of his teaching on the source and operation of the will: his treatise Against the Collator, written around 432 and examining twelve propositions from Cassian's thirteenth Conference, simply cited texts of his own choosing in refutation of those quoted by Cassian but without mentioning him by name, another echo of Augustine's tactics in his first reactions to Pelagius' teaching, and it was as

[34] PL 49, 898–954.
[35] Faustus is described as a Briton, ortu Britannum, in Avitus, Letter to Gundobadus, MGH vi. 2, p. 30, which may have led N. K. Chadwick, 1959, 26ff., 254ff., to develop her 'curious theory' that he was of aristocratic birth, the son of Vortigern by the daughter of Magnus Maximus, dismissed by Hanson, 1968, 64, as 'so unlikely as to be impossible'. He may just as well have been a Breton.
[36] Harnack, 321, n. 2. The term 'Semi-Pelagian' was first applied to the Molinists in the polemic of their opponents but it could have been used just as appropriately to describe medieval theologians such as William of Ockham; see Adams, 370ff., Pelikan, I, 319.
[37] Jacquin, 300.
[38] PL 51, 77–90; 91–148.

much a parody of Cassian's theology as the writings of his opponents were held to be a caricature of Augustine's.[39] Its contribution to the debate was minimal, and a second appeal to Rome, this time addressed to Celestine's successor, Sixtus III, met with as little success as the earlier one. 'In one sense', comments Owen Chadwick, 'the *Contra Collatorem* marked the beginning of the end of the controversy. It is probably the earliest document in which Prosper abandoned the attempt to preach predestination and irresistible grace.'[40] No doubt he had by now realised that the Massilians had displayed considerable shrewdness in concentrating their attack on these two, linked aspects of Augustine's teaching as his Achilles' heel, and Faustus of Riez continued to exploit their weakness, bringing about their condemnation by local synods around 475. But he was really no more a Pelagian in the strict sense of the word than his master Cassian had been; indeed, he had demonstrated this fact by writing a treatise *On Grace and Free Choice*, which was specifically directed against Pelagianism and in which Pelagius himself was described as a 'pestilential doctor'.[41]

As for Cassian, despite his monumental influence on the spirituality of western Europe through his teaching on the ascetic life – 'the first theologian of the religious orders' and 'in the high Middle Ages the chief "doctor" of the monks'[42] – his criticism of Augustine was never to be forgotten, let alone forgiven. Though the Council of Orange in 529, summoned and presided over by Caesarius of Arles, who was himself strongly opposed to the Semi-Pelagians and had written a treatise to refute Faustus' *On the Grace of God and Free Choice*,[43] condemned the doctrine that some are predestined to evil as anathema, it also reaffirmed the Augustinian teaching on grace and free will and rejected Cassian's theory of the successive operation of will and grace. And its canons or, at least, the first eight of them on justification, mainly taken from Augustine's works and supported by a statement of the bishops' own creed, were confirmed by Pope Boniface II. Furthermore, the so-called Gelasian decree, listing Cassian among those whose writings lacked the approval of the Church, was later to be incorporated in the Church law of the high medieval period. 'Such was the penalty for opposing Augustine's doctrine of grace.'[44]

Yet this was the man who could write: 'We may first show to our brethren true humility from the very bottom of our heart, assenting to nothing which will sadden or hurt them. . . . Then, next after this, we must maintain with

---

[39] *Against the Collator* (PL 51, 213–76); *Responses* (PL 51, 155–74, 177–86) – these were replies to Augustine's critics, especially the author of the so-called *Vincentian Objections*, though we cannot be quite certain that Vincent was the author. Wermelinger comments that Prosper's booklist is an almost complete list of Augustine's anti-Pelagian works with the exception of the controversial works written for the monks of Hadrumetum and for Hilarius and Prosper – *GFC, RG, PS* and *GP* (248 and n. 158).

[40] O. Chadwick, 1968, 134.

[41] PL 58, 783–836.

[42] O. Chadwick, 1968, 158.

[43] *The opinions of the lord Caesarius against those who explain why God gives grace to some but not to others* (Morin, ed.).

[44] O. Chadwick, 1968, 152.

the utmost firmness this same humility towards God. And this will be fulfilled by us in such a way as not only to acknowledge that we are powerless to accomplish anything relating to the perfecting of virtue without his assistance and grace, but also to believe honestly that our being worthy to comprehend this is in fact a gift from him.' And again: 'Experience proves that all the good in everyone is the work of the God of the universe. . . . The God of all must be held to be working all goodness in everyone, stirring up, protecting, strengthening; but not in such a way as to destroy the free will which is in our gift.'[45] His writings show him to have been one of the most attractive of the Western Fathers, a humble Christian and a dedicated teacher of his monks, and he deserved better treatment at the hands of posterity – perhaps 'a little generous prudence, a little forbearance and some grain of charity', qualities which John Milton once commended for those who sought 'to join and unite into one general and brotherly search for truth'.[46] Like Pelagius, who might justifiably have hoped for a better fate than excommunication from the Church which he loved, he too fell a victim to the same 'prelatical tradition of crowding free consciences and christian liberties into canons and precepts of men' that Milton so deplored. Such was the temper of the fifth-century Church and of Augustine, the man who impressed his individual stamp upon it and upon western theology for centuries to come.

Meanwhile, before Cassian's death and while Prosper was still pursuing his campaign against Semi-Pelagianism, ominous signs began to appear of the spread of the dreaded virus even farther afield. As early as 432 Prosper commends Pope Celestine's diligence in 'freeing Britain from this same disease by shutting off from that remote corner of the ocean certain enemies of grace who were occupying the soil of their native land'. And, in his *Chronicle* written many years later in Rome, he names Agricola, son of Bishop Severian, as one of those enemies of grace who had 'corrupted the churches of Britain by introducing his own dogma into them'.[47] At the suit of the deacon Palladius, Celestine sent Germanus of Auxerre to Britain as his representative, and he 'dislodged the heretics from their stronghold and guided the Britons back to the catholic faith'. Now it is important to note that these two references, brief and terse as they are, represent in fact the only first-hand evidence for Pelagianism in fifth-century Britain which we possess and the only evidence in which we can place any confidence. The rest is intelligent or not so intelligent guesswork, based on secondary sources, most prominent among them being Constantius' *Life of Germanus*, written about 480. In it Constantius, who was 'a hagiographer, not an historian' and whose sole purpose in writing was not to give a report on contemporary Britain but 'to glorify Germanus',[48] includes a vivid but almost wholly unreliable account of the visit of 429, adding that the saint was accompanied by another, Lupus of

[45] *Institutes* XII, 32f. (PL 49, 474ff.), as translated by N. K. Chadwick, 1955, 223.
[46] *Areopagitica*, 554 (Complete Prose Works II, 1643–8, Oxford, 1959).
[47] *Against the Collator* 21, 2 (PL 51, 271); *Chronicle*, year 429 (PL 51, 594f.) (Stevenson, 351). On Agricola see now Markus, 1986, 201ff.
[48] Thompson, 1984, 85f.

Troyes. He attributes the visit not to a decision of the Pope, as does Prosper, but to one taken by a Gallican Synod of which we have no mention elsewhere, and he also recounts a second visit made by Germanus between 441 and 448, this time accompanied by Severus of Trier, to which Prosper does not refer at all.[49] Not everyone has been willing to accept the historicity of this second visit: Nora Chadwick, for example, suggested that 'the second journey looks suspiciously like a duplication of the first, possibly incorporating a variant tradition'.[50] The two accounts could well be different versions of the same story, later used and embellished by Nennius and others in order to enhance the reputation of legendary heroes like Germanus and Lupus as a part of 'their strategy of bringing the Welsh Church at the turn of the eighth and ninth centuries under the newly introduced Roman order'.[51] If the account of the second visit has an historical basis, as most historians seem ready to accept, then it is hard to reconcile the apparently overwhelming success credited to the first visit with a need for Germanus to make a second for the same purpose less than twenty years later. Whether the second visit did take place and, if so, at what date is a question which will continue to be debated; in the present context it is important only as a possible indication of the strength of British Pelagianism in the fifth century and of the duration of its survival.

As to the first visit, much could be and indeed has already been said about the omissions from Constantius' admittedly colourful description of it – about the absence of any mention of British bishops at the debate with the Pelagians, about the lack of any reference to Roman officials except 'a man with tribunician authority', whatever that may be taken to mean, and about the writer's failure to tell his readers when or where the debate took place or the great battle against the Picts and Saxons which was fought after it and in which Germanus led the Britons to a glorious 'Alleluia Victory' on Easter Day.[52] Such omissions are attributable only to Constantius' almost complete

---

[49] Constantius, *Life of Germanus*, 12ff., 25ff. (Krusch and Levison VII, 247ff.). Thompson, op. cit., 55ff., after noting that there is general agreement with a date in the 440s and that most place it between 444 and 448, suggests 437 for the second visit, 'a possible, even a probable date' and withdraws his earlier preference (1957, 135ff.) for 444 with the wry comment – *horresco referens*!

[50] N. K. Chadwick, 1955, 255ff.; 1958, 23; 1963, 142; cf. J. Evans, 177. But Thompson, 1984, 4, thinks that Chadwick 'goes too far' and that Hanson, 1968, 50 is nearer the mark when he concludes that Constantius may have known only that a second visit took place but almost no details of what happened in the course of it.

[51] Hanson, 1968, 52; see also N. K. Chadwick, 1955, 268ff., Loyer, 24, Hardinge, xiii and G. Williams, 1f.

[52] Thompson, 1984, 50ff., tentatively suggests the London area as a possible site for the debate but with the caveat that this is 'only make-believe'. As for the battle, Welsh tradition locates it at Maes Garmon, 'Garmon's Field', in Mold, and Morris, 1965, 162ff., in the Vale of Llangollen on the Dee, provoking Alcock, 102, to remark that it could just as well have been 'a valley in the Chilterns'! And he, Kirby, 49f., and Dumville, 1977, 186, rightly warn that it is impossible to reconcile Germanus of Auxerre with the Welsh Garmon, who is 'the dynastic or territorial saint of Powys' (Dumville) or 'a Welsh ecclesiastic of that name' (Alcock). No wonder that Saunders Lewis in his play *Buchedd Garmon* (Aberystwyth 1937) abandons historical 'fact' for poetic licence by bringing two Welsh saints Paulinus and Illtud to Auxerre to supplicate for Germanus' help and Germanus himself first to Caerleon on the Usk and finally to Maes Garmon to confront and defeat his British opponents on Easter Day! But at least he never claimed to be a historian.

ignorance of events in Britain at the time and of its religious state some fifty years before he wrote his *Life*, whereas his picture of events in Gaul is rich in detail and clearly drawn from personal knowledge. His account of the visits of Germanus to Britain, on the other hand, contains 'practically no details . . . because he knew none'.[53] All he appears to have known was that such visits took place, and the only detail which most of our authorities accept as historical is the visit of Germanus and Lupus to the shrine of Alban at Verulamium. But even this, it has recently been suggested, may have been no more than an attempt to associate the cult of the British martyr with continental orthodoxy: Constantius' *Life* must be used with caution as an historical source and should be regarded as 'primarily an allegory'.[54]

Trying to ascertain the true facts about fifth-century Pelagianism in Britain is like trying to make bricks without straw or at least almost without straw, if we accept, as we surely must, that at least Prosper's references to it are reliable. From those references we might conclude that the movement which Germanus was commissioned to extirpate was a religious one, probably activated by Pelagian exiles in flight from the continent after the condemnation of their leaders and the subsequent persecution of the remnant, among them Agricola, who need not necessarily have been a cleric himself. On the same premisses the phenomenon would not have been of long duration – about ten years or, if the second visit is accepted, about thirty: Prosper believed that one visit was sufficient to bring it to an end, Constantius that a second was needed to do so, adding that the Pelagians were then sent into exile.[55] Thompson maintains that, by the time when Gildas was writing around the middle of the sixth century, 'Pelagianism was dead, buried and forgotten':[56] certainly Gildas makes no mention of it, although he laments that British Christians of his time were plagued by Arianism. But it has often been pointed out that Gildas' silences are notorious and may mean nothing, and it has also been suggested that 'perhaps some lingering Pelagian influences, may be detected in Gildas himself'.[57] But, as Thompson has observed, the passages quoted do not bear out this opinion: the brief sentence from the Pelagian tract *On Virginity* which Gildas repeats and which is found also with a slight change of wording in another Pelagian work from the same period had already been cited by others and could well have become an ethical commonplace by then. Gildas attributes it to *quidam nostrum*, 'one of ours', which is open to many

[53] Thompson, op. cit., 13. Others have been less cautious: for example, G. A. Williams, 22, goes so far as to state that 'Germanus debated with their (*sc.* the Pelagians') spokesman, the son of a bishop', presumably Agricola, not mentioned by Constantius, and that Aetius 'sent Germanus with the Bishop of Troyes to Britain', referring to Vortigern as 'another opponent of Germanus'.

[54] Wood, 14; but he, 8, may have misunderstood Prosper's reference to Agricola, attributing the British heresy not to the latter, as does Prosper, but to his father.

[55] Thompson, 1984, 28ff., comments that it is odd they should have been sent into exile by the congregation and finds the description of their destination – *ad mediterranea* – as hard to explain as others before him.

[56] Thompson, 1979, 211; cf. 1985, 54f.

[57] W. H. Davies, 140 and 149, n. 105; Myres, 1951, 227f., takes a similar view.

interpretations, and he would not have used it if he had been aware that it was unorthodox.[58] Thompson concludes that extracts from Pelagian writings may well have been circulating in the sixth century without being recognised as heretical. More recently, a contributor to a collection of essays on Gildas has cited other passages in his *On the Ruin of Britain* which might be explained as echoes of Pelagianism but has suggested that they reveal only that Pelagian texts and ideas were still in circulation in Britain at the time when Gildas was writing, 'nothing more'.[59] And if Pelagianism was still remembered in the middle of the sixth century, though no longer a force to be reckoned with, it is just possible that its roots in Britain were stronger then either Prosper or Constantius realised.

Such a possibility provided the basis for a novel theory, advanced by Myres and developed by Morris, that the outbreak of Pelagianism which Germanus was sent to quell was much more than simply an offshoot of the heresy.[60] Myres used the popular meaning of *gratia* in the Theodosian Code, that is, of 'judicial corruption in the courts, official hanky-panky of all kinds in public life' as the starting-point for his argument that 'Pelagius and his friends may have been attempting, however confusedly, an attack upon the social corruption inherent in a totalitarian regime, rather than initiating, as Augustine insisted, a barefaced assault on the fundamentals of the Christian faith', going on to link this attack with the political situation in early fifth-century Britain. Morris, following another path but in the same general direction, re-examined a batch of Pelagian documents from the same period and concluded that Britain was the home not only of Pelagius himself but also of a group of young radicals, one of whom, 'the Sicilian Briton' now in exile, was the author of the documents concerned. Britain had thus provided the soil in which Pelagianism first took root as early as the mid-nineties of the fourth century, when Victricius of Rouen was summoned to Britain to settle differences which had arisen between the British bishops. 'Poor Victricius', comments Charles Thomas, 'continually, if marginally, found, interred in speculative footnotes'.[61]

Myres's thesis was that early British Pelagianism represented a conscious effort to shake off the last shackles of imperial rule and revive older Roman virtues by men who resented the intrusion of Augustinian orthodoxy as the alien doctrine of a foreign government, and this was taken on board by Morris

[58] Thompson, 1979, 212f. The reference to *On Virginity*, 6 (PL 30, 167) is in Gildas, *On the Ruin (and Conquest) of Britain* II, 38, 2: *non agitur de qualitate peccati sed de transgressione mandati*, 'it is not a question of the nature of the sin but of the fact of having disobeyed an order', a quotation repeated in *On Works*, 13, 1 (PLS 1, 1438f.) with the minor change of *agitur* to *actum est*. The same sentiment appears also in the Pelagian letter *Honorificentiae tuae*, 1 (PLS 1, 1689).

[59] Wood, 8. O'Sullivan, 180, dates *On the Ruin of Britain c.* 515–20 but 'with a real possibility remaining that it was written within a decade before the earlier or after the later date'; Dumville, 1984, 84, prefers the second quarter of the sixth century or possibly the third.

[60] Myres, 1960, 21ff.; Morris, 1965, 26ff.; see also Myres, 1968, 6, and Morris, 1968, 61ff.

[61] A. C. Thomas, 1981, 51. Victricius' visit to Britain at the request of his fellow-bishops there is recorded in his *On the Praise of the Saints*, 1 (PL 20, 443), and Pope Innocent's letter to him in the Peterborough text of the *Anglo-Saxon Chronicle* is 'a Latin interpolation under the year 403' often linked with this visit but without any implication 'that it had anything to do with Pelagianism in Britain' (Thomas, op. cit., 55).

as an early example of a British tendency towards political radicalism and social egalitarianism. The common basis which they shared was a conviction that there was much more to British Pelagianism than had hitherto been realised and that, far from being a relatively brief and insignificant offshoot of a continental heresy, it was a factor of considerable importance in the social and political history of Britain in the early decades of the fifth century, especially around the 'time of troubles' in 409/10 and probably even earlier in the nineties of the preceding century. But there are several differences in detail, as there are in the sources employed by the two scholars, and it is difficult to reconcile Myres's well-to-do landowners, the 'well-dressed and well-heeled' audience of Constantius' account,[62] with Morris's young radical thinkers: 'by any textbook definition', the latter argues, 'the crisp argumentation' of the Pelagian treatise *On Riches* is socialism, 'socialism of a coherence and urgency that was hardly to be met again before the nineteenth century, or at earliest the end of the eighteenth'. In support of his case he presents a number of quotations from his 'Sicilian Briton', including this striking passage: 'They do not understand that the reason why the poor exist is that the rich own too much. Abolish the rich and you will not be able to find the poor. If no one possesses more than he needs, all will have as much as they need. For it is those who are rich that are the reason for the many who are poor.'[63]

But despite the patent enthusiasm with which Myres and Morris propounded their theses and the unquestionable skill with which they deployed their arguments they were to find very few supporters,[64] and they soon came under attack from all sides, as theologians, archaeologists and historians of Roman Britain began to discover weaknesses in the evidence employed to build up this new and exciting scenario for Romano-British politics in the early fifth century. In the first place, Pelagius never saw himself as heading a movement for social reform nor is there a shred of evidence that he and his immediate circle sought to exploit the popular sense of the word *gratia* as 'graft' in order to boost their own theological opinions. On the contrary, Pelagius' main defence of his orthodoxy was the claim that he was *not* an 'enemy of grace': Pelagianism, as we have emphasised, was an ascetic movement in origin, and its appeal was for better Christians and not for a more democratic form of government. Nor do the Pelagian tracts and letters from the early fifth century which gave Morris the evidence for his thesis show any noticeable trace of the catastrophical events taking place in Britain at the time when they were written, and Morris's attempt to link the Pelagian letter

    [62] Johnson, 116.

    [63] *On Riches*, 12, 2 (PLS 1, 1401); Morris, 1965, 50f. The six Pelagian documents first published by Caspari consisted of two letters and four tracts, three of these also in letter form: *Honorificentiae tuae, Humanae referunt litterae, On Riches, On Evil Doctors and Works of Faith and Future Judgement,* usually cited as *On Works, On the Possibility of Not Sinning,* and *On Chastity* (PLS 1, 1687–94, 1375–80, 1380–1418, 1418–57, 1457–64 and 1464–1504 respectively). Plinval attributed all six to Pelagius but Caspari to Agricola and Morris to his 'Sicilian Briton'.

    [64] For example, Salway, 443, 727; Frere, 376; Ward, 284f.; D. S. Evans, 1971, 3, n. 10.

Humanae referunt litterae with the unrest of 409 and 410 has been shown to depend on an incorrect interpretation of the phrase 'perpetual consulate' in the last sentence of the letter. As for the authorship of the tracts *On the Christian Life* and *On Virginity*, attributed by Morris to 'Fastidius' and his 'Sicilian Briton' respectively, they are far more likely to have been the work of Pelagius himself. Moreover, even if we are prepared to accept that all the Caspari documents were written by the same man, there is good reason to doubt whether he was a Briton at all. And the attempt to cast Vortigern in the rôle of arch-Pelagian and leading opponent of Germanus has absolutely no evidence to support it.[65]

After a judicious summary of the pros and cons of the Myres–Morris theses, Thomas concludes that it is doubtful if heresies like Pelagianism *'were* ever applied socially to the extent where they governed or modified history'.[66] He aptly reminds us of the warning given by A. H. M. Jones that nationalist and socialist theories applied to heresies seem to be based 'on a radical misapprehension of the mentality of the Later Roman Empire': modern historians who so apply them are 'retrojecting into the past the sentiments of the present age'.[67] Jones was referring, of course, to Arianism, Donatism and Monophysitism but his salutary warning might equally have been addressed to Myres and Morris and their interpretation of Pelagianism in Britain. This tendency to explain the past by analogies with the present, though already visible in nineteenth-century historians of the ancient world, was perhaps never more prevalent than in those heady decades immediately following the Second World War, when many historians appeared to have forgotten that they were dealing with periods of history during which political ideology still hovered back in the wings, awaiting the opportunity to make its entrance on-stage several centuries later.

Nevertheless it would be a great mistake – and it would also be unjust – to dismiss the investigations of Myres and Morris as entirely without merit: Myres deserves credit for having forced others to re-examine the evidence for the rise of Pelagianism in Britain in the early fifth century against the backcloth of the political situation at the time, and Morris for having made a significant contribution to the problem of the authorship of the Pelagian tracts and letters written in that period. Whereas the founders of Pelagianism produced works wholly free from political undertones, much of the literature first brought to our attention by Caspari was written by individuals deeply conscious and strongly critical of the social and political inequalities of

---

[65] I have culled these criticisms from Liebeschuetz, 1963, 237, 1967, 446; Thompson, 1977, 314 and n. 42; Cameron, 215; R. F. Evans, 1968(a), 37ff.; Bonner, 1972, 5f.; Hanson, 1968, 19. They have been aptly summed up by Jarrett, 1983, 25: 'the evidence justifies, and perhaps compels, agnosticism'. Brown, 1972, 184, n. 1, also comments: 'It is impossible to veil my disagreement with these two scholars'; but, in fairness to them, he goes on to add: 'It would be ungrateful not to record how much my own interest in the Pelagian controversy owes to their erudition and freshness of approach.'

[66] A. C. Thomas, 1981, 59.

[67] A. H. M. Jones, 1959, 295, in an article which should be compulsory reading for historians writing about the heresies of the early Christian Church.

contemporary society and utilising Pelagian theology in order to highlight the need for social justice. But that does not entitle us to claim that these Pelagian converts were the force behind the appearance of the heresy in Britain in the second quarter of the fifth century, much less that they represented a radical party in Romano-British politics as early as 409, or even earlier in the last decade of the fourth century. When the 'evidence' adduced by Myres and Morris is subjected to closer examination, Victricius, 'Fastidius', that *fantôme indécis*,[68] the Sicilian 'Briton' and all the other extras in 'this insubstantial pageant faded' melt into thin air and leave not a rack behind! We are left with what we started – Prosper's references to Agricola as instigator of the Pelagian unrest and to the first visit of Germanus in 429: Germanus came to Britain at the request of the Pope to nip Pelagianism in the bud. He fulfilled this task, and, if we are prepared to place any confidence at all in Constantius' farrago of folklore, legend and allegory, he *may* have become involved in a minor skirmish with Picts and Saxons. But his activities were confined to the south-eastern corner of the island and, if he did make a second visit, he certainly did not travel via Brittany to the western regions or venture as far as North Wales or northern Britain.[69]

But we are not yet out of the wood: even if Germanus did not extend his second mission to the western regions, we cannot rule out the possibility that the ghost of Pelagius, well and truly laid in the south-eastern corner of Britain, was still haunting the Celtic fringe and, in particular, that part of it which many in the past have held to be his homeland – Wales, if it is 'meaningful to talk of Wales before England exists'.[70] In his *magnum opus*, his *Life of St. David*, the eleventh-century Welsh scholar Rhigyfarch (Ricemarch) refers to Germanus' second visit to Britain and records that, even after this visit, 'the Pelagian heresy was recovering its vigour and obstinacy, implanting the poison of a deadly serpent in the innermost regions of our country'.[71] To combat this threat to true belief a synod of 'all the bishops of Britain' assembled at Brefi, now Llanddewi Brefi in Dyfed, and was attended by 'one

[68] Plinval, 1943, 46, applying the same description to Agricola as well.

[69] J. Evans, 185, with whom Thompson, 1984, 47f., now agrees, withdrawing his earlier suggestion (1979, 215) that Germanus went 'to a more westerly point' on his second visit. Plinval, 146, sent him to the borders of Scotland and Candida Casa, and Meissner I, 84, to the north of Britain. But they, unlike Saunders Lewis, lacked the benefit of poetic licence.

[70] Jarrett, 1983, 35.

[71] Rhigyfarch, *Life of St. David*, 49 (J. W. James, 21, 43). He uses the same metaphor to describe Pelagianism, 'the serpent's poison', as Gildas, *On the Ruin of Britain* I, 12, 3 (Winterbottom, 20, 93), does in writing of Arianism; this metaphor was, of course, a traditional one to apply to any heresy in the early Christian Church but its occurrence in both contexts does prompt the rather naughty thought that neither Rhigyfarch nor Gildas knew the difference between Pelagianism and Arianism. In a lecture which is eminently sane and judicious, yet not without its touches of quiet humour, my former colleague Simon Evans describes the situation facing anyone who tries to uncover the facts of David's life as one in which 'it is not easy to distinguish between saga and history' (10f.), and the tremendous literary activity of the period in which Rhigyfarch wrote as 'works that are full of the marvellous, the miraculous and the incredible' (12). Particularly relevant to the present context is his conclusion that Rhigyfarch's *Life* was intended to contribute to his father Bishop Sulien's diplomacy (14) by establishing the priority of the church of Dewi over those of Bangor and Llandaff and of Dewi himself over Patrick, Gildas, Teilo, Daniel and Dyfrig, as well as his ascendancy over the Irish and the Cornish (15ff.).

hundred and eighteen bishops and an innumerable multitude of priests, abbots, clergy of other ranks, kings, princes and lay men and women'. So vast was the assembled throng that none of the bishops was able to make himself heard, and, on the advice of Paulinus, David was summoned from somewhere nearby and preached from a hill which rose miraculously beneath his feet. Such was his eloquence that the heresy was at once overcome and the true faith restored; later, a second synod, the 'Synod of Victory', was summoned and reaffirmed the decisions of the first. If Rhigyfarch is recording an historical event, then surely, it is argued, no better location could have been chosen for the holding of a synod to suppress a recrudescence of Pelagianism than Brefi, 'situated in what would have been a focal area of some importance in the days of St. David, at a convergence of minor routes among the hills'.[72]

As one reads the narrative of the Synod of Brefi, one has a strong feeling of *déjà lu*, evoked by the many reminiscences in it of Constantius' account of Germanus' missions to Britain: the totally one-sided debate with the Pelagians in which no Pelagian either spoke or is even named, the vast multitude present, the accompanying miracles, the overwhelming success of the defender of orthodoxy, the second occasion needed to confirm the result of the first, and even the name given to it, recalling the 'Alleluia Victory'. Is it inconceivable that Rhigyfarch adapted Constantius' account to the greater glory of David, in order to demonstrate that a Celtic saint could be just as effective in uprooting heresy as any imported saint from Gaul, however prestigious? He was writing in the eleventh century, when Lanfranc and Anselm pursued their campaign to extend the jurisdiction of their Church and when, despite the general acceptance of catholic views in Wales by 768, it might still be of some tactical importance for the Welsh to establish that the Celtic Church had a tradition founded on sound orthodoxy, even before that other Augustine came to Britain to convert the Angli and made his abortive attempt to persuade the representatives of Celtic Christianity to accept Roman practices and discipline.

Some will find it incredible that Rhigyfarch, a highly respected scholar with family connections in Llanbadarn Fawr in Dyfed through his father Sulien, twice Bishop of St. David's, could have invented this revival of Pelagianism and adapted Constantius to suit his own purposes, even supplying Paulinus, traditionally a fellow-student of David and a friend of Germanus, with a major rôle in his narrative of the synod of Brefi. But we do have to take account on the other side of the balance sheet of three countervailing items: Prosper's assertion that Germanus eliminated the heresy in 429, Constantius' that he finally did so in the middle of the fifth century, and Gildas' failure to mention Pelagianism in the middle of the sixth. One would certainly have expected Prosper not to miss an opportunity of referring to his *bête noire* if it still existed in Britain in the mid-fifth century, bearing in mind that his

---

[72] Bowen, 1983, 59; elsewhere (1982, 31) he describes it as 'a veritable Piccadilly Circus in Early Christian Times', and G. A. Williams, 5, as 'a veritable Crewe Junction of the sea-routes which laced the Irish Sea and the Western Approaches'.

Chronicle extended to 455. But Prosper, it will be countered, is not infallible and, in any case, was far away in Rome by that time, Constantius is *capable de tout*, and Gildas' silences are no more than signs of his ignorance. Might not Rhigyfarch have been resurrecting a folk-memory of an earlier recurrence of the heresy in an area with which he was thoroughly familiar? Is it quite unthinkable that it could have infiltrated into south-west Wales in the fifth century and exerted a continuing influence in popular religious thought there until the sixth? After all, a heresy does not need to be fully articulated in precise theological terms in order to survive and retain its grasp on the imagination of the unlearned.

In fact, there is archaeological evidence which may be interpreted as suggesting that there *were* Pelagians in that same area of Wales around the same period and that they had come there not from south-eastern Britain but from Ireland, thus linking the synod of Brefi with the Irish settlements in south-west Wales between the late fourth and early sixth centuries.[73] Much has been written about these settlements and, in particular, about a batch of ogham and ogham/Latin inscriptions attributed to their influence and found on tombstones and other memorials in the fifth and sixth centuries.[74] These inscriptions have been discovered in Dumnonia, Brycheiniog, Gwynedd and even in north Scotland, as it now is, but the heaviest concentration is in Dyfed. Most of them include a filiation-formula using the word *maqqi* or its Latin equivalent *filius* or both, unlike the Latin inscriptions predominating in Gwynedd during the same period, which employed the same formula as the bulk of Romano-Christian inscriptions on the continent and omitted the patronymic in deference, it has been suggested, to the Gospel injunction to 'call no man your father on earth'.[75] But in the case of the Dyfed memorials, it has been argued, the inclusion of the filiation-formula is rather an indication of Pelagianism and of a conscious rejection of the doctrine of original sin. In North Wales in the same period, on the other hand, there is a markedly lower proportion of inscriptions which include a filiation-formula, most of them in Latin and very few in ogham, and the predominance of the formula *hic iacit (iacet)* there may be due to a closer relationship with the continent – though one must add that it could equally well be attributed to the fact that, unlike the Déisi, who came to south-west Wales from southern Ireland, the Féni, who came from central Ireland to north Wales, never succeeded in establishing themselves to anything like the same extent, 'their memorial being little more than the survival of their name in its British form'.[76] However that may be, David, we are told, 'bore a traditional hostility to the Irish invaders' of his

---

[73] Bowen, 1982, 23ff., 1983, 61ff.

[74] Nash-Williams, 3ff. A revised edition of this work is currently being prepared, and I am indebted to one of the joint editors, W. Gwyn Thomas, for the advance information that, though Nash-Williams suggested that some of the relevant inscriptions may be early fifth century, it does not now seem likely for any with the filiation formula.

[75] Nash-Williams, 6, quoting Le Blant, *Inscriptions de la Gaule* I, 126, a quotation repeated by many others since.

[76] Powell, 173.

own area and would have had no truck with any perverse practices or unorthodox views with which they were associated.[77] As for Gildas, who seems to have known nothing of the outbreak of Pelagianism in south-eastern Britain, he is just as unlikely to have heard of a recurrence in south-western Wales, since the synod of Brefi was no more than a tribal gathering, not even remotely resembling the grand ecclesiastical convention of British Christians recorded by Rhigyfarch half a millennium later.

From this standpoint there is nothing inherently impossible in the idea of a Pelagian influence which was still a force to be reckoned with in south-west Wales a century after its elimination from south-eastern Britain; and if there was such an influence, then we should look for its source not on the continent but in Ireland, since there had long been a two-way traffic between Wales and Ireland. The ogham script, now generally accepted to have been 'based on a fourth-century classification of the Roman alphabet, as used by grammarians in the late empire', was invented either in Ireland itself or 'in south Wales by an Irish immigrant exposed to Roman schooling'.[78] And the *maqqi*-formula too is found in Ireland: after an exhaustive analysis of all the instances of its occurrence which he was able to discover in Ireland, Kenneth Jackson counted over three hundred, the great majority from Kerry, Cork and Waterford, and it was from these very areas that the Irish settlers came to south Wales from the late fourth to the early sixth centuries, members of the Déisi and Uí Líathain tribes of southern Ireland who presumably brought their filiation-formula with them.[79]

But are we justified in assuming that the use of such a formula is an indication of Pelagian influence, or is it rather no more than a relic of an earlier pagan practice long discarded by Christians elsewhere? As Jackson reminds us, the practice of 'defining a man's name by adding his father's' is 'absolutely typical of all Celtic languages at all periods': such a formula is 'distinctive of the lands bordering on the Irish Sea' and 'rightly at home in a pagan tribal society, where descent was a major factor in a person's status'.[80] A similar formula in Latin has also been found on some continental memorials up to the middle of the fifth century, pagan as well as Christian. But many of the memorials in ogham or ogham/Latin in south-west Wales contain words or terms with a specifically Christian flavour and some of them are marked with an early form of the cross; not all of them can be proved to be Christian

[77] Bowen, 1982, 25; 1983, 65f.
[78] A. C. Thomas, 1981, 299. In his article contributed to *Hermathena* in 1943 my old friend L. J. D. Richardson recalled the theory of R. A. S. Macalister that ogham writing was derived from an early form of the Greek alphabet and argued a strong case for accepting it and for holding that the word Ogham itself was also Greek in origin and derived from the forgotten Greek letter *agma*. Lacking Richardson's great knowledge of comparative philology and being no longer, regrettably, able to consult him, I record this divergence from the conventional view as a matter of interest and *honoris causa*.
[79] Jackson, 1953, 152; more recently Coplestone-Crow, 1ff., has suggested that there were two distinct waves of settlers, the first in the late fourth and early fifth century and the second in the late fifth and early sixth.
[80] Jackson, 1953, 168; Alcock, 241f.

but most of them are, certainly the later ones.[81] Nevertheless, even if the literacy which they imply can have come only from association with a Romano-Christian society, the filiation-formula itself may still have been an echo of an earlier pagan background.

Were the Irish immigrants Christians when they arrived in Wales? If so, by whom had they been converted in Ireland? And could they have been Pelagians on arrival? The simple, straightforward answer to the first two questions would be that they were Christians on arrival and that they had been converted by Patrick or his successors. But such an answer would beg many questions: as Nora Chadwick once commented somewhat ruefully, 'Every question connected with St. Patrick bristles with difficulties.'[82] For example, 'Patrick seems to write as if all the Irish were heathens on his arrival';[83] but Prosper, though he describes Ireland as 'the barbarous island' as opposed to Britain, 'the Christian island', also tells us that in 431 Pope Celestine gave it its 'first bishop', Palladius.[84] This was certainly the same Palladius who had persuaded the Pope to send Germanus on his first mission to Britain, and the decision to appoint him 'first bishop of the Irish' may have been taken after consultation with him on his return to Auxerre, if, as has been suggested, he had accompanied Germanus to Britain.[85] But Prosper categorically states that he was sent to 'the Irish who believed in Christ', and this statement would be consistent with the practice of the Church at Rome at this time not to despatch missionaries to pagan areas.[86]

And that is Prosper's last word on the subject of Palladius' mission to Ireland: he has nothing to say about its duration, its success or its failure. Later Irish writers, however, were not short of ideas as to what happened to him: he was forced to leave Ireland prematurely by the antagonism of the Irish bishops, whoever they may have been at this time, or because he was

[81] A. C. Thomas, 1981, 299, 1971, 106; cf. Jackson, 168, Alcock, 241f. I am grateful to W. Gwyn Thomas for the following comment based on his revision of the section in Nash-Williams which is concerned with these memorials: 'Leaving aside those inscriptions referring to *presbyter*, *sacerdos*, *in pace* or with early forms of a cross (and even some of the undatable Irish ogam-inscribed stones include *bendacht*, *ab* (for 'abbot'), *aspog* and *isgob*, *grimitir* (= *cruimther*, *presbyter*) as well as many with *anm* (name) which is reckoned to be specifically Christian), the basic question would be whether British or Irish inscriptions would have been made without a Christian context. I would have thought the implied literacy could have come only from an ecclesiastical source.' This, he emphasises, is a 'subjective view'. Cf. Jackson, 1953, 176, n. 1: 'There is no reason to suppose that there was anything about the Ogam script essentially repugnant to Christianity and that an Ogam inscription means that the man commemorated must have been a pagan.' Richards, 151f., also observes that many of them 'had distinguishing Christian symbols'.

[82] N. K. Chadwick, 1961, 19. D. S. Evans, 1984, 10f., makes a similar remark about David: 'When we go back as far as Saint David, we find that every corner is dark.'

[83] Hughes, 1966, 31.

[84] *Against the Collator* 21, 2 (PL 51, 271); *Chronicle*, under the year 431 (PL 51, 595); Stevenson, 351.

[85] O'Rahilly, 1942, 19; see Hanson, 1968, 54, n. 2.

[86] In a letter addressed to 'all the bishops of the provinces of Vienne and Narbo' (*Letters* 4, V, 7 in PL 50, 434) Pope Celestine himself declares: 'Let no bishop be given to those who are unwilling [to receive him]; let the agreement of the clergy, common people and men of standing be required.' As Thompson, 1985, puts it: 'The idea of a Catholic missionary bishop did not yet exist in the early fifth century.'

homesick, or that he was martyred by the Irish, or that he did not reach Ireland at all but died 'in the extremities of Britain' or 'in the land of the Picts'; 'the variety of these stories', comments Hanson, 'shows the ignorance of their authors'.[87] It is probable that 'Palladius left very little impression on folk-memory in Ireland',[88] and that his mission was of no long duration and became confused by some elements of later Irish tradition with that of Patrick, perhaps for lack of evidence, perhaps deliberately in order to enhance the latter's reputation as the *bona fide* founder of Irish Christianity, 'the Apostle of the Irish', while other elements of the same tradition may have been just as anxious to preserve at least the memory of Palladius as evidence of an historical link with the Church at Rome – though it is not impossible that they believed Patrick to have been sent by the Pope also.[89] Incidentally, Patrick does not mention Palladius; but neither Prosper nor Bede mention Patrick, although Bede twice refers to Palladius' mission, presumably on Prosper's authority.[90]

The only tenable explanation of Prosper's failure to record Patrick's mission to Ireland is that he knew nothing of it, since it was authorised and promoted not by the Pope but by the bishops of Britain. On the subject of his appointment Patrick too is silent: his own version of the reason for his return to Ireland is that he was summoned in a dream by a man called Victoricus, who came 'as it were, from Ireland with countless letters', including one entitled 'The Voice of the Irish', pleading with him to return to them.[91] Even the date of that return is based only on the conjectures of later Irish writers, who may well have plumped for the first year available after Prosper's date for the mission of Palladius on the assumption that, after its failure or abandonment, Patrick was sent his successor. But the question of the date of Patrick's return as bishop to Ireland is one of those which 'bristles with difficulties': some have argued for a considerably later date in the middle of the century, and there is even a theory of 'two Patricks', the one earlier, the

[87] Hanson, 1968, 182ff.; cf. Thompson, 1985, 173.

[88] Binchy, 143.

[89] As in the letter of Columbanus to Pope Boniface IV in 613 (Sancti Columbani Opera, ed. Walker), quoted by Binchy: 'The catholic faith, as it was first delivered *by you* (my emphasis), is maintained unbroken.'

[90] Bede, *Ecclesiastical History* i. 13, 24 (Everyman's Library, London 1970, 20, 281); Bede uses the same phrase as Prosper, 'to the Scots (*sc.* Irish) that believed in Christ'. 'Patrick', comments Binchy, 168f., 'was buried in a mysterious silence for the century and a half which followed his death' – a silence for which ample compensation has since been made! Thompson, 1985, adds: 'Patrick was almost completely unknown on the Continent in his lifetime and for centuries after it.'

[91] *Confession*, 23 (Stevenson, 352). Patrick concludes his account of this dream with the words: 'Thanks be to God that after very many years the Lord granted to them according to their cry.' If his return to Ireland as bishop was an answer to the appeal, then it would have been long delayed. But Thompson, 1985, maintains that Patrick may well have responded much earlier by returning to Ireland as a deacon in 431 'or even earlier' and suggests that he may have served as a deacon under Palladius (39, 175). The only direct reference which Patrick himself makes to his appointment as bishop is in his *Letter to the Soldiers of Coroticus*, 1 (Stevenson, 356): 'I, Patrick, a sinner and unlearned, declare that I am indeed a bishop, resident in Ireland.'

other later and also called 'Patricius'.[92] There is indeed confusion in the little isle! 'Of the origin of Irish Christianity we know absolutely nothing', commented Charles Plummer writing in 1896, and a more recent writer, quoting him, adds the question: 'Are we really much wiser now than then?'[93] On the basis of linguistic evidence revealing a number of loanwords borrowed into Irish from Latin and mainly religious or ecclesiastical Jackson concluded that 'the early development of Irish Christianity was fostered mainly from Britain' and that 'small communities of Christians may have existed in parts of Ireland already by the beginning of the fifth century, presumably founded by British missionaries'; but he then went on to add that 'if so, they were of little importance in a nation whose religion was still overwhelmingly pagan' and that 'the real conversion of Ireland began with the mission of St. Patrick in 432'.[94]

Whatever the date of Patrick's return may have been, the regions in which he operated were the north and north-east, not those from which Irish settlers started out for south-west Wales, and, in any case, despite attempts to unearth traces of anti-Pelagianism in his writings or to argue that his emphasis on the need to obey the call of the free will was Pelagian in origin,[95] there is no good reason to believe that he was consciously either Pelagian or anti-Pelagian: he was a fisher of human souls, not a spinner of theological webs. As for Palladius, whose mission is traditionally located in the south or central-east regions from which the settlers came, he was too closely associated with Germanus to have been a Pelagian or crypto-Pelagian and would hardly

[92] O'Rahilly, 1942, 8 and 48, n. 5; Carney, 1961, 1ff., 26ff., 114ff.; Binchy, 114, 129ff. After examining the 'evidence', Hanson, 1968, 191, concludes that 'all strictly dichotomous two – Patrick theories must be abandoned'. Thompson, 1985, 166–75, devotes an Appendix to Patrick's chronology, in which he dates his appointment as bishop 'some years, let us say, after 434'; in his Introduction, xiii, he dismisses 'the value of the Lives and the Irish annals and other later documents': 'It cannot be stressed too often that Patrick's own writings contain all the valid evidence about his life and thought which we possess.' This seems to me to be a fair comment on the 'small mountain of guesswork, mythology and political and ecclesiastical propaganda . . . which grew up about his name'.

[93] Plummer, II, 26, cited by Harrison, 307, who makes the apt comment. Thompson, 60, also remarks: 'If we ask, then, how Christianity had reached Ireland before 431, the answer is very obscure', and he does well to remind us (61, n. 10) that 'there is no direct evidence for Christianity in Ireland in the fourth century'.

[94] Jackson, 1953, 122; Thompson, on the other hand, adheres to the statement of Prosper and maintains that 'the bulk of the Christians in Ireland in 431 were Irish, not immigrants from Britain' (1985, 56, 64f.). He further suggests the possibility that it was in Patrick's earlier period as a deacon in Ireland that he began his work as a missionary and that this was with the permission or even encouragement of Palladius, whom 'it is not easy to visualise as a great missionary' (174f.). Nor does he see Patrick as Palladius' immediate successor: he may well have been 'at best the third Catholic bishop to go to Ireland', having succeeded the man who was appointed bishop on the occasion when he himself was rejected by his 'seniors' in Britain (170, 68ff.).

[95] Traces of anti-Pelagianism and Pelagianism in Patrick have been found by Nerney, 97f., 106ff., and criticised by Hanson, 1968, 173ff., and Hardinge, 29ff., respectively. I am glad to find that Thompson, 1985, 36, agrees with me: 'Although four popes had thundered against it, it seems to have passed Patrick by' – referring, of course, to Pelagianism. And, elsewhere, 54, n. 4, he reminds us that 'Patrick was not familiar with Augustine's Confessions', citing O'Meara, 1956, 190ff., and 1976, 44ff. In that case it is hardly likely that he had become familiar with the fifteen anti-Pelagian treatises.

have been sent to Ireland by the Pope as its 'first bishop' if he had been. Thus, if it was Pelagian influence which motivated the use of the filiation-formula found in memorials from Pembrokeshire and the neighbouring areas, neither Patrick nor Palladius could have been responsible for it. No doubt there were Christians in Ireland at the time of Palladius' mission, as Prosper tells us and as the busy two-way traffic between Wales and Ireland would lead us to expect, the descendants or successors of fourth-century traders or British slaves snatched from their homeland by raids like that of which Patrick himself was a victim but probably not, *pace* Jackson, the converts of British missionaries. The Irish settlers who came to south-west Wales or, at least, some of them may well have been members of these small Christian communities; but there is no evidence to prove that they were Pelagians. At the end of a characteristically animated exposition of his views on the subject Emrys Bowen once dismissed my mild reservations with the Parthian shot: 'The trouble with you historians is that you simply won't listen to what the archaeologists have to tell you!' Well, we have listened to them and re-examined the archaeological data, and we have found that the evidence is far from conclusive.

Bowen's thesis would have been much more sympathetically received at the turn of the century, when modern research into Pelagianism was only just burgeoning, when a writer on the Celtic Church could confidently assert that Pelagius was 'a Goidelic Celt educated at the monastery of Bangor Iscoed' and that 'the faith of the Goidelic Celts . . . is usually called, from its great exponent, Pelagianism', and when a great historian was propounding his theory that Pelagius 'descended from Irish settlers in Somerset, Devonshire or the south-west coast of Wales'.[96] It was also the time when Zimmer's *Pelagius in Irland* appeared and was rightly applauded by Souter and others for its seminal contribution to the establishment of a reliable text of Pelagius' commentary on the Pauline Epistles. Zimmer reminded his readers that the Irish Church was being blamed for a resurgence of Pelagianism as early as 640 in a letter from Pope John IV and that an Irish collection of canons dated around 700 twice cites Pelagius as an authority.[97] The *Book of Armagh*, a codex

[96] Willis Bund, 108; Bury, 1904, 26ff., 1905, 43, 296.

[97] The papal letter, written to the clergy of northern Ireland by John as Pope-elect and three other members of the Roman *curia*, has long been something of a puzzle, not least to me. But Cróinín, 505ff., has demonstrated that Bede's repetition of it in *Ecclesiastical History*, 2, 19 is based on a misunderstanding of the true reason for the letter, which was to censure the Irish for celebrating Easter, as Rome supposed, on the fourteenth day of the moon *contra orthodoxam fidem*; by doing this, the letter continues, they were 'trying to revive a new heresy from an old'. This old heresy was, of course, Pelagianism! But, as Cróinín rightly remarks, 'even the Romans realised that a Pelagian revival in Ireland would be a curious development, for they pointed out themselves *non solum per istos CC annos abolita est, sed et cotidie a nobis perpetua (sic) anathemate sepulta damnatur*' – 'Pelagianism has not only been dead for these two hundred years but also buried, being daily condemned by us under perpetual anathema'. John and his colleagues were replying to a letter sent from Ireland to Pope Severinus and attributed the error of the northern Irish to Pelagian denial of grace, since the celebration of Easter on the fourteenth day of the moon 'preempted the pasch and, by the same token, denied the efficacy of the Resurrection as the true instrument of man's redemption'. Bede, citing only excerpts from the letter, fell into the same trap and, as Cróinín points out, again links the same two errors in his *De temporum ratione*, 6. I am

dating from the late eighth or early ninth century, also contains several references to Pilagius (*sic*) as the author of a commentary on the Pauline Epistles, and, on the eve of completing his book, Zimmer had the great personal satisfaction of discovering the St Gall MS of that commentary, catalogued before 900.[98] The later Irish Church certainly reveals a considerable respect for the Pelagian commentary, which 'was popular in Irish circles for a long period when it was unknown (under that name) elsewhere'; but even Zimmer was forced to admit that the St Gall MS was composite in character and apparently the work of some Irish medieval scholar.[99] But he allowed his enthusiasm to carry him too far – 'his historical sense failed him'[100] – when he tried to retroject Pelagius' later popularity with the Irish into the period of his lifetime by arguing that he was an Irishman himself and began to formulate his teaching before leaving his native land – as did Esposito a little later with his 'curious theory' that Pelagius was not only Irish but may have converted Patrick before his departure from Ireland.[101]

'When the tide set from Ireland to the continent, the Irish missionaries took their Pelagius with them.'[102] Very true: there is evidence of the existence of manuscripts of the Pelagian commentary in three libraries on the continent, all of them connected with the Irish mission and one of them being St Gallen.[103] But that was a long time after the Irish immigrants set out for Wales and, according to Bowen's theory, brought *their* Pelagius with them. No one would be more pleased than the present writer if it were possible to establish that Pelagius' journey started in Ireland, that his Pelagianism began there and that its influence outlived him both there and in Wales into the sixth century. On the evidence at present available, however, such a conclusion would be pure fantasy, best left in the Celtic twilight to which it properly belongs.

not qualified to assess Croínín's case that the northern Irish were using the table of Victorius of Aquitaine and not the eighty-four-year cycle, as scholars have hitherto held; but his general conclusion may well be correct. If so, J. F. Kelly's remark, cited by Croínín, that 'Bede's intriguing and puzzling reference must remain just that' is no longer true, and yet another of Zimmer's bubbles has at last been pricked. The papal letter is not evidence for a seventh-century revival of Pelagianism in northern Ireland.

[98] Turner, 1902–3, 137. The first leaf of *Codex Sangallensis* 73, containing the author's name and prologue, was lost between the ninth and nineteenth centuries.

[99] Souter, 1907, 431. Turner, 1902–3, 138f., comments that the MS reveals a considerable degree of contamination and 'is not a faithful reproduction of the original Pelagius'. But, as Loyer, 79, reminds us, the choice of commentaries at this date must have been very limited; cf. Croínín, 505, n. 2.

[100] E. James, 362, recalling Kenney, 77: 'Heinrich Zimmer, the Ishmael of Celtic Studies', whose hand was against every man's'. Turner, 132, describes *Pelagius in Irland* as 'not so much about Pelagius as about his Commentary on St. Paul's Epistles, and not so much about Ireland as about Irish scholars and manuscripts on the continent'. Poor Zimmer seems to have been the cause of much wit in others; but it was he and Souter who laid the foundations for our present text of the commentary, and Souter generously acknowledged his debt to the pioneer work of his predecessor.

[101] Esposito, 134f.; Hanson, 1968, 38, n. 3.

[102] Turner, 1902–3, 137, citing *inter alia* Sedulius Scotus' reference to Pelagius' exposition of Romans 1, 17.

[103] Souter, 1922–31, 418.

A more plausible explanation of the persistence of Pelagianism in Britain has been recently advanced by Markus.[104] 'Is there any reason', he asks, 'why the British Church should not have been as inhospitable to the newly forged Augustinian orthodoxy as was Italy, or as indifferent as, apparently, that part of the Greek Church which was not positively sympathetic to Pelagius? The British Church might, for all we know, have been more hostile.' He suggests that there may have been 'a pre-Pelagian tradition' in Britain, 'perhaps containing a range of views similar to that found in Italy, perhaps even more drawn towards the Pelagian end of the spectrum'. The appeal for help against the British 'Pelagians' may have come from a new, 'orthodox' group – 'orthodox' in the new, African and Continental sense – opposed by Agricola on his return from the Continent to defend the faith of his father, Bishop Severianus, because it represented 'new-fangled ideas' imported from that quarter perhaps very recently. Markus stresses the conjectural nature of his suggestion; but it would tie in well with the opposition of Julian and his supporters in Italy, the hostility of some of the monks at Hadrumetum to Augustine's extreme views on free will and predestination, and the similar reaction of Cassian and the Semi-Pelagians. It might also explain the 'total disappearance from the subsequent record of a "heresy" which only an isolated and probably small group had ever recognised as a "heresy" in Britain'. This pre-Pelagian tradition, of course, could not be described as 'Pelagian' before the Pelagian controversy made explicit those elements in it which thereafter became known as 'Pelagian'.

What then have we gained by our long, hesitant trek across the Roman Empire from the eastern shores of the Mediterranean to the western isles in our pursuit of the last, lingering manifestations of Pelagianism in the years immediately following the condemnation of its eponymous 'founder'? Precious little, it must be admitted, in terms of hard, historical fact. But our journey will not have been in vain if we have at least succeeded in demonstrating that the heresy, 'the proudest heresy of all', continued to exercise a strong appeal far beyond the small circle of discredited ascetics with whom it originated. In the monasteries of southern Gaul it spoke to the condition of men of the stature of John Cassian, Vincent and Faustus, and it still speaks to all those who, like them, find themselves unable to endorse the doctrines of Augustine in their most uncompromising form; and, though driven out of Africa, Palestine, Italy, Asia Minor and Gaul and stifled almost at birth in Britain, it lived on to fight another day.

In the monasteries of the continent the old controversy went on simmering and disturbing the peace of the monks many centuries later, as in the debate between Henry of Lausanne and William of St. Thierry from 1133 to 1135, when Henry's rejection of 'the medieval rôle of the clergy as dispensers of God's grace in favour of the responsibility of the individual' was 'carried to extreme lengths involving Pelagianism: original sin was rejected . . . [and]

---

[104] Markus, 1986, 199ff.

baptism could not be conferred on infants without understanding'.[105] But the next great battle in England was to come in the fourteenth century, when that 'Doctor Profundus', Archbishop Thomas Bradwardine, wrote his *De Causa Dei* 'in revulsion against emphasis on free will and disregard of divine grace as preached in the schools' with William of Ockham as his main target.[106] 'The word Pelagian once again became common currency', and 'it is hard to know what the outcome would have been had not the Black Death of 1348–50 supervened, carrying off the greater part of the participants, Bradwardine included'.[107] It has been argued that even Langland's theological outlook in *Piers Plowman* is in fact Semi-Pelagian and that, in adopting it, he was merely accepting 'the standard solution to the problem of justification in his day' as advanced by Ockham and his followers.[108] But though the main issues around which controversy centred in the fourteenth century were still grace, free will and predestination, the original boundaries between Augustinianism and Pelagianism had by then become hopelessly blurred as scholars searched for a more contemporary statement of definitions, and names of existing heresies, such as Pelagianism, Donatism and Manicheism, were used almost indiscriminately to brand ideas which appeared to be unorthodox.[109] And thereby hangs another tale – for others to tell.

---

[105] Lambert, 50; for the full text of this debate see, for example, Moore, 46ff.

[106] Leff, 1957, 13.

[107] Leff, 1967, I, 302.

[108] Adams, 369, 374ff., and, for passages in the *Pardon* which are suggestive of Semi-Pelagianism, 377, 385, 390f., 393, 394f., 401.

[109] As, for example, in Albert the Great's *Compilatio de novo spiritu* (Leff, 1967, I, 311).

Recessional

'It is not easy to feel any deep emotion when Tweedledum defeats Tweedledee.'

E. A. Thompson[1]

'Oh, will it boote thee
To say a Philip or a Gregory,
A Harry, or a Martin taught thee thus?
Is not this excuse for mere contraries,
Equally strong? Cannot both sides say so?'

John Donne[2]

'What if Pelagius after all were more right than his detractors?'

H. D. Lewis[3]

It is quite understandable that Edward Thompson, reflecting on the controversy between Augustine and Pelagius and accustomed to marshalling and analysing historical data, should find himself out of sympathy with the manner in which such theological debate tends to be conducted, with the apparent unreality of the issues involved and with the ambivalence of the conclusions reached. 'The mountains will go into labour, and there will be born – an absurd little mouse', he might well exclaim with the Roman poet or repeat the famous question with which the African Church Father began his attack on the 'stupidities of the philosophers': 'What has Athens to do with Jerusalem, the Academy with the Church?'[4] It is inevitable that, to a twentieth-century observer, Augustine and Pelagius must often seem to be as irrelevant and as unreasonable as Lewis Carroll's ineffectual siblings, when they hurl chunks of scripture at each other in turn, following these up with

---

[1] Thompson, 1984, 25. The eighteenth-century minor poet John Byrom seems to have felt much the same when he wrote his *Epigram on the Feuds between Handel and Bononcini*:

'Strange that such high dispute shou'd be
'Twixt Tweedledum and Tweedledee.'

But this is not the time or place to discuss the origins of these two gentlemen and their history before Alice met them!

[2] *Satyres* III, 95–9, in *The Poems*, ed. H. J. C. Grierson, Oxford 1933, 139f. It may be of interest to note that, in the same century, the Quaker George Fox addressed a similar question to an Anglican congregation at Ulverstone: 'You will say, Christ saith this and the apostles say this, but what canst thou say?' (*Journal*, ii. 512).

[3] *Morals and the New Theology*, London 1947, 138; I am indebted to the author for locating the precise reference for me. Its context is a defence of Tennant and 'other liberal thinkers' at the end of a discussion of Tennant's book *The Concept of Sin*, referred to in n. 3 to my *Introit*. 'To dismiss their books with contempt as "Pelagian treatises"', comments Lewis, 'is sheer evasion.'

[4] Horace, *Ars Poetica*, 139; Tertullian, *De Praescriptione Haereticorum* vii. 9 (PL 2, i. 23).

lengthy and tedious exegeses which prove only that their chosen citations, far from being conclusive, are capable of being interpreted in at least two different ways. Unable to perceive that 'arguments about scripture achieve nothing but a stomach-ache or headache',[5] they generally end up by dismissing each other's arguments with 'Nohow' or 'Contrariwise'. Their *modus pugnandi* reminds one of Stephen Leacock's two embattled knights, who believed that the best way to settle their differences was to lie down in turn and allow their adversary to jump upon them in full battle-order, until the demands of honour were satisfied and they themselves resembled a pair of flattened sardine-tins!

My second quotation suggests that Thompson is in very good company, that of the 'metaphysical' poet who became Dean of St. Paul's. Other poets too, relying on their imagination rather than reasoned argument or intellectual speculation, have shown irritation with theological debate and its consequences. We have already had occasion to note how, in the same century as Donne, John Milton expressed his irritation at 'the prelatical tradition of crowding free consciences and Christian liberties into canons of men'; elsewhere in the same work he complains of 'troublers and dividers of unity, who neglect and permit not others to unite those dissever'd pieces which are wanting to the body of Truth'.[6] A little earlier, Edmund Spenser was just as critical of the 'deep learning' which led to 'doubts among Divines and difference of texts' and so to a 'diversitie of sects and hateful heresies'.[7] Pascal, as I have commented before, though no poet, as far as I am aware, found the intellectual antics of the learned theologians of the Sorbonne so distasteful that he abandoned analytical reasoning for intuitive faith. Modern theologians too sometimes display impatience with the controversies of their forerunners and even their peers: Rahner, one of the foremost theologians of the present century, once warned of 'the danger of wild and empty conceptual acrobatics',[8] and Richard Hanson describes the behaviour of Jerome over Pelagius and of Theophilus over Chrysostom as an example of 'the magnifying of fairly trivial faults' as 'part of the stock-in-trade of ecclesiastical warfare in the fifth century'.[9] Theology, for all its uses, is not an exact science, and trying to treat it as if it were leads only to confusion and exposes it to derision; nowhere is this more likely to happen than in that grey area where saints and heretics have fought their battles to win the prize of orthodoxy.[10]

Orthodoxy was the prize for which Augustine and Pelagius fought their

---

[5] Wilken, 42, citing Tertullian, op. cit., xvi. 2 (PL 2, i. 35).

[6] *Areopagitica*, 550f.; see my n. 12 to c. II.

[7] *Prosopopoia or Mother Hubberds Tale*, 385, Globe ed., London/New York 1893, 516.

[8] Lampe, 1977, 228, quoting K. Rahner, *The Trinity*, London 1970, 48.

[9] Hanson, 1968, 136, n. 1.

[10] This is not a cheap gibe at theologians, many of whom are among my best friends; but not all of them seem to be aware of the risks involved in trying to draw fine distinctions between heretics and saints. 'The conflict between heresy and orthodoxy is not one between an established and generally accepted doctrinal tradition and attempts to subvert, change or modify it by innovations but between elements crystallised out of a pre-existing, undifferentiated range of acceptable doctrinal opinions' (Markus, 1986, 198).

battle in the fifth century, but the issues which they debated were by no means as trivial as they may now appear to have been: in their eyes such issues were, on the contrary, of paramount importance to the Christian Church. Modern theologians have a wide range of contemporary problems from which to pick and choose as possible subjects for their discussions – creation and the 'Big Bang', evolution and 'creationism', liberation theology and racism, sexism and feminism and homosexuality, abortion and artificial insemination, ecology and the state of the inner cities and so on, quite apart from more traditional topics in the fields of doctrine, Church history and biblical scholarship. Augustine and Pelagius, on the other hand, did not debate appropriate issues of their own choice; yet those which they did debate were every bit as real, as crucial and as relevant in the fifth century as those of present-day theology are in the late twentieth, and some of them were being given a thorough airing for the first time in the history of the Church. In handling these issues they were able to draw upon a legacy of doctrine which was common to both of them, and consequently, there were many basic assumptions which they shared and never thought it necessary to question. For example, both argued on the basis that the scriptures were infallible as long as they were correctly interpreted; both adhered to the classical idea of divine and human nature as static and unchanging; both were natural ascetics, so obsessed with the problem of sin that, whichever of them won the day, their debate would leave the Church in the West dominated by sin for centuries to come; both were so preoccupied with the salvation of the individual that they neglected to explore that healthier and saner dimension of corporate salvation which is a recurrent theme in both Old and New Testaments. But both remained convinced that the issues which united them were far less in need of discussion than those which kept them apart, and, once their battle-lines had been joined, neither was prepared to give an inch to his opponent, neither was able to conceive it possible that he was mistaken.

And so Tweedledum went on complaining that Tweedledee had 'spoiled his nice, new rattle', and Tweedledee was just as adamant in maintaining that he had done no such thing. Augustine's 'nice, new rattle' was, of course, his doctrine of grace, which he believed Pelagius to be deliberately spoiling by his excessive emphasis on the freedom of the will; Pelagius, on the other hand, held it to be an 'overvalent idea',[11] because it threatened to restrict or even destroy that freedom. The other issues which they debated were all peripheral

[11] I noted this phrase in the course of my reading but have been unable to track down its provenance; nor have I been able to find the word 'overvalent' in the dictionaries which I have consulted. But its meaning is clear, and it can be applied to Augustine's doctrine of grace in two ways: more obviously, of course, to the extreme positions which it led him to adopt but also to one of the more unhappy results of this doctrine over the centuries in the Western Church, namely, its neglect of the doctrine of the Holy Spirit. It is ironical that the man whose treatise *On the Trinity* is held by many to have been his greatest doctrinal work should have contributed to much to this neglect by failing to give the Holy Spirit its proper place in his doctrine of grace and thus, albeit unintentionally, causing it to become the Cinderella of Western theology. Fortunately, much has been done to redress the damage in recent years, especially by Charles Raven and Geoffrey Lampe in this country.

to the central issue at stake, and, in their treatment of the relationship of divine grace to human freedom, both made the same mistake, that of attempting to define the undefinable. Grace is not something that we can define: it is something that we can only experience. Human freedom too is 'just a fact of experience', and nothing that we can learn from physics or psychology will ever prevent us from using it as a working hypothesis in our daily lives. In the last of his Reith Lectures John Searle, from whom I have just quoted, after satisfying himself that he had been able to keep both his commonplace conceptions and his scientific belief in his discussions of the relationship between mind and body, had to admit that he was unable to reconcile the two sides of the 'characteristic philosophical conundrum' presented by the perennial question of freedom and determinism: He concludes that 'neither this discussion nor any other will ever convince us that our behaviour is unfree'.[12] If Searle, a Professor of Philosophy with a vast range of modern knowledge at his disposal, has in the end to confess himself unable to solve this conundrum, what chance had Augustine and Pelagius of solving it with their much more limited resources?

It might be interjected that they had at least at their disposal a weapon which the Reith Lecturer of 1984 seems to have discarded; they could invoke the Christian doctrine of grace. But it was precisely this doctrine which was the nub of the matter for them, and both Pelagius and, later, the Semi-Pelagians maintained that Augustine had distorted it by arguing for a form of predestination, even double predestination, which was contrary to the teaching of the Church. His justifiable insistence on the absolute priority of the divine initiative in the work of human salvation appeared to them to have led him to adopt an extreme position which threatened to undermine the whole foundation of the Christian life as an active and loving co-operation between God and man. All that he had succeeded in doing, albeit unwittingly and 'in the grip of his daimon', was to replace the Christian God with the Nature of the Stoics, endowed with the superhuman faculties of omnipotence, omniscience and omnipresence but robbed of the infinite power of love. Whether by Nature or God, man was programmed from the beginning of the world to find his freedom only by sacrificing it to the laws of the one or to the will of the other. Pelagius argued that Augustine had deprived man of his freedom to respond to God, Augustine that it was only by surrendering his apparent freedom that man could be truly free. By winning the argument in the end, Augustine left God to play 'the ancient rôles of Clotho the spinner of life-threads or Lachesis the dispenser of lots'[13] – to which I venture to add 'or Atropos the irresistible or all three working together in harmony'.[14]

But if this was how the Doctor of Grace may have appeared to his critics, Pelagius left nimself just as open to the charge of having pushed his argument

[12] My quotations are taken from Searle's final lecture, 'The Freedom of the Will', as published in *The Listener* of 13 December 1984, 10ff.

[13] L. Dewart, 212, n. 35.

[14] The idea of the *Fates* or *Moirai* as a group of three daughters of Zeus appears as early as Hesiod, *Theogony*, 904–6, and reappears in Plato, *Republic* X, 614b–21d and especially in 617c.

to unacceptable extremes in the view of his opponents, who happened to include the leaders of the Western Church at that time. In his anxiety to stress the human rôle in the pursuit of righteousness he failed to give the divine rôle what they considered to be its proper place; instead, by his over-emphasis on the freedom of the human will and on its ability to cope with the problems presented by human weakness when faced by day-to-day pressures, he gave the appearance of having lapsed into a kind of naturalism. He believed in divine grace, however inadequately he may have defined it; he believed in it as a means of redemption and as a means of salvation available to all men and women alike; but either he had no doctrine of infused grace or he was unable to make it explicit. He was 'not a notably adroit theologian in the midst of controversy',[15] and his argument that the human will was itself a form of interior grace was totally rejected by his critics. It may be true that, as Frend suggests, 'in circumstances other than those of the first decades of the fifth century, his teaching might have provided a basis for a Christian ethic which would have set the seal on the conversion of the empire; medieval Europe might possibly have been built on different and more optimistic foundations.'[16] It may also be true that, even if he would not have been willing to admit it openly, he at least offered just a hint of a possible compromise by the care which he took to qualify his own emphasis on the ability of men to choose good by adding the phrase 'with the assistance of God' both at Diospolis and in his confession of faith presented to the Pope. But he was faced by an adversary who could not admit the possibility of any compromise on a matter which he believed to be of vital importance for the survival of the Christian Church, one whose 'worst enemy was his pursuit of controversy to the bitter end and his inability to concede the least right to an opponent'.[17] In his dealings with Pelagius, Augustine followed his normal practice of identifying his opponent's main weakness and of concentrating his attention upon it. The protagonists in the Pelagian controversy had stumbled upon one of the 'bundle of paradoxes' comprising our understanding of providence, 'which Christians also know as grace', 'religious truth which may be stated only as antinomy'.[18] 'If either of the symbolic positions espoused in Pelagianism and Augustinianism is taken by itself without the modifications that the other demands, if they are simply pitted against each other in an either/or fashion with no attempt at integration, one will inevitably be led to the untenable extremes that each position implies.'[19] This is a salutary warning, which John Cassian in the fifth century acknowledged at great personal cost, and we, in the late twentieth century, when the Christian Church is again at the

[15] R. F. Evans, 1968(a), 106.
[16] Frend, 1984, 675. More recently (1985, 139f.), Frend sums up the controversy between Augustine and Pelagius as follows: 'So, Augustine in arguing for the solidarity of mankind and making that bond of association sin was asserting a lasting truth. But this is not the whole truth about humanity. Pelagius was equally right in asserting the dignity and responsibility of man.'
[17] Frend, 1984, 676.
[18] I am quoting here from a most interesting article by J. S. Whale in *The Times* of 9 March 1985, entitled 'Paradoxes of Providence'.
[19] Haight, 42.

crossroads, ignore only at our own peril. We might also agree with the same writer's conclusion that 'because Christianity has unanimously judged that Augustine's is *essentially* the Christian doctrine, his view must provide the key to how this integration is to be effected, how the two poles will relate to one another.'[20] But Augustine and Pelagius were born into a world not yet ready to perceive and accept the truth of such a conclusion and the need for such an integration, and neither, engaged as he was in a heated debate, would have regarded it as anything other than a betrayal of his most cherished and fundamental beliefs.

For them it was a fight to a finish, and at the end of the day it was Augustine's high standing as an acknowledged leader of the Church and his proven skill as a controversialist that won the battle. After the Synod of Diospolis had announced its verdict in favour of Pelagius, Augustine's determination to destroy his opponent and all that he stood for hardened into an obsession. It was he who revived the subject of Pelagius' orthodoxy as soon as the records of Diospolis were made available for examination; it was he who masterminded the all-out campaign of the African Church to enlist the support of the Emperor and the Pope of Rome and to overcome the latter's reluctance to endorse an unambiguous condemnation of Pelagius and Celestius;[21] it was he who, indefatigable as ever, picked off Pelagius' main supporters one by one and reduced them to silence;[22] and it was he who continued the witch-hunt into the far corners of the Empire by ensuring that there would be no area of the Church in which Pelagius and his friends might be able to find asylum.[23]

Hans Küng, who has also experienced what it means to be submitted to treatment almost amounting to persecution at the hands of the leaders of his Church, though without, in his case, having to undergo the ultimate penalty for internal dissent, once made the pertinent comment that 'any heresy involves both a strengthening and a weakening of the Church': what is gained in certainty by a more precise formulation of doctrine is lost in vitality by trying to make this formulation too dogmatic.[24] It is a matter of opinion whether or not Augustine's treatment of Pelagius was, to say the least, uncharitable; it was certainly not in keeping with his usually kindly and sympathetic behaviour when dealing with fellow-Christians and may be excused as a justifiable reaction to provocation. But it was in keeping with the spirit and temper of theological debate in the fifth century, when white was white and black was black, when theologians had yet to learn and admit that there is more than one path leading to truth, that 'doctrine is not an end but a

---

[20] Ibid.; the emphasis is mine. The chapter from which I have quoted, entitled 'Augustine: grace and autonomy', is an admirable summary of the main issues in the Pelagian controversy as they relate to contemporary society.

[21] Patout Burns, 1979(b), analyses the part played by Augustine in this phase of controversy.

[22] Wermelinger, 210.

[23] H. Chadwick, 1983, 428ff. and 440, summarises and discusses the relevant letters – 4, 6 and 10 – in Divjak's collection.

[24] Küng, 1964, 99.

beginning'.[25] It would have been naïve of Pelagius to expect any better treatment than, for example, Priscillian of Avila and Rufinus of Aquileia had received before him. But it can be argued that, when the Church in its wisdom decided in the last resort to excommunicate him, it lost a potential source of vitality: it was depriving itself of the services of a committed Christian who had much to offer through his teaching and example to ordinary folk like the monks of Hadrumetum and Southern Gaul, incapable of fully appreciating a doctrine of grace which seemed to them to endanger the freedom of choice essential to their Christian way of life.

Oh, what a fall was there! Yes, and some of us must feel 'the dint of pity' for Pelagius.[26] For myself, I have to admit that, in trying to recount the vicissitudes of his star-crossed career, I may have shown more sympathy for him than the strict demands of historical objectivity permit. My thoughts have often strayed to his last days in Egypt – or wherever he may have been forced to spend them – and I have dared to hope that at the end there was someone who was not afraid to grant him that communion of which his Church had deprived him and the loss of which must have been for him 'the most unkindest cut of all'. He wanted above all else to be a good Christian, working for the reform of the Christian Church from within, he sincerely believed that his teaching was orthodox and consistent with that Church's tradition, and it was in order to prove this to his critics that he allowed himself to become involved in an arduous and prolonged controversy for which he was by ethos and training quite unsuited. And I have been reminded of how, in the midst of a time of even greater turmoil for the Church, Erasmus wrote to Jodocus Jonas of Erfurt to discourage him from too close an association with Martin Luther and to urge him to work instead for reform from within the Church. In his second letter he draws Jonas' attention to the shining example of two such reformers, whom he considered to have been true and sincere Christians. The first of these was Johan Vitrier, whom he had met in 1501 at the Franciscan house of St Omer in Artois, and after commenting that his 'jewel of a Vitrier' had indicated to him in the course of their conversation that he had found no theologian whose genius he admired more than Origen, he remarked that, when he had teased Vitrier by expressing some surprise that he should take pleasure in the writings of a heretic, he had received this prompt reply: 'The mind that produced so many learned works written with such fervour could not but have been the dwelling-place of the Holy Spirit.'[27]

[25] Haight, 42.

[26] Frend, 1985, 11, for example, confesses to 'an instinctive sympathy for history's runners-up', numbering Pelagius among them.

[27] *Erasmi Epistulae* IV, 1211, 508; Allen, 1918, 89ff. Bainton, 1977, 85, claims that 'he [Vitrier] was for Erasmus the perfect exemplification of the *philosophia Christi*' and also points out that 'Vitrier passed into oblivion' unlike the second of Erasmus' two reformers, John Colet. He may not have suffered that fate but 'he constantly inveighed against ecclesiastical abuses and, though he never challenged the doctrines of the Christian Church, was often accused of heresy' (Livingstone, 117). I am indebted to my friend Ceri Davies for reminding me of this passage in Erasmus.

This is true of Origen, whom Jerome himself once described as 'the greatest teacher of the Church since the apostles',[28] and of whom Henry Chadwick writes: 'If the meaning of orthodoxy is to wish to believe as the Church believes, then there can be virtually no hesitation in pronouncing Origen as orthodox. . . . The model of Christ himself is always before his eyes.'[29] It is true of Luther, of whom Erasmus may well have been reminded by Vitrier's judgement of Origen. And although his works fall short of those of Origen and Luther both in number and in quality, it is surely true also of Pelagius. 'What if Pelagius after all were more right than his detractors?' It is possible that our re-examination of the strengths and weaknesses of both sides in the Pelagian controversy may have persuaded some that he was or, at least, that his theology of grace could be adjudged no less 'orthodox' than that of Augustine. But in trying to arrive at an objective decision when both sides are in some respects right and, in others, wrong it would be more prudent to keep an open mind. The principal significance of the Pelagian controversy lies, after all, not in the personalities who were involved in it nor even in the arguments which they advanced but in the issues which were raised and which are as important today as they were in the fifth century of the Christian era, 'the very mainspring of the Christian religion and life'.[30] But 'now we have talked enough about this problem to satisfy a sensible man.'[31]

[28] H. Chadwick, 1966, 97; Jerome, pref. to *Onomasticon* or *Liber de nominibus Hebraicis* (PL 23, 772): *post apostolos ecclesiarum magistrum.*

[29] H. Chadwick, 1966, 122. Chadwick comments that Origen 'wanted to be a Christian, not a Platonist'; Pelagius wanted to be known as a Christian, not a Stoic, and saw himself as a traditionalist, defending the true faith against the innovations of Augustine. Wilken, 178ff., maintains that Arius too could be said to have been the traditionalist in the Nicene controversy and Athanasius and his supporters the innovators, adding that 'all heresies are backward-looking'.

[30] Sell, 143.

[31] William of St Thierry; the translation is that of Moore, 51.

Appendix I
Works attributable to Pelagius

At first glance this list may seem to be an impressive one but closer inspection
will reveal that only seven works listed have survived intact; the remainder
are either lost or represented only by fragments. Many others have been
attributed to Pelagius at various times in the past but must now be declared
to be either *adespota* or attributable to other writers of the Pelagian persuasion;
they have not been included in my list nor have the statements made by
Pelagius at the Synod of Diospolis, which will be found in full in Appendix II.

Uncertainty as to Pelagian authorship was an inevitable result of the
excommunication of the Pelagians and the general attempt to suppress their
opinions in the aftermath of the controversy. As a result works of Pelagius in
circulation in the fifth century and those immediately following it tended to be
attributed *faute de mieux* to more reputable authors. The earlier editors of
Migne's *Patrologia Latina* had therefore to be content with tacking them on to
the works of Hilary, Athanasius, Ambrose, Jerome, Paulinus of Nola, Sulpicius
Severus and, save the mark!, even Augustine. But when interest in Pelagius
began to revive and scholars to react to the patent hostility with which he
seemed to have been treated by their predecessors, some of them took this as
the signal for a free-for-all: Plinval, for example, published a list which
contained almost every work which could be attributed to Pelagius on any
conceivable ground, though he later found it necessary to recant and remove
a number of them after more careful consideration.

In this list readers will find only the basic references which will enable them
to locate Pelagius' works in the main collections of the writings of the Fathers
of the Church. For more detailed information as to their provenance and
exegetical history they are referred to the bibliographies contained in PLS 1,
1101–9 and the most recent volume of the *Dictionnaire de spiritualité, ascetique,
mystique, doctrine et histoire* (Vol. 12B, 2889–942), which is more up-to-date and
also more comprehensive and reliable.

A. Extant works

1. *Commentary on the Epistles of Paul (Expositiones XIII Epistularum Pauli
    Apostoli)*: PLS 1, 1110–374; CPL 728.

2. *Letter to Demetrias (Epistula ad sacram Christi virginem Demetriadem)*: PL
    30, 15–45; 33, 1099–120; CPL 737 = 633, 1.

3. *Confession of Faith* (*Libellus fidei ad Innocentium papam*): PL 45, 1716, 18; 48, 488–91; CPL 731 = 368, 236 = 633, 16.

4. *On the Christian Life* (*Liber de vita christiana*): PL 40, 1031–46; 50, 383–402; CPL 730.

5. *Letter to Celantia* (*Epistula ad Celantiam*): PL 22, 1204–29; 61, 723–36; CSEL 29, 436–59; 56, 329–56; CPL 745.

6. *On the Divine Law* (*Epistula ad Thesiphontem de scientia divinae legis*: PL 30, 105–16; CPL 740.

7. *On Virginity* (*Epistula ad Claudiam de virginitate* or *Ad Mauritii filiam laus virginitatis*): PL 18, 77–90; 20, 227–42; 30, 163–75; 56, 329–56; 103, 671–84; CSEL 1, 225–50; CPL 741.

B. Fragments

8. *On the Trinity* (*Libri tres de fide Trinitatis*): PL 39, 2198–200; PLS 1, 1544–60; CPL 748a–f.

9. *Extracts from the Divine Scriptures* (*Eclogarum ex divinis scripturis Liber*): PL 23, 519–26; 48, 594–6; CSEL 42, 52–107; 60, 547; CPL 750.

10. *To the Widow Livania* (*Libellus exhortatorius ad quandam Livaniam viduam*): PL 48, 598; CPL 754.

11. *On Nature* (*Liber de natura*): PL 48, 599–606; CSEL 42, 190–200; 60, 231–99, 456f.; CPL 753.

12. *Letter (II) to Augustine* (*Epistula ad Augustinum episcopum* or *Chartula defensionis suae*): PL 48, 608; CSEL 42, 111–13.

13. *Letter to a Friend* (*Epistula ad amicum suum quendam presbyterum*): PL 48, 609; CPL 749b.

14. *In Defence of Free Will* (*Pro libero arbitrio libri IV*): PL 48, 611–13; PLS 1, 1539–43; CSEL 42, *passim*; CPL 749.

15. *Letter to Pope Innocent* (*Epistula purgationis ad Innocentium papam*): PL 20, 608–11; 48, 610–11; CSEL, 42, 150–81; CPL 749a.

16. *Fragments from the Collection of Sedulius Scotus* (*Fragmenta e collectione Sedulii Scoti*): PLS 1, 1570; CPL 756.

17–18. *Pelagian Fragments of Vienna* (*Fragmenta pelagiana Vindobonensia*): PLS 1, 1561–70; CPL 755.

19. *To a Widow* (*Liber primus ad viduam*): PL 23, 586; 44, 329; CSEL 42, 68.

C. Lost Works

20. *Letter to Paulinus* (*Epistula ad sanctum virum Paulinum episcopum*): v. PL 44, 378; CSEL 42, 154.

21. *Letter to Constantius* (*Epistula ad sanctum Constantium episcopum*: ibid.

22. *Letter (I) to Augustine* (*Epistula ad Augustinum episcopum*): v. PL 48, 606; CSEL 42, 104.

Appendix II
The Synod of Diospolis

At the Synod of Diospolis in A.D. 415 Pelagius was confronted with a number of statements which he was alleged to have made in his writings as well as others attributed to Celestius. These are given below together with his replies and the comments of the Synod. The Latin text will be found in *PP* i. 2–xx. 44 (PL 44, 320–46) (CSEL 42, 51–99), and the translation is my own, as elsewhere in this book except where otherwise indicated.

1. A man cannot be without sin, unless he has acquired a knowledge of the Law.
   Pelagius: I did indeed say this but not in the sense in which they understand it. I did not say that a man who has acquired a knowledge of the Law cannot sin, but that by knowledge of the Law he is helped not to sin, as it is written: 'He hath given them a law for help.'
   Synod: What Pelagius has said is not inconsistent with [the teaching of] the Church.

2. All men are governed by their own will.
   P.: This I stated on account of free will, which God helps when it chooses good; man, however, when he sins, is himself to blame as of free will.
   S.: Nor is this inconsistent with the teaching of the Church.

3. In the day of judgement the unrighteous and sinners are not to be spared but to be consumed in eternal fires.
   P.: I stated this in accordance with the Gospel, in which it is said of sinners: 'These shall go away into eternal punishment but the righteous to life eternal.' And if anyone believes differently, he is an Origenist.
   S.: This too is not inconsistent with [the teaching of] the Church.

4. Evil does not enter our thoughts.
   P.: This I did not state in this way. What I did state was that the Christian ought to take pains not to think evil thoughts.
   S.: [This, as was proper, the Bishops approved.]

5. The kingdom was promised even in the Old Testament.
   P.: This can be proved by the Scriptures but heretics deny it in disparagement of the Old Testament. I, however, said this following the authority of the Scriptures, since it is written in the prophet Daniel: 'The

135

saints shall receive the kingdom of the Most High.'

S.: Nor is this inconsistent with the faith of the Church.

6. A man can be without sin, if he wishes.

P.: I did indeed say that a man can be without sin and keep the commandments of God, if he wishes, for this ability has been given to him by God. However, I did not say that any man can be found who has never sinned from his infancy up to his old age, but that, having been converted from his sins, he can be without sin by his own efforts and God's grace, yet not even by this means is he incapable of change for the future.

[Other statements alleged to have been made by Pelagius in a letter and another work addressed to a widow were also cited against him.]

P.: The rest of the statements cited are not in my works nor have I ever said such things.

S.: Since you deny having written such things, would you anathematise those who hold them?

P.: I anathematise them as fools but not as heretics, since there is no dogma [respecting these opinions].

S.: Since Pelagius has now anathematised with his own utterance this foolish talk which has been introduced, rightly replying that a man can be without sin with the help and grace of God, let him now reply to the other points in the accusation.

7. [Statements were then cited which were said to have been found in the teachings of Celestius:]

(a) Adam was created mortal and would have died whether he sinned or not.

(b) Adam's sin injured only himself and not the human race.

(c) The Law sends us to the kingdom no less than the Gospel.

(d) There were men without sin before Christ's coming.

(e) New-born infants are in the same state as Adam was before his transgression.

(f) The whole human race neither dies through Adam's death or transgression nor rises again through the resurrection of Christ.

[Further points were next introduced in connection with a mention of Augustine's name, having been transmitted to him by Catholic brethren in Sicily:]

(g) A man can be without sin, if he wishes.

(h) Infants have eternal life, even if unbaptised.

(i) Rich men who have been baptised, unless they renounce everything, are not credited with any good that they may seem to have done nor can they possess the kingdom of God.

P.: On the statement that man can be without sin I have spoken earlier; however, on the statement that there were men without sin before the Lord's coming I also say that before Christ's coming some men lived holy and righteous lives according to the teaching of the Holy Scriptures. As for the rest of the statements, even by their own testimony they were not made by me, and I am not obliged to satisfy them on these counts; yet, for the satisfaction of the Holy Synod, I anathematise those who hold or have ever held such opinions.

S.: To these points aforesaid Pelagius, who is present, has given us adequate and proper satisfaction by anathematising those which were not his.

8.   The Church here is without spot or wrinkle.

P.: I have said this but in the sense that the Church is cleansed by the laver from every spot and wrinkle and that the Lord wishes it to remain so.

9.   [Statements were then cited from a book by Celestius chapter by chapter but rather according to the sense than the actual words, since the accusers had been unable to adduce all the words:]

(a) We do more than is commanded in the Law and the Gospel.

P.: This they have set down as my statement; what I said, however, was consistent with what Paul states on the subject of virginity: 'I have no commandment of the Lord.'

S.: This too the Church accepts.

(b) God's grace and help are not given for single actions but consist in free will or in the Law and teaching.

(c) God's grace is given according to our merits, since he seems to be unjust if he gives it to sinners.

[By these words, according to Augustine, he implied: For that reason grace itself has been located in my will according as I have been worthy or unworthy of it. For if we do all things by grace, it is not we who are overcome by sin when we are overcome by sin but the grace of God, which wished to help us by all means and was not able to do so.

(d) If it is the grace of God when we overcome sin, then He Himself is at fault when we are overcome by sin, because He has been either unable or unwilling entirely to protect us.

P.: It is for those who say that these are the opinions of Celestius to look to it whether they really are his. I, however, have never held such views and I anathematise the man who does hold them.

S.: The Holy Synod accepts this condemnation of yours of these false statements.

(e) Every man is able to possess all virtues and graces [and this implies the removal of the diversity of graces which the Apostle teaches].

P.: I have said it but they have made an accusation which is both malicious and inept; for I do not remove the diversity of graces but I say that God gives all graces to him who has been worthy to receive them, even as He bestowed them on Paul.

S.: Your interpretation of the gift of graces, which are concentrated in the Holy Apostle, conforms to the interpretation of the Church.

(f) Men cannot be called sons of God, unless they have been made completely free from sin.

137

(g) Forgetfulness and ignorance are not subject to sin, since they occur not according to the will but according to necessity.

(h) Will is not free if it stands in need of God's help, since everyone has it in his own will either to do or not to do something.

(i) Our victory comes not from God's help but from free will. [Augustine adds that he, that is, Celestius, was said to have made this inference in the following words: 'The victory is ours, since we took up arms of our own will, just as the fault is ours when we are overcome, since we neglected to arm ourselves of our will.' And, Augustine goes on to say, he cited as evidence from the Apostle Peter 'we are partakers of the divine nature', from which he formed this conclusion: 'for if our soul is not without sin, therefore God too is subject to sin, since part of him, that is, our soul, is beholden to sin.']

(j) Pardon is not given to the repentant according to the grace and mercy of God but according to the merit and efforts of those who have become worthy of mercy through repentance.

S.:   What does the monk Pelagius say in reply to these points which have been read out? For the Holy Synod and God's Holy Catholic Church condemn them.

P.:   I say again that these opinions are not mine by their own testimony, and I am not obliged to give satisfaction for them. Those statements, however, which I have admitted to be mine I maintain to be correct; but those which I have said not to be mine I condemn according to the judgement of the Holy Church, pronouncing anathema on everyone who opposes and contradicts the teachings of the Holy Catholic Church. For I believe in the Trinity of the one substance and in all things in accordance with the teaching of the Holy Catholic Church. If anyone has opinions, however, which are different from hers, let him be anathema.

S.:   Now since we have received satisfaction in respect of the charges brought against the monk Pelagius in his presence and since he gives his assent to sound doctrines but condemns and anathematises those contrary to the faith of the Church, we adjudge him to belong to the communion of the Catholic Church.

Pelagius was thus acquitted on the basis of his replies to the charges concerned with statements which he admitted to have been his own and of his condemnation of those which he denied ever having made. But to complete the picture and to explain why it was that Augustine was so dissatisfied with the outcome of the Synod we need to read the latter's comment at the end of his account of the proceedings as recorded in *PP* xxi. 45 (PL 44, 346) (CSEL 42, 99):

They judged him as one of whom they knew nothing, especially in the absence of those who had drawn up the indictment against him, a man whom they were thus quite unable to judge with greater care; yet, in spite of this, they utterly destroyed the heresy itself. Those, however, who know what Pelagius has been in the habit of teaching or who have resisted his arguments or who congratulate themselves on having been set free of his error, how can they possibly not regard him as suspect, when they read his disingenuous confession condemning his past errors but so expressed as to imply that he never held opinions different from those to which approval was given by his judges on the basis of his replies?

In other words, Pelagius went scot-free; but his heresy stands condemned!

Appendix III

The Pelagian controversy: a summary

c. 380   Pelagius arrives in Rome and gains a high reputation as an ascetic, spiritual mentor and moral reformer.

390–9   He meets Celestius and, towards the end of the decade, Rufinus the Syrian.

c. 402–5   He expresses strong dissent from the view of grace revealed in Book X of Augustine's *Confessions* and writes his *On the Trinity* and *Extracts*.

406–9   He writes his *Commentary on the Pauline Epistles*.

c. 409   He leaves Italy and arrives in Palestine via Carthage.

411/12   Celestius, who stays in Carthage, is condemned by the Council there for his heretical opinions; he leaves soon after for the East. Augustine attacks the teachings of Celestius and Rufinus the Syrian on original sin and infant baptism in his *On the Merits and Forgiveness of Sins and Infant Baptism*.

412   He follows this up with his *On the Spirit and the Letter*.

413   Pelagius comes under attack from Jerome in Palestine. He writes his *Letter to Demetrias* but Jerome also writes to her, taking the opportunity to warn her against adherents of Origenism, among whom he now counts Pelagius.

c. 414   Pelagius defends himself in his treatise *On Nature*.

415   Augustine writes his *On Nature and Grace* in reply. He also sends Orosius to Jerome, armed with two important letters and an anti-Pelagian dossier to alert Jerome against the Pelagians. Jerome refers to them unfavourably in his *Commentary on Jeremiah* and redoubles his efforts to discredit them in his *Letter to Ctesiphon* and, later, his *Dialogue against the Pelagians*, begun about this time.

Orosius' charges against Pelagius and Celestius are dismissed as not proven by the Synod of Jerusalem, and he responds with his *Book in Defence against the Pelagians*. Pelagius is accused of heresy by Heros and Lazarus but is acquitted by the Synod of Diospolis. Celestius is ordained priest at Ephesus but Augustine renews his attack with his *On the Perfection of Man's Righteousness*.

c. 416	Pelagius writes his treatise *In Defence of Free Will* in response to the attacks of Orosius, Jerome and Augustine.
416	Pelagius and Celestius are condemned by Councils at Milevis and Carthage. Pope Innocent responds to three letters from the African bishops and the news of an attack on Jerome's monastery allegedly by Pelagians by excommunicating Pelagius and Celestius, while giving Pelagius an opportunity to justify himself either by appearing before him in Rome or by letter. Pelagius sends him a *Letter in Justification* and *Confession of Faith*, supported by a letter of commendation from Praylius, John's successor as Bishop of Jerusalem. Innocent dies early in 417, and the documents are received by Zosimus, his successor.
417	Augustine gives wide circulation to his work *On the Proceedings of Pelagius*. Expelled from Constantinople by the Patriarch Atticus, Celestius now appeals to Pope Zosimus, submits his *Confession of Faith* to him and appears before a tribunal at Rome. Zosimus reserves judgement for two months pending the appearance before him of Celestius' accusers but informs the African bishops that he is acquitting Pelagius for lack of firm evidence against him and asks them to recognise that Pelagius and Celestius have not yet been finally cut off from the Church.
418	Augustine responds with his treatise *On the Grace of Christ and Original Sin*, and the African bishops by again writing to Zosimus, respectfully asking him to confirm the decision of his predecessor. The Emperor Honorius now intervenes from Ravenna, alarmed by the news of an assault by Pelagians on a retired official in Rome and reports of unrest there. He issues an imperial rescript in which he condemns all those who deny the Fall and orders the banishment of Pelagius and Celestius from Rome, assuming them to be still there. The Council of Carthage passes a series of nine canons against Pelagianism, and Zosimus, now under great pressure from the African bishops as well as the opponents of the Pelagians in Rome, publishes and circulates an *Epistula Tractoria* condemning Pelagius and Celestius and excommunicating them. After further intervention by Augustine, Pelagius is expelled from Jerusalem and then from Palestine and, possibly after a brief stay in Antioch, seeks refuge in Egypt with a small number of his remaining supporters, who are already there. In the meantime eighteen Italian bishops, led by Julian of Eclanum, refuse to subscribe to Zosimus' *Epistula*, their appeal is rejected, and they are condemned, deposed from office, and, after a final refusal to subscribe, excommunicated and banished from the towns of Italy.
419	Julian at once begins to attack Augustine's 'neo-Manicheism', and Augustine responds with Book I of his *On Marriage and Concupiscence*

and *On the Soul and its Origin*. Julian replies to the former with his four books *To Turbantius*.

420–1 On receipt of Julian's *To Turbantius*, *Letter to Rufus* and *Letter to the Romans* Augustine publishes the second book of his *On Marriage and Concupiscence* and his work *Against Two Letters of the Pelagians*. Julian replies with his *To Florus* in eight books, written in Cilicia while he is under the protection of Theodore of Mopsuestia.

421–2 Augustine writes six books *Against Julian* to refute the charges made in *To Turbantius*.

426–7 Augustine sends his treatises *On Grace and Free Will* and *On Rebuke and Grace* to allay the doubts of the monks at Hadrumetum.

c. 428 Julian, forced to leave Cilicia, arrives with three other Italian bishops in Constantinople and appeals to the Emperor there and the Patriarch Nestorius; the latter writes to Pope Celestine at Rome for confirmation of the condemnation of the Italian bishops and is asked by the Pope to condemn them and confirm the sentence passed on them by the Church in Rome. His response is pre-empted by an imperial degree expelling Julian and his supporters from the city and mainly brought about by the submission by Marius Mercator of a *Memorandum on the Name of Celestius*.

428–9 Augustine responds to Prosper's and Hilary's anxiety about the monks of Provence with his treatises *On the Predestination of the Saints* and *On the Gift of Perseverance*.

430 Augustine dies, leaving his reply to Julian's treatise *To Florus* unfinished.

431 The Council of Ephesus condemns 'the opinions of Celestius' and confirms the deposition of Julian and his supporters. Julian again flees and returns to Italy, where he is refused permission to receive communion by Pope Sixtus III.

c. 443–5 Julian dies in Sicily.

The Drinking Song of Pelagius

Pelagius lived in Kardanoel
And taught a doctrine there,
How whether you went to Heaven or Hell,
It was your own affair;
How whether you found eternal joy
Or sank forever to burn,
It has nothing to do with the Church, my boy,
But was your own concern.
Oh, he didn't believe
In Adam and Eve,
He put no faith therein!
His doubts began with the fall of man,
And he laughed at original sin!
With my row-ti-tow, ti-oodly-ow,
He laughed at original sin!

Whereat the Bishop of old Auxerre
(Germanus was his name),
He tore great handfuls out of his hair,
And he called Pelagius Shame:
And then with his stout Episcopal staff
So thoroughly thwacked and banged
The heretics all, both short and tall,
They rather had been hanged.
Oh, he thwacked them hard, and he banged them long,
Upon each and all occasions,
Till they bellowed in chorus, loud and strong,
Their orthodox persuasions.
With my row-ti-tow, ti-oodly-ow,
Their orthodox persuasions.

Now the Faith is old and the devil is bold,
Exceedingly bold indeed;
And the masses of doubt that are floating about
Would smother a mortal creed.
But we that sit in a sturdy youth

And still can drink strong ale,
Oh – let us put it away to unfallible truth,
Which always shall prevail!
And thank the Lord
For the temporal sword,
And howling heretics too,
And whatever good things
Our Christendom brings,
But especially barley brew!
With my row-ti-tow, ti-oodly-ow,
Especially barley brew!

After subjecting my readers to many *longueurs* in the course of this little book, I feel obliged to offer them by way of compensation this ditty from the pen of one who could find humour in any person or subject, Hilaire Belloc. It comes from his *farrago* entitled *The Four Men* and is elsewhere found under a different title: 'Song of the Pelagian Heresy for the Strengthening of Men's Backs and the very Robust Outthrusting of Doubtful Doctrine and the Uncertain Intellectual'. I am indebted to my friends Lisbeth David and Lou Matthews for drawing my attention to it and subsequently unearthing it along with the music to which it can be sung. Even Pelagius has his funny side.

Short Reading List

The books listed below will give readers who may wish to extend their knowledge of the various aspects of the Pelagian controversy a reasonably comprehensive introduction. They are listed in order of publication but the bibliography must be consulted for the full details.

J. Burnaby, *Amor Dei*
G. de Plinval, *Pélage: ses écrits, sa vie et sa réforme*
J. J. O'Meara, *The Young Augustine*, p/b
J. Ferguson, *Pelagius*
H. I. Marrou, *St Augustine and His Influence through the Ages*
E. Gilson, *The Christian Philosophy of St Augustine*
F. van der Meer, *Augustine the Bishop*
G. Bonner, *Augustine: Life and Controversies*
P. R. L. Brown, *Augustine of Hippo: a Biography*, p/b
R. F. Evans, *Pelagius: Inquiries and Reappraisals*
E. TeSelle, *Augustine the Theologian*
G. Bonner, *Augustine and Modern Research on Pelagianism*
R. A. Markus, ed., *Augustine: a Collection of Critical Essays*, p/b
P. R. L. Brown, *Religion and Society in the Age of St Augustine*
J. N. D. Kelly, *Jerome: His Life, Writings and Controversies*
E. Portalié, *A Guide to the Thought of St Augustine*
O. Wermelinger, *Rom und Pelagius*
D. Bentley-Taylor, *Augustine: Wayward Genius*
H. I. Marrou (with A.-M. La Bonnardière), *St Augustin et l'augustinisme*, p/b
W. T. Smith, *Augustine: His Life and Thought*, p/b
G. R. Evans, *Augustine on Evil*
W. H. C. Frend, *Saints and Sinners in the Early Christian Church*, p/b
H. Chadwick, *Augustine*, p/b

Translations

A Select Library of the Nicene and Post-Nicene Fathers, Michigan, 1974
The Works of Aurelius Augustinus, Edinburgh, 1871–6
Ancient Christian Writers, Westminster, Maryland/London, 1946–
Fathers of the Church, New York/Washington, 1948ff., 1960ff.
Library of the Christian Classics, Philadelphia, 1953, 1955

145

The Essential Augustine, ed. V. J. Bourke, Indianopolis, Indiana, 1964
Confessions, City of God, Harmondsworth, 1961, 1964 (Penguin Classics)
Confessions, City of God, Select Letters, London/Cambridge, Mass., 1957ff.
   (Loeb Classical Library)
Walking in the Light: The Confessions of St Augustine, D. Winter, London/
   Wheaton, Illinois, 1986 (paraphrased selection)

Abbreviations

(a) Works of Augustine cited:

B	On Baptism, VII (De baptismo contra Donatistas)
C	Confessions, XIII (Confessiones)
CD	Against Cresconius the Donatist, IV (Contra Cresconium grammaticum partis Donati)
CG	On the City of God, XXII (De civitate Dei)
E	Enchiridion on Faith, Hope and Charity (Enchiridion ad Laurentium de fide, spe, caritate)
FC	On Free Choice, III (De libero arbitrio)
GC	On the Grace of Christ (De gratia Christi)[1]
GFC	On Grace and Free Choice (De gratia et libero arbitrio ad Valentinum)
GP	On the Gift of Perseverance (De dono perseverantiae)
H	On Heresies (De haeresibus ad Quodvultdeum)
IWJ	Incomplete Work against Julian, VI (Opus imperfectum contra Iulianum)
J	Against Julian, VI (Contra Iulianum haeresis Pelagianae defensorem)
L	Letters (Epistolae)
LCG	Literal Commentary on Genesis, XII (De Genesi ad litteram)
LParm	Against the Letter of Parmenian, III (Contra epistolam Parmeniani)
LPet	Against the Letters of Petilian, III (Contra epistolas Petiliani Donatistae)
MBC	On the Moral Behaviour of the Catholic Church and of the Manichees, II (De moribus Ecclesiae Catholicae et de moribus Manichaeorum)
MC	On Marriage and Concupiscence, II (De nuptiis et concupiscentia)
MFS	On Merits and Forgiveness of Sins and Infant Baptism, III (De peccatorum meritis et remissione et de baptismo parvulorum)
NG	On Nature and Grace against Pelagius (De natura et gratia contra Pelagium)
OS	On Original Sin (De peccato originali)[1]
PMR	On the Perfection of Man's Righteousness (De perfectione iustitiae hominis)
PO	Against the Priscillianists and Origenists (Contra Priscillianistas et Origenistas ad Orosium)

[1] I have listed the two volumes of the treatise On the Grace of Christ and on Original Sin separately for convenience.

PP	On the Proceedings of Pelagius (*De gestis Pelagii*)[2]
PS	On the Predestination of the Saints (*De praedestinatione Sanctorum*)
R	Retractations, II (*Retractationes*)
RG	On Rebuke and Grace (*De correptione et gratia*)
S	Sermons (*Sermones*)
SL	On the Spirit and the Letter (*De spiritu et littera*)
SO	On the Soul and its Origin, IV (*De anima et eius origine*)
T	On the Trinity, XV (*De Trinitate*)
TLP	Against Two Letters of the Pelagians, IV (*Contra duas epistolas Pelagianorum ad Bonifacium Papam*)
VQS	On Various Questions for Simplicianus (*De diversis quaestionibus VII ad Simplicianum*)

---

[2] The title of the treatise *De Gestis Pelagii* has appeared in various forms. Augustine himself refers to it in *OS* 15 as *De Gestis Palaestinis*, and Prosper, *Against the Collator*, also describes it thus, while Possidius names it as *Contra Gesta Pelagii*. It is sometimes entitled *On the Activities of Pelagius* in modern works.

(b) Journals and works of reference:

AB	*Analecta Bollandiana*
AC	*Archaeologia Cambrensis*
ACant	*Archaeologia Cantiana*
AM	*Augustinus Magister*
AS	*Augustinian Studies*
AThA	*Année théologique augustinienne*
ATR	*Anglican Theological Review*
BA	*Bibliothèque Augustinienne, Oeuvres de Saint Augustin*
BTRL	*Bulletin of the John Rylands Library*
BSR	*Biblioteca di Scienze Religiose*
CC	*Corpus Christianorum, series Latina*
CMCS	*Cambridge Medieval Celtic Studies*
CPL	*Clavis Patrum Latinorum*
CQR	*Church Quarterly Review*
CR	*Clergy Review*
CRAI	*Comptes rendus de l'Académie des Inscriptions et Belles Lettres*
CSEL	*Corpus Scriptorum Ecclesiasticorum Latinorum*
CTJ	*Calvin Theological Journal*
DR	*The Dublin Review*
DTC	*Dictionnaire de Théologie Catholique*
EHR	*English Historical Review*
ET	*Expository Times*
HJ	*Hibbert Journal*
HTR	*Harvard Theological Review*
IER	*Irish Ecclesiastical Record*
IHS	*Irish Historical Studies*
JBAA	*Journal of the British Archaeological Association*
JEH	*Journal of Ecclesiastical History*
JRIC	*Journal of the Royal Institute of Cornwall*
JRS	*Journal of Roman Studies*
JRSAI	*Journal of the Royal Society of Antiquaries in Ireland*
JTS	*Journal of Theological Studies*
KTR	*King's Theological Review*
PAPS	*Proceedings of the American Philosophical Society*
PBA	*Proceedings of the British Academy*

PCA	*Proceedings of the Classical Association*
PG	*Patrologiae cursus completus, series Graeca*
PL	*Patrologiae cursus completus, series Latina*
PLS	*Patrologiae cursus completus, series Latina, supplementum*
RA	*Recherches augustiniennes*
RB	*Revue bénédictine*
RE	*Real-Encyclopädie der klassischen Altertumswissenschaft*
REA	*Revue des études augustiniennes*
REL	*Revue des études latines*
RHE	*Revue d'histoire ecclésiastique*
RPh	*Revue de philologie, de littérature et d'histoire anciennes*
RPThK	*Realencyclopädie für protestantische Theologie und Kirche*
RSR	*Recherches de science religieuse*
RThAM	*Recherches de théologie ancienne et mediévale*
SC	*Studia Celtica*
SH	*Studia Hibernica*
SP	*Studia Patristica*
STL	*Studia Theologica Lundensia*
TC	*The Churchman*
TCR	*The Contemporary Review*
ThL	*Theologische Literaturzeitung*
ThQ	*Theologische Quartalschrift*
THSC	*Transactions of the Honourable Society of Cymmrodorion*
UJA	*Ulster Journal of Archaeology*
VC	*Vigiliae Christianae*
WHR	*Welsh History Review*
ZCP	*Zeitschrift für Celtische Philologie*
ZKG	*Zeitschrift für Kirchengeschichte*

Bibliography

I cannot claim to have compiled a comprehensive list of works relating to Pelagius and the Pelagian controversy. This bibliography is no more than a hotchpotch consisting of books and articles which I have read or consulted in preparing this monograph, though I dare to hope that it may serve as a useful guide for any who may be interested enough to want to pursue their own enquiries into the subjects discussed. Where there are two or more editions of the same work, I have cited only those which I have consulted myself.

ADAM, K. *'Causa finita est'*, *Festgabe Albert Erhard*, ed., A. M. Köeniger, Bonn–Leipzig, 1922, 1–23.

ADAMS, R. 'Piers's Pardon and Langland's Semi-Pelagianism', *Traditio* 39, 1983, 367–418.

ALCOCK, L. A. *Arthur's Britain: History and Archaeology, A.D. 367–634*, London, 1971.

ALLEN, P. S. *Selections from Erasmus²*, Oxford, 1918.

—— and H. M. Edd., *Erasmi Epistolae* I–XII, Oxford, 1906–58.

ALTANER, B. 'Der *Liber de Fide*, ein Werk des Pelagianers Rufinus des "Syrers"', *ThQ* 130, 1950, 422–49.

ANTIN, P. 'Rufin et Pélage dans Jérôme, *Prologue I in Hieremiam*, *Latomus* 22, 1963, 792–4.

ARMSTRONG, A. H. *An Introduction to Ancient Philosophy*, London, 1947.

—— Ed., *The Cambridge History of Later Greek and Early Medieval Philosophy²*, Cambridge, 1970.

—— 'St Augustine and Christian Platonism' in MARKUS, R. A., ed., 1972, 3–37 (The Saint Augustine Lecture 1966, Villanova, 1967).

ARMSTRONG, C. B. 'St Augustine and Pelagius as religious types', *CQR* 162, 1961, 150–64 (summary in *PCA* 57, 1960, 27–8).

ARMSTRONG, K. *The First Christian: St Paul's Impact on Christianity*, London, 1983.

AUSTIN, A. W. 'Are religions enabling methods for survival?', *Zygon* 15, 1980, 193–201.

BABCOCK, W. S. 'Augustine's interpretation of Romans (A.D. 394–9)', *AS* 10, 1979, 55–74.

—— 'Augustine and Tyconius: a study in the Latin appropriation of Paul', *SP* 17, 1982, iii, 1209–16.

BADHAM, P. and L. *Immortality or Extinction*, London, 1982.

BAINTON, R. H.   *Here I Stand: a Life of Martin Luther*, New York/London, 1950.

—— *Erasmus of Christendom*, New York/London, 1977.

BARLEY, M. W. and HANSON, R. P. C.   Edd., *Christianity in Britain, 300–700*, Leicester, 1968.

BARNARD, L. W.   'Pelagius and early Syriac Christianity', *RThAM* 35, 1968, 193–6.

BARTHOLOMEW, D. J.   *God of Chance*, London, 1984.

BAUER, W.   *Orthodoxy and Heresy in Earliest Christianity²*, London, 1972.

BEATRICE, P. F.   *Tradux Peccati*, Milan, 1978.

BENTLEY-TAYLOR, D.   *Augustine: Wayward Genius*, London, 1980.

BERGER, P. L.   *The Heretical Imperative: Contemporary Possibilities of Religious Affirmation*, London, 1980.

BETHELL, D. L. T.   'The originality of the Early Irish Church', *JRSAI* 110, 1981, 36–49.

BETHUNE-BAKER, J. F.   *An Introduction to the Early History of Christian Doctrine²*, London, 1954.

BETTENSON, H.   *The Later Christian Fathers*, Oxford, 1970.

BEZZANT, J. S.   'Intellectual Objections' in VIDLER, A. R., ed., 1963, 79–111.

BIELER, L.   'The Mission of Palladius', *Traditio* 6, 1948, 1–32.

—— *The Life and Legend of St Patrick*, Dublin, 1949.

—— *Libri Epistolarum Sancti Patricii Episcopi*, Dublin, 1952.

—— *St Patrick and the Coming of Christianity*, Dublin, 1967.

—— 'St Patrick and the British Church' in BARLEY, M. W. and HANSON, R. P. C., edd., 1968, 123–30.

BINCHY, D. A.   'Patrick and his biographers, ancient and modern', *SH* 2, 1962, 7–173.

BLIC, J. de   'Le péché originel selon Saint Augustin', *RSR* 16, 1927, 512–31.

BOGAN, M. I.   Ed. and trans., *Retractationes*, Catholic University of America, 1968.

BOHLIN, T.   *Die Theologie des Pelagius und ihre Genesis*, Uppsala/Wiesbaden, 1957.

BONNER, G.   '*Libido* and *concupiscentia* in St Augustine', *SP* 6, iv, 1962, 303–14.

—— *St Augustine of Hippo: Life and Controversies*, London, 1963, repr. Norwich, 1986.

—— 'How Pelagian was Pelagius?: an examination of the contentions of Torgny Bohlin', *SP* 9, 1966, 350–8.

—— 'Les origines africaines de la doctrine augustinienne sur la chute et le péché originel', *Augustinus* 12, 1967, 97–111.

—— 'Rufinus of Syria and African Pelagianism', *AS* 1, 1970, 31–47.

—— *Augustine and Modern Research on Pelagianism* (The Saint Augustine Lecture, 1970), Villanova, 1972.

—— 'Augustine's Conception of Deification', *JTS* n.s. 37, 1986(a), 369–86.

—— 'Adam', *Augustinus-Lexicon* I, ed. C. Mayer, Basel/Stuttgart, 1986(b), 63–87.

152

BORIUS, R.   Ed. and trans., *Constance de Lyon: Vie de saint d'Auxerre*, Paris, 1965.

BOURKE, V. J.   *The Essential Augustine²*, Indianopolis, Indiana, 1974.

BOUWMAN, G.   *Des Julian von Aeclanum Kommentar zu den Propheten Osee, Joel und Amos: ein Beitrag zur Geschichte der Exegese (Analecta Biblica 9)*, Rome, 1958.

BOWEN, E. G.   *The Settlements of the Celtic Saints in Wales*, Cardiff, 1956.

—— *Saints, Settlements and Seaways in the Celtic Lands*, Cardiff, 1969.

—— *The St David of History: Dewi Sant, our Founder Saint* (Address given to the Friends of St David's Cathedral, 1981), Aberystwyth, 1982.

—— *Dewi Sant: Saint David*, Cardiff, 1983.

BROOKS, E. C.   'The translation techniques of Rufinus of Aquileia (343–411)', *SP* 17, i, 1982, 357–64.

BROWN, P. R. L.   'Religious dissent in the Later Roman Empire: the case of North Africa', *History* 46, 1961, 83–101 (*Religion and Society in the Age of St Augustine*, London, 1972, 237–59).

—— 'Aspects of the Christianization of the Roman Aristocracy', *JRS* 61, 1961, 1–11 (*Religion and Society*, 161–82).

—— 'Religious coercion in the Later Roman Empire: the case of North Africa', *History* 48, 1963, 283–305 (*Religion and Society*, 301–31).

—— 'Saint Augustine', in Smalley, B., ed., *Trends in Medieval Political Thought*, 1963, 1–21 (*Religion and Society*, 25–45).

—— 'St Augustine's attitude to religious coercion', *JRS* 54, 1964, 107–16 (*Religion and Society*, 260–78).

—— *Augustine of Hippo: a Biography*, London, 1967.

—— 'Pelagius and his supporters', *JTS* n.s. 19, i, 1968, 93–114 (*Religion and Society*, 183–207).

—— 'The diffusion of Manichaeism in the Roman Empire', *JRS* 59, 1969, 92–103 (*Religion and Society*, 94–118).

—— 'The patrons of Pelagius', *JTS* n.s. 21, i, 1970, 56–72 (Religion and Society, 208–26).

—— *The World of Late Antiquity*, London, 1971.

—— *Religion and Society in the Age of St Augustine*, London, 1972.

—— 'Sexuality and Society in the Fifth Century A.D.: Augustine and Julian of Eclanum', in Garba, E., ed., *Tria Corda: scritti in onore di Arnaldo Momigliano*, Como, 1983(a), 50–69.

—— 'Augustine and Sexuality', in *Center for Hermeneutical Studies in Hellenistic and Modern Culture, Protocol Series of the Colloquies*, 1983(b), 1–13.

BRUCKNER, A.   *Julian von Eclanum, sein Leben und seine Lehre*, Leipzig, 1897.

BU'LOCK, J. D.   'Early Christian Memorial Formulae', *AC* 105, 1956, 133–41.

—— *The Life of the Early Celtic Church*, Edinburgh, 1963.

BURKITT, F. C.   *The Religion of the Manichees*, Cambridge, 1925.

BURNABY, J.   *Amor Dei: a Study of the Religion of Saint Augustine* (The Hulsean Lectures for 1938), London, 1938.

—— 'The *Retractationes* of Saint Augustine: self-criticism or apologia?', *AM* 1, 1954, 85–92.

BURY, J. B. 'The origins of Pelagius', *Hermathena* 13, 1904, 26–35.

—— *The Life of St Patrick and His Place in History*, London, 1905.

—— *A History of the Later Roman Empire from the Death of Theodosius I to the Death of Justinian, A.D. 395 to A.D. 565*, London, 1923.

CAMERON, A. 'Celestial consulates: a note on the Pelagian letter *Humanae referunt*', *JTS* n.s. 19, 1968, 213–15.

CAMPBELL, D. T. 'The conflict between social and biological evolution and the concept of original sin', *Zygon* 10, 1975, 234–49.

—— 'On the conflict between biological and social evolution and between psychology and moral tradition', *Zygon* 11, 1976, 167–208.

CAPANAGA, V. *La teologia agustiniana de la gracia*, Madrid, 1933.

CAPPS, W. H. and WRIGHT, W. M. *Silent Fire*, New York, 1978.

CARNEY, J. *Studies in Irish Literature and History*, Dublin, 1955.

—— 'A new chronology of the Saint's life' in RYAN, J., ed., 1958, 24–37.

—— *The Problem of St Patrick*, Dublin, 1961, 1973.

CASEY, P. J. Ed., *The End of Roman Britain*, Oxford, 1979.

CASPARI, C. P. *Briefe, Abhandlungen und Predigten aus den zwei letzten Jahrhunderten des kirklichen Altertums und den Anfang des Mittelalters*, Brussels, 1964 (*Christiania*, 1890).

CAVALLERA, F. *Saint Jérôme: sa vie et son oeuvre*, Louvain/Paris, 1922.

CHADWICK, H. *Origen contra Celsum*, Cambridge, 1953.

—— *The Sentences of Sextus: a Contribution to the History of Early Christian Ethics* (Texts and Studies, n.s. V), Cambridge, 1959.

—— *Early Christian Thought and the Classical Tradition*, Oxford, 1966.

—— *The Early Church*, Harmondsworth, 1967.

—— *Priscillian of Avila: the Occult and the Charismatic in the Early Church*, Oxford, 1976.

—— 'New Letters of St Augustine', *JTS* n.s. 34, 1983, 425–52.

—— *Augustine*, Oxford, 1986.

CHADWICK, N. K. *Poetry and Letters in Early Christian Gaul*, London, 1955.

—— Ed., *Studies in the Early British Church*, Cambridge, 1958.

—— Ed., *Studies in Early British History*, Cambridge, 1959.

—— *The Age of Saints in the Early Celtic Church*, Oxford, 1961.

—— *Celtic Britain*, London, 1963.

CHADWICK, O. 'Euladius of Arles', *JTS* 46, 1945, 200–5.

—— *John Cassian*², Cambridge, 1968.

CHAPMAN, J. 'The Holy See and Pelagianism', *DR* 120, 1897, 88–111; 121, 1897, 99–124,

CHARLESWORTH, M. P. *The Lost Province or The Worth of Britain*, Cardiff, 1949.

CHÉNÉ, J. 'Les origines de la controverse semi-pélagienne', *AThA* 13, 1953, 56–109.

CLARK, M. T. *Augustine, Philosopher of Freedom*, New York, 1958.

COCHRANE, C. N. *Christianity and Classical Culture: a Study of Thought and Action from Augustus to Augustine*, New York, 1957.

COHEN, J. 'Original Sin as the Evil Inclination', *HTR* 72/3, 1979/80, 496–520.

COLLINGWOOD, R. G. and MYRES, J. N. L. *Roman Britain and the English Settlements*², Oxford, 1937.

COOPER, T. 'On praying to God in English', *CR* 65, 2, 1980, 41–51.

COPLESTONE-CROW, B. 'The dual nature of the Irish colonization of Dyfed in the Dark Ages', *SC* 16/17, 1981/2, 1–24.

COURCELLE, P. 'Paulin de Nole et Saint Jérôme', *REL* 25, 1947, 250–80.

—— *Les Confessions de Saint Augustin dans la tradition littéraire, antécédents et postérité*, Paris, 1963.

—— *Recherches sur les Confessions de Saint Augustin*, Paris, 1968.

CROÍNÍN, D. Ó. 'New Heresies for Old: Pelagianism in Ireland and the Papal Letter of 640', *Speculum* 60, 1985, 505–16.

CROSS, F. L. Ed., *The Oxford Dictionary of the Christian Church*², corr. repr. 1977.

CUPITT, D. *The Nature of Man*, London, 1979.

—— *Only Human*, London, 1985(a).

—— *Crisis of Moral Authority*², London, 1985(b).

DANIÉLOU, J. *The Development of Christian Doctrine before the Council of Nicaea*, II, ed. and trans. J. A. Baker, London/Philadelphia, 1973.

—— and MARROU, H. I. *The Christian Centuries*, trans. V. Cronin, London, 1964.

D'ARCY, M. Ed., *St Augustine*, New York, 1957.

DAVIDS, J. A. *De Orosio et Sancto Augustino Priscillianistarum adversariis commentatio historica et philosophica*, Diss., The Hague, 1930.

DAVIES, W. *Wales in the Early Middle Ages: Studies in the Early History of Britain*, Leicester, 1982.

DAVIES, W. H. 'The Church in Wales' in BARLEY, M. W. and HANSON, R. P. C., edd., 1968, 131–50.

DAWKINS, R. M. *The Selfish Gene*, Oxford, 1976.

——'In defence of selfish genes', *Philosophy*, 1981, 556–73.

DEMPSEY, J. J. *Pelagius's Commentary on St Paul*, Rome, 1937.

DEVRESSE, R. *Essai sur Théodore de Mopsueste*, Studi e Testi 141, Rome, 1948.

DEWART, J. McW. 'The Influence of Theodore of Mopsuestia on Augustine's *Letter* 187', *AS* 10, 1979.

—— 'The Christology of the Pelagian Controversy', *SP* 17, iii, 1982, 1221–44.

DEWART, L. *The Future of Belief*, London, 1967.

DIDIER, J. C. 'Saint Augustin et la baptême des enfants', *REA* 2, 1956, 109–29.

DILLON, M. 'The Irish Settlements in Wales', *Celtica* 12, 1977, 1–11.

—— and CHADWICK, N. K. *The Celtic Realms*, London, 1967.

DINKLER, E. 'Pelagius' in *RE* 1937, 226–42.

DIVJAK, J. *Epistolae S. Aurelii Augustini*, CSEL 88, 1981, 32–8.

DIXON, N. *Troubled Waters*, London, 1979.

DODDS, E. R. 'Augustine's *Confessions*: a study of spiritual maladjust-ments', *HJ* 26, 1927/8, 459–73.

—— *Pagan and Christian in an Age of Anxiety*, Cambridge, 1965.

DUCHESNE, L. *Histoire ancienne de l'Eglise*, III, Paris, 1910.

DUMVILLE, D. N. 'Sub-Roman Britain: history and legend', *History* n.s. 62, 1977, 173–92.

—— 'The chronology of the *De Excidio Britanniae*, I' in LAPWIDGE, M. and DUMVILLE, D., edd., 1984, 61–84.

—— 'Late-seventh or eight-century evidence for the British transmission of Pelagius', *CMCS* 10, 1985, 39–52.

DUVAL, Y.-M. 'Julien d'Eclane et Rufin d'Aquilée: du concile de Rimini à la repression pélagienne', *REA* 24, 1978, 248–9.

—— 'Pélage est-il le censeur inconnu de l'*Adversus Iovinianum* à Rome en 393' *ou* 'Du "Portrait-Robot" de l'hérétique chez S. Jérôme', *RHE* 75, 1980, 525–57.

ELLIS, I. '*Essays and Reviews* reconsidered', *Theology* 74, 1971, 396–404.

ESPOSITO, M. 'The Patrician problem and a possible solution', *IHS* 10, 38, 1956/7, 131–55.

EVANS, D. S. *Stori Dewi Sant*, Llandybie, 1959.

—— Ed., *Buchedd Dewi²*, Cardiff, 1965.

—— Ed., *Lives of the Welsh Saints by G. H. Doble*, Cardiff, 1971.

—— *Historia Gruffud vab Kenan*, Cardiff, 1977.

—— 'Ychwaneg am Ddewi Sant – ei fuchedd a'i fywyd', *THSC*, 1984, 9–29.

EVANS, G. R. *Augustine on Evil*, Cambridge, 1982.

EVANS, J. 'St Germanus in Britain', *ACant* 80, 1965, 175–85.

EVANS, R. F. 'Pelagius, Fastidius and the Pseudo-Augustinian *De Vita Christiana*, *JTS* n.s. 13, 1962, 72–98.

—— 'Pelagius's veracity at the Synod of Diospolis' in J. Sommerfeld, ed., *Studies in Medieval Culture*, Kalamazoo, Mich., 1964, 21–30.

—— *Pelagius: Inquiries and Reappraisals*, London, 1968(a).

—— *Four Letters of Pelagius*, London, 1968(b).

FAIRWEATHER, E. R. 'St Augustine's interpretation of infant baptism', *AS* 2, 1954.

FERGUSON, E. 'Inscriptions and the origin of infant baptism', *JTS* n.s. 30, 1979, 37–46.

FERGUSON, J. *Pelagius: a Historical and Theological Study*, Cambridge, 1956, repr. New York, 1978.

—— 'In defence of Pelagius', *Theology* 83, 1980, 114–19.

FERRARI, L. C. 'The Boyhood Beatings of Augustine', *AS* 5, 1974, 1–14.

FISHER, J. D. C. *Christian Initiation: Baptism in the Medieval West*, London, 1965.

FLOËRI, F. 'Le pape Zosime et la doctrine augustinienne du péché originel', *AM* 2, 1954, 755–61.

—— 'Remarques sur la doctrine augustinienne du péché originel', *SP* 9, iii, 1963, 416–21.

FOAKES-JACKSON, F. J. *History of the Christian Church from the Earliest Times to A.D. 461*, Cambridge, 1947.

FOSTER, I. L. and DANIEL, G. *Prehistory and Early Wales*, London, 1965.

FREDERIKSEN, P. 'Paul and Augustine: conversion narratives, orthodox traditions, and the retrospective self', *JTS* n.s. 37, 1986, 3–34.

FREEMAN, A. *The Benn Heresy*, London, 1982.

FREND, W. H. C. 'The Christianization of Roman Britain' in BARLEY, M. W. and HANSON, R. P. C., edd., 1968, 37–50.

―― *The Donatist Church: a Movement of Protest in Roman North Africa*, Oxford, 1971.

―― *The Early Church: from the Beginnings to 461*, London, 1982.

―― *The Rise of Christianity*, London, 1984.

―― *Saints and Sinners in the Early Church: Differing and Conflicting Traditions in the First Six Centuries*, London, 1985.

FRERE, S. S. *Britannia: a History of Roman Britain*, London, 1967.

GARCIA-ALLEN, C. A. *Pelagius and Christian Initiation: a Study in Historical Theology*, Washington, 1978.

―― 'Was Pelagius influenced by Chromatius of Aquileia?', *SP*, iii, 1982, 1251–7.

GAUDEL, A. 'Péché originel' in *DTC* 12/1, 275–624.

GILSON, E. *Introduction a l'étude de Saint Augustin³*, Paris, 1949.

GLOUBOKOWSKY, N. N. 'The Greek Fathers' in WHITLEY, W. T., ed., 1932, c.II.

GOODWIN, R. P. Ed. and trans., *Selected Writings of St Thomas Aquinas*, Indianopolis, Indiana, 1965.

GREENE, D. 'Some linguistic evidence relating to the British Church' in BARLEY, M. W. and HANSON, R. P. C., edd., 1968, 75–86.

GRESHAKE, G. *Gnade als konkrete Freiheit: eine Untersuchung zur Gnadenlehre des Pelagius*, Mainz, 1972.

GRIMES, W. F. Ed., *Aspects of Archaeology in Britain and Beyond*, London, 1951.

GROSJEAN, P. 'Notes d'hagiographie celtique', *AB* 63, 1945, 65–130; 70, 1953, 312–26; 75, 1957, 158–226.

―― 'The Confession of St Patrick' in RYAN, J., ed., 1958, 81–94.

GROSSI, V. 'Il battesimo e la polemica pelagiana negli anni 411–413', *Augustinianum* 9, 1969, 30–61.

GUNTON, C. 'The theologian and the biologist', *Theology* 77, 1974, 526–8.

HAIGHT, R. *The Experience and Language of Grace*, Dublin, 1979.

HALL, S. 'Sub-Christian prayer: Pelagian didacticism in the Alternative Service Book 1980', *KTR* 4, 1, 1981, 1–7.

HAMMAN, A. 'Orosius de Braga et le pélagianisme' in *Bracara Augusta* 21, 1967, 346–55.

HAMMOND, C. P. 'The last ten years of Rufinus's life and the date of his move from south Aquileia', *JTS* n.s. 28, 1977, 327–429.

HANSON, R. P. C. *Origen's Doctrine of Tradition*, London, 1954.

―― *St Patrick, a British Missionary Bishop*, Nottingham, 1965.

—— *Saint Patrick: his Origins and Career*, Oxford, 1968.

—— *Mystery and Imagination*, London, 1976.

—— 'The Date of St Patrick', *BJRL* 61, 1978/9, 60–77.

—— and BLANC, C. *Saint Patrick: Confession et Lettre a Coroticus*, Paris, 1978.

—— *The Life and Writings of the Historical St Patrick*, New York, 1983.

HARDINGE, L. *The Celtic Church in Britain*, London, 1972.

HARDY, A. *The Living Stream* (Gifford Lectures, 1963/4), London, 1965.

—— *The Divine Flame* (Gifford Lectures, 1964/5), London, 1966.

—— *The Biology of God*, London, 1975.

—— *Darwinism and the Spirit of Man*, London, 1984.

HARNACK, A. von *History of Dogma*, trans. J. Millar, London, 1961.

HARRISON, K. 'Episodes in the history of Easter cycles in Ireland' in WHITELOCK, D., McKITTERICK, R. and DUMVILLE, D., edd., 1982, 307–19.

HEDDE, R. and AMANN, E. 'Pélagianisme' in *DTC* 12, 692ff.

HEFELE, C. J. *A History of the Christian Councils*, London, 1871–96.

HENRY, P. 'Why is contemporary scholarship so enamoured of ancient heretics?', *SP* 17, i, 1982, 123–6.

HICK, J. *Evil and the God of Love*, London/New York, 1966.

—— *Death and Eternal Life*, London, 1976.

—— *The Second Christianity*, London, 1983(a).

—— and M. GOULDER *Why Believe in God?*, London, 1983(b).

HODGSON, L. *The Grace of God in Faith and Philosophy*, London, 1936.

—— *For Faith and Freedom* (Gifford Lectures, 1954/6), London, 1968.

HUBER, K. C. *The Pelagian Heresy: observations on its social context*, Ann Arbor, 1984.

HUGHES, K. *The Church in Early Irish Society*, London, 1966.

—— *Early Christian Ireland: Introduction to the Sources*, London, 1972.

HUNT, E. D. *Holy Land Pilgrimages in the Later Roman Empire, A.D. 312–460*, Oxford, 1982.

JACKSON, K. H. 'Notes on the Ogam inscriptions of southern Britain' in Fox, C. F. and Dickins, B., edd., *Early Cultures of North-west Europe*, Cambridge, 1950, 197–213.

—— *Language and History in Early Britain*, Edinburgh, 1953.

JACKSON, M. 'Home cooking: British theology and the Universal Church', *Theology* 82, 1979, 244–51.

JACQUIN, M. 'Questions de prédestination aux Ve et VIe siecles', *RHE* 5, 1904, 266ff.

JAMES, E. 'Ireland and Western Gaul' in WHITELOCK, D., McKITTERICK, R. and DUMVILLE, D., edd., 1982, 362–86.

JAMES, J. W. *Rhigyfarch's Life of St David*, Cardiff, 1967.

JARRETT, M. G. 'Magnus Maximus and the end of Roman Britain', *THSC*, 1983, 22–35.

—— and DOBSON, B. edd., *Britain and Rome: Essays Presented to Eric Birley on his Sixtieth Birthday*, Kendal, 1965.

JOAD, C. E. M. *God and Evil*, London, 1942.

JOHNSON, S. *Later Roman Britain*, London, 1980.

JOLIVET, R. *Le problème du mal d'après saint Augustin²*, Paris, 1936.

JONES, A. H. M. 'Were ancient heresies national or social movements in disguise?', *JTS* n.s. 10, 1959, 280–98.

—— *The Later Roman Empire, 284–602: a Social, Economic and Administrative Survey*, Oxford, 1964.

—— 'The Western Church in the fifth and sixth centuries' in BARLEY, M. W. and HANSON, R. P. C., edd., 1968, 9–18.

JONES, O. W. *Rowland Williams, Trivium* Suppl., 1971.

JUNG, C. G. *Memories, Dreams and Reflections*, London, 1967.

KEE, A. *Constantine versus Christ: the Triumph of Ideology*, London, 1982.

KELLY, J. F. 'Pelagius, Pelagianism and the Early Christian Irish', *Mediaevalia* 4, 1978, 99ff.

KELLY, J. N. D. *Jerome: His Life, Writings and Controversies*, London, 1975.

—— *Early Christian Doctrines⁵*, New York, 1978.

KENNEY, J. F. *The Sources for the Early History of Ireland: I, Ecclesiastical*, New York, 1929.

KIDD, B. J. *History of the Christian Church to A.D. 461*, III, Oxford, 1922.

KIRBY, D. P. 'Bede's native sources for the *Historia Ecclesiastica*', *BJRL* 48, 1966, 341–71.

KOOPMANS, J. H. 'Augustine's first contact with Pelagius and the dating of the condemnation of Caelestius at Carthage', *VC* 8, 1954, 149–63.

KRUSCH, B. and LEVISON, W. Edd., *Vita Sancti Germani Episcopi Autissiodorensis* in *Passiones vitaeque sanctorum aevi merovingici*, VII, Hannover, 1919/20.

KÜNG, H. *Justification*, trans. T. Collins, E. E. Tolk and D. Grandskou, London, 1964.

—— *On Being a Christian*, trans. E. Quinn, London, 1977.

LACHOIX, B. *Orose et ses idées*, Montreal, 1965.

LAMBERT, M. D. *Medieval Heresy: Popular Movements from Bogomil to Hus*, London, 1977.

LAMPE, G. W. H. 'Salvation: traditions and reappraisals' in *Explorations in Theology* 8, London, 1981 (repr. from J. M. Turner, ed., *Queen's Essays*, Birmingham, 1980).

—— *God as Spirit* (Bampton Lectures, 1976), Oxford, 1977.

LAPIDGE, M. 'Gildas' education and the Latin culture of Sub-Roman Britain' in LAPIDGE, M. and DUMVILLE, D., edd., 1984, 27–50.

—— and DUMVILLE, D. edd., *Gildas: New Approaches*, Studies in Celtic History V, Woodbridge, 1984.

LEFF, G. A. *Bradwardine and the Pelagians*, Cambridge, 1957.

—— *Heresy in the Latin Medieval Age* I, Manchester, 1967.

LEVISON, W. 'Bischof Germanus von Auxerre und die Quellen zu seiner Geschichte', *Neues Archiv der Gesellschaft für ältere deutsche Geschichtskunde* 29, 1904, 95–175.

LEWIS, H. D. *Morals and the New Theology*, London, 1947.

LIEBESCHUETZ, W. 'Did the Pelagian movement have social aims?', *Historia* 12, 1963, 227–41.

—— 'Pelagian evidence on the last period of Roman Britain', *Latomus* 26, 1967, 436–47.

LIVINGSTONE, E. A. Ed., *The Concise Oxford Dictionary of the Christian Church*, corr. repr., Oxford, 1980.

LLOYD, J. E. *A History of Wales from the Earliest Times to the Edwardian Conquest³*, London, 1939.

LOOFS, F. 'Pelagius' in *RPThK*, 15, 1904³, 747–74; 24, 1913, 310–12.

LORENZ, R. 'Der Augustinismus Prospers von Aquitanien' *ZKG* 73, 1963, 217–52.

—— 'Gnade und Erkenntnis bei Augustinus', *ZKG* 75, 1964, 21–78.

LOT, F. *La fin du monde antique et le début du Moyen Age*, Paris, 1927.

LOUTH, A. 'Messalianism and Pelagianism', *SP* 17, i, 1982, 127–35.

LOYER, O. *Les Chrétientés Celtiques*, Paris, 1965.

LUBAC, H. de *Augustinianism and Modern Theology*, London, 1969.

LUCAS, J. R. *The Freedom of the Will*, Oxford, 1970.

—— 'Pelagius and St Augustine', *JTS* n.s. 22, 1971, 73–85.

—— *Freedom and Grace*, London, 1976.

LUMSDEN, C. J. and WILSON, E. O. *Genes, Mind and Culture*, Harvard, 1981.

MACKIE, J. L. 'The Law of the jungle: moral principles and principles of evolution', *Philosophy*, 1978, 455–64.

—— 'Genes and egoism', *Philosophy*, 1981, 553–5.

MACMULLEN, R. *Christianizing the Roman Empire*, Yale, 1984.

MACQUARRIE, J. *Existentialism*, Harmondsworth, 1973.

—— *Thinking about God*, London, 1975.

—— *In Search of Humanity*, London, 1982.

MADEC, G. 'Connaissance de Dieu et action de grâces', *RA* 2, 1962, 273–309.

MANSON, T. W. 'Grace in the New Testament' in WHITLEY, W. T., ed., 1932, c.I.

MARKUS, R. A. *Saeculum: History and Society in the Theology of St Augustine*, Cambridge, 1970.

—— Ed., *Augustine: a Collection of Critical Essays*, New York, 1972.

—— *Christianity in the Roman World*, London, 1974.

—— 'Pelagianism: Britain and the Continent', *JEH* 37, 2, 1986, 191–204.

MARROU, H. I. *Saint Augustine and his Influence through the Ages*, New York, 1957.

—— *S. Augustin et la fin de la culture antique⁴*, Paris, 1958.

—— 'Les attaches orientales du Pélagianisme', *CRAI* 1969, 459–72.

—— (with A.-M. BONNARDIÈRE) *St Augustin et l'augustinisme*, Paris, 1980.

MARTINETTO, G. 'Les premières réactions antiaugustiniennes de Pélage', *REA* 17, 1971, 83–117.

MATTHEWS, J. *Baptism, Eucharist and Ministry: Seven Studies*, London, 1982 (based on *Faith and Order Paper* No. 111, of the World Council of Churches).

MAUSBAEK, J. von *Die Ethik des heiligen Augustinus*, Freiburg, 1929.

MIDGELEY, M. 'Gene-juggling', *Philosophy*, 1979, 439–58.

—— *Evolution as a Religion: Strange Hopes and Stranger Fears*, London/New York, 1985.

MILLER, M. 'Bede's use of Gildas', *EHR* 90, 1975, 241–61.

—— 'The last British entry in the "Gallic Chronicles"', *Britannia* 9, 1978, 315–18.

MILLER, M. W. *Rufini Presbyteri liber de fide: a Critical Text with Introduction and Commentary*, Washington, 1964.

MOMIGLIANO, A. Ed., *The Conflict between Christianity and Paganism in the Fourth Century*, Oxford, 1963.

MOMMSEN, T. *Chronica Minora*, 3 vols., Berlin, 1891–8.

MONOD, J. *Chance and Necessity*, trans. A. Wainhouse, London, 1979.

MONTEFIORE, H. *The Probability of God*, London, 1985.

MOORE, D. Ed., *The Land of Dyfed in Early Times*, Cardiff, 1964.

MOORE, R. I. *The Birth of Popular Heresy: Documents of Medieval History 1*, London, 1975.

MORIN, G. 'Lettre inédite de l'évêque Evodius aux moines d'Adrumète sur la question de la grâce', *RB* 13, 1896, 481–5.

MORRIS, J. R. 'Pelagian Literature', *JTS* n.s. 16, 1965, 26–60.

—— 'Dark Age Dates' in JARRETT, M. G. and DOBSON, B., edd., 1965, 145–84.

—— 'The Dates of the Celtic Saints', *JTS* n.s. 17, 1966, 342–91.

—— 'The Literary Evidence' in BARLEY, M. W. and HANSON, R. P. C., edd., 1968, 55–73.

—— *The Age of Arthur: a History of the British Isles from 350 to 650*, London, 1973.

MOSS, H. St L. B. *The Birth of the Middle Ages*, London, 1947.

MOZLEY, J. B. *A Treatise on the Augustinian Doctrine of Predestination²*, London, 1878.

MUNZ, P. 'John Cassian', *JEH* 9, 1960, 1–22.

MURPHY, F. X. *Rufinus of Aquileia (345–411): his Life and Works*, Washington, 1945.

—— 'Melania the Elder: a biographical note', *Traditio* 5, 1947, 59–77.

MURRAY, J. C. *The Problem of God*, Yale, 1964.

MYRES, J. N. L. 'The *Adventus Saxonum*' in GRIMES, W. F., ed., 1951, 221–41.

—— 'Pelagius and the end of Roman rule in Britain', *JRS* 50, 1960, 21–36.

—— 'Introduction' to BARLEY, M. W. and HANSON, R. P. C., edd., 1968, 1–8.

NASH-WILLIAMS, V. E. *The Early Christian Monuments of Wales*, Cardiff, 1950.

NERNEY, D. S. 'A Study of St Patrick's sources, III', *IER*, 5th ser. 72, 1949, 14–26, 97–110, 265–80.

NEWMAN, J. H. *Apologia pro Vita Sua*, London, 1949.

NOCK, A. D. *Conversion: the Old and the New in Religion from Alexander the Great to Augustine of Hippo*[3], 1961.

NORREGAARD, J. 'Grace in St Augustine' in WHITLEY, W. T., ed., 1932, c.IV.

NORRIS, R. A. *Manhood and Christ: a Study in the Christology of Theodore of Mopsuestia*, Oxford, 1963.

NUVOLONE, F. G. and SOLIGNAC, A. 'Pélage et Pélagianisme' in *Dictionnaire de spiritualité, ascetique, mystique, doctrine et histoire*, Vol. 12B, 1986, 2889–942.

NYGREN, G. 'Das Prädestationsproblem in der Theologie Augustins', *STL* 12, 1956.

OBERMAN, H. O. *Archbishop Thomas Bradwardine: a Fourteenth-Century Augustinian*, Utrecht, 1957.

O'MEARA, J. J. 'The Confession of St Patrick and the Confessions of St Augustine', *IER*, 5th ser., 85, 1956, 190–7.

—— *The Young Augustine: an Introduction to the Confessions of St Augustine*[2], London/New York, 1980.

O'RAHILLY, T. F. *Ireland and Wales: their Historical and Literary Relations*, London, 1924.

—— *The Two Patricks: a Lecture on the History of Christianity in Fifth-Century Ireland*, Dublin, 1942.

—— *The Two Patricks*, Dublin, 1957.

O'SULLIVAN, T. D. *The De Excidio of Gildas: its Authenticity and Date* (*Columbia Studies in the Classical Tradition* vii), Leiden, 1978.

PANNENBERG, W. *Faith and Reality*, trans. J. Maxwell, London, 1977(a).

—— *Human Nature, Election and History*, Philadelphia, 1977(b).

PAPE, W. and BENSELER, G. *Wörterbuch der griechischen Eigennamen*, Graz, 1959.

PASSMORE, J. *The Perfectibility of Man*, London, 1970.

PATOUT BURNS, J. 'The interpretation of Romans in the Pelagian controversy', *AS* 10, 1979, 43–54(a).

—— 'Augustine's role in the imperial action against Pelagius', *JTS* n.s. 30, 1979, 67–83(b).

PATTERSON, L. *Theodore of Mopsuestia and Modern Thought*, London, 1926.

PELIKAN, J. *The Christian Tradition: a History of the Development of Doctrine* I, Chicago/London, 1971.

PETERS, E. Ed., *Heresy and Authority in Medieval Europe: Documents and Translations*, London, 1980.

PHIPPS, W. W. 'The Heresiarch: Pelagius or Augustine?', *ATR* 62, 1980, 124–33.

PIGANIOL, A. *L'Empire chrétien* (*Histoire romaine* IV, 2), Paris, 1947.

PINCHERLE, A. *La formazione teologica di S. Agostino*, Rome, 1947.

PIRENNE, R. *La morale de Pélage*, Rome, 1961.

PITTENGER, N. *Picturing God*, London, 1982.

PLUMMER, C. *Venerabilis Baedae Opera Historica*, Oxford, 1896.

PLINVAL, G. de 'Recherches sur l'oeuvre littéraire de Pélage', *RPh* 60, 1934, 10–42.

—— 'La problème de Pélage sous son dernier état', *RHE* 35, 1939, 5–21.

—— *Pélage, ses écrits, sa vie et son reforme*, Lausanne, 1943.

—— *Essai sur le style et la langue de Pélage (Collectanea Friburgensia* 31), Fribourg, 1947.

—— 'Julien d'Éclane devant la Bible', *RSR* 47, 1959, 345–66.

—— *La crise pélagienne*, I. Introductions, traductions et notes par G. de Plinval et J. de la Tullaye, *BA* 21, Paris, 1966.

—— 'L'heure est-elle venue de redécouvrir Pélage?', *REA* 19, 1973, 158–62.

POPE, H. *St Augustine of Hippo*, London, 1937.

PORTALIÉ, E. 'Augustin, Saint' in *DTC*², I, 1923, 2268–472.

—— *A Guide to the Thought of Saint Augustine*², trans. R. J. Bastian, Westport, Conn., 1975.

POWELL, T. G. E. *The Celts*, London, 1958.

PRESTIGE, G. L. *Fathers and Heretics*, London, 1963.

PRETE, S. *Pelagio e il pelagianesimo (Biblioteca di Scienze Religiose* X, 5), Brescia, 1961.

PRICE, D. T. W. *A History of Saint David's University College*, I, Cardiff, 1977.

PUECH, H. C. *Le Manichéisme: son fondateur, sa doctrine*, Paris, 1949.

RADFORD, C. A. R. 'The earliest Irish Churches', *UJA* 40, 1977, 1–11.

REES, B. R. 'The conversion of Saint Augustine', *Trivium* 14, 1979, 1–17.

REFOULÉ, F. 'Datation du premier concile de Carthage contre les Pélagiens et du *Libellus Fidei* de Rufin', *REA* 9, 1963(a), 41–9.

—— 'La distinction "Royaume de Dieu-Vie éternelle" est-elle pélagienne?', *RSR* 51, 1963(b), 247–54.

—— 'Julien d'Éclane, théologien et philosophe', *RSR* 52, 1964, 42–84, 233–47.

—— 'Julien d'Éclane', *Catholicisme* 6, 26, 1966, 1236–9.

RICHARDS, M. 'The Irish settlements in South-West Wales: a topographical approach', *JRSAI* 90, 1960, 133–52.

RICHARDSON, A. Ed., *A Dictionary of Christian Theology*, London, 1969.

RIST, J. M. 'Augustine on free will and predestination', in MARKUS, R. A., ed., 1972, 218–52.

RIVIÈRE, J. 'Hétérodoxie des pélagiens en fait de rédemption?', *RHE* 41, 1946, 5–43.

ROBINSON, J. A. T. *The Roots of a Radical*, London, 1980.

RONDET, H. *Gratia Christi*, Paris, 1948.

—— *Le péché originel dans la tradition patristique et théologique*, Paris, 1967.

—— 'Rufin de Syrien et le *Liber de Fide*', *Augustiniana* 22, 1972, 531–9.

ROWE, W. L. 'Augustine on foreknowledge and free will' in MARKUS, R. A., ed., 1972, 209–17.

RYAN, J. Ed., *Saint Patrick* (Thomas Davis Lectures), Dublin, 1958.

SAGE, A. 'La prédestination chez S. Augustin d'après une thèse récente', *REA* 6, 1960, 37.

—— 'Faul-il anathématiser la doctrine augustinienne de la prédestination?', *REA* 8, 1962, 240.

——— 'Praeparatur voluntas a Domino', *REA* 10, 1964, 1–20.

——— 'Péché originel: naissance d'un dogma', *REA* 13, 1967, 211–48.

——— 'Le péché originel dans la pensée de Saint Augustin de 421–430', *REA* 15, 1969, 75–112.

SALWAY, P. *Roman Britain*, Oxford, 1981.

SAWYER, P. H. *From Roman Britain to Norman England*, London, 1978.

SCHLEIERMACHER, F. D. E. *The Christian Faith*, trans. H. R. Mackintosh and J. S. Stewart, London, 1928.

SCHNITZER, J. 'Orosio e Pelagio', *Religio* 8, 1937, 336–43.

SELL, A. P. F. 'Augustine versus Pelagius: a cautionary tale of perennial importance', *CTJ* 12, 1977, 117–43.

SHARPE, R. 'Gildas as a Father of the Church' in LAPWIDGE, M. and DUMVILLE, D., edd., 1984, 193–205.

SHAW, B. D. 'The Family in Late Antiquity: the experience of Augustine', *Past & Present*, 115, May 1987, 3–51.

SHELDON-WILLIAMS, I. P. 'The Cappadocians' in ARMSTRONG, A. H., ed., 1970, 432–56.

SIMONE, R. J. de 'Modern research on the sources of St Augustine's doctrine of original sin', *AS* 11, 1980, 205–27.

SIMS-WILLIAMS, P. 'The evidence for vernacular Irish influence on early medieval Welsh literature' in WHITELOCK, D., McKITTERICK, R. and DUMVILLE, D., edd., 1982, 235–57.

SINGER, P. *The Expanding Circle: Ethics and Sociology*, Oxford, 1981.

SMITH, A. J. 'The Latin sources of the Commentary of Pelagius on the Epistle of St Paul to the Romans', *JTS* 19, 1917/18, 162–230; 20, 1919, 55–65.

——— 'The Commentary of Pelagius on "Romans" compared with that of Origen–Rufinus', *JTS* 20, 1919, 127–77.

——— 'Pelagius and Augustine', *JTS* 31, 1929/30, 21–35.

SMITH, W. and WACE, H. Edd., *A Dictionary of Christian Biography, Literature, Sects and Doctrines*, London, 1877–87.

SMITH, W. T. *Augustine: His Life and Thought*, Atlanta, Georgia, 1980.

SONNTAG, F. 'Augustine's metaphysics and free will', *HTR* 60, 1967, 297–306.

SOUTER, A. 'The Commentary of Pelagius on the Epistles of Paul: the problem of its restoration', *PBA* 2, 1905/6, 409–39.

——— 'Another new fragment of Pelagius', *JTS* 12, 1910/11, 32–5.

——— 'Freiburg fragments of an MS of the Pelagian Commentary on the Epistles of St Paul', *JTS* 13, 1911/12, 515–19.

——— 'New Manuscripts of Pelagius', *ThL* 38, 1913, 442.

——— 'Pelagius and the Pauline text in the *Book of Armagh*', *JTS* 16, 1914/15, 105.

——— 'Pelagius' doctrine in relation to his early life', *Expositor* 1, 1915, 180–2.

——— 'The character and history of Pelagius' Commentary on the Epistles of St Paul', *PBA* 7, 1915/16, 261–96.

——— 'Pelagius' text of Romans v.12 with commentary', *ET* 28, 1916/17, 42–3.

—— 'The earliest surviving book of a British author', *TCR* 115, 1919, 76–82.

—— *Pelagius's Expositions of the Thirteen Epistles of St Paul* (*Texts and Studies* IX), Cambridge, 1922/31.

SPARROW-SIMPSON, W. J. *The Letters of St Augustine*, London, 1919.

STEVENS, C. E. 'Gildas Sapiens', *EHR* 56, 1941, 353–73

STEVENSON, J. Ed., *A New Eusebius: Documents Illustrative of the History of the Church to A.D. 337*, London, 1965.

—— Ed., *Creeds, Councils and Controversies: Documents Illustrative of the History of the Church, A.D. 337–461*, London, 1966.

STOKES, W. Ed. and trans., *The Tripartite Life of St Patrick and Other Documents Relating to That Saint*, II, London, 1887.

TAYLOR, J. V. *The Go-Between God*, London, 1972.

TENNANT, F. R. *The Concept of Sin*, Cambridge, 1912.

TESELLE, E. *Augustine the Theologian*, London, 1970.

—— 'Rufinus the Syrian, Caelestius, Pelagius: explorations in the prehistory of the Pelagian controversy', *AS* 3, 1972, 61–95.

THEISSEN, G. *Biblical Faith: an Evolutionary Approach*, London, 1984.

THOMAS, A. C. 'The evidence from North Britain' in BARLEY, M. W. and HANSON, R. P. C., edd., 1968, 93–122.

—— *Britain and Ireland in Early Christian Times, A.D. 400–800*, London, 1971.

—— 'Irish colonies in post-Roman Western Britain: a survey of the evidence', *JRIC* n.s. 6, 1972, 251–74.

—— 'Saint Patrick and fifth-century Britain: an historical model explained' in CASEY, P. J., ed., 1979, 81–101.

—— *Christianity in Roman Britain to A.D. 500*, London, 1981.

THOMAS, J. F. *Saint Augustin s'est-il trompé?: essai sur la prédestination*, Paris, 1959.

THOMPSON, E. A. 'Zosimus on the end of Roman Britain', *Antiquity* 30, 1956, 163–7.

—— 'A chronological note on St Germanus of Auxerre', *AB* 75, 1957, 135–8.

—— 'Britain A.D. 406–410', *Britannia* 8, 1977, 303–18.

—— 'Gildas and the history of Britain', *Britannia* 10, 1979, 203–26

—— *St Germanus of Auxerre and the End of Roman Britain* (*Studies in Celtic History* 6), Woodbridge, 1984.

—— *Who was St Patrick?*, Woodbridge, 1985.

THONNARD, F.-J. 'La prédestination augustinienne et l'interprétation de O. Rottmaner, *REA* 9, 1983, 259–87.

—— 'La prédestination augustinienne: sa place en philosophie augustinienne', *REA* 10, 1964, 97–123.

—— 'L'aristotélisme de Julien d'Éclane et saint Augustin', *REA* 11, 1965, 296–304.

—— 'La notion de "nature" chez saint Augustin: son progrès dans la polémique antipélagienne', *REA* 11, 1965, 239–65.

THORPE, W. H. *Purpose in a World of Chance: A Biologist's View*, Oxford, 1978.

TODD, J. H.   *St Patrick, Apostle of Ireland*, Dublin, 1864.

TOYNBEE, J. M. C.   'Christianity in Roman Britain', *JBAA*, 3rd ser., 16, 1953, 1–24.

TOYNBEE, P.   *Towards the Holy Spirit*, London, 1982.

TRIGG, J. W.   *Origen: the Bible and Philosophy in the Third-Century Church*, Atlanta, Georgia, 1983.

TRIGG, R.   *The Shaping of Man: Philosophical Aspects of Sociology*, Oxford, 1982.

TURNER, C. H.   'Pelagius' Commentary on the Pauline Epistles and its history', *JTS* 4, 1902/3, 132–41.

——   'Curiosities of the Latin interpretation of the Greek Testament', *JTS* 12, 1911, 273–5.

UNAMUNO, M. de   *The Tragic Sense of Life*, trans. J. E. Crawford-Flitch, London, 1967.

VALERO, J. B.   'El estoicismo de Pelagio', *Estudios Eclesiasticos* 57, 1982, 39–63.

VAN DER MEER, F.   *Augustine the Bishop: the Life and Work of a Father of the Church*[2], trans. B. Battershaw and G. R. Lamb, London, 1978.

VANDERVELDE, G.   *Original Sin: Two Major Trends in Contemporary Reinterpretation*, Amsterdam, 1975.

VIDLER, A. R.   Ed., *Objections to Christian Belief*, London, 1963.

WADE-EVANS, A. W.   *Life of St David*, London, 1923.

WALLACE-HADRILL, D. S.   *Christian Antioch: a Study of Early Christian Thought in the East*, Cambridge, 1982.

WAND, J. W. C.   *A History of the Early Church to A.D. 500*, London, 1963.

WARD, J. H.   'Vortigern and the end of Roman Britain', *Britannia* 3, 1972, 276–89.

WATSON, E. W.   'The Latin Fathers' in WHITLEY, W. T., ed., 1932, c.III.

WEBB, C. C. J.   *Problems in the Relations of God and Man*, London, 1911.

WERMELINGER, O.   *Röm und Pelagius: die theologische position der römischen Bischöfe im pelagianischen Streit in den Jahren 411–432 (Päpste und Papsttum VII)*, Stuttgart, 1975.

WEST, R.   *St Augustine*, London/New York, 1933, repr. in *Rebecca West: a Celebration*, Harmondsworth, 1978, 157–236.

WHITELOCK, D., McKITTERICK, R. and DUMVILLE, D.   Edd., *Ireland in Early Medieval Europe*, Cambridge, 1982.

WHITLEY, W. T.   Ed., *The Doctrine of Grace*, London, 1932.

WIDENGREN, G.   *Mani and Manichaeism*, trans. C. Kessler, London, 1965.

WILES, M.   *The Remaking of Christian Doctrine*, London, 1974.

——   *Faith and the Mystery of God*, London, 1982.

WILKEN, R. L.   *The Myth of Christian Beginnings*, London, 1979.

WILLIAMS, G.   *The Welsh Church from Conquest to Reformation*, Cardiff, 1962.

WILLIAMS, G. A.   *When was Wales?*, Harmondsworth, 1985.

WILLIAMS, H.   Ed. and trans., Gildas, *De Excidio Britanniae*, London, 1899/1901.

—— 'Heinrich Zimmer on the history of the Celtic Church', *ZCP* 4, 1903, 527–74.

—— *Christianity in Early Britain*, Oxford, 1912.

WILLIAMS, H. A. 'Psychological Objections' in VIDLER, ed., 1963, 35–56.

—— *Some Day I'll Find You*, London, 1982.

WILLIAMS, N. P. *The Ideas of the Fall and of Original Sin* (Bampton Lectures, 1924), London, 1927.

—— *The Grace of God*, London, 1930.

WILLIS BUND, J. W. *The Celtic Church in Wales*, London, 1897.

WILSON, E. O. *Sociobiology: the New Synthesis*, Cambridge, Mass., 1975.

WILSON, P. A. 'Romano-British and Welsh Christianity: continuity or discontinuity?', *WHR* 3, 1966/7, 5–21, 103–20.

—— 'St Patrick and Irish Christian origins', *SC* 14/15, 1979/80, 344–80.

WINTERBOTTOM, M. Ed. and trans., *Gildas: the Ruin of Britain and Other Works* (Arthurian Sources 7), Phillimore/London/Chichester, 1978.

WOLFSON, H. A. 'Philosophical implications of the Pelagian controversy', *PAPS* 103, 1959, 554–62.

WOOD, I. 'The End of Roman Britain: continental evidence and parallels' in LAPWIDGE, M. and DUMVILLE, D., edd., 1984, 1–25.

WOODS, H. *Augustine and Evolution: a Study in the Saint's De genesi ad litteram and De Trinitate*, New York, 1924.

WRIGHT, D. F. 'Pelagius the Twice-Born', *TC* 82, 1972, 6–15.

YOUNG, D. 'Ethology and the evolution of human behaviour, 1: an introductory review', *Theology* 77, 1974(a), 394–404.

—— 'Ethology and the evolution of human behaviour, 2: suggestions for theology', *Theology* 77, 1974(b), 470–8.

YOUNG, F. M. 'Did Epiphanius know what he meant by Heresy?', *SP* 17, i, 1982, 199–205.

—— *Can These Dry Bones Live?*, London, 1982.

—— *From Nicaea to Chalcedon: a Guide to the Literature and its Background*, London, 1983.

ZIEGLER, K. and SONTHEIMER, W. Edd., *Der kleine Pauly: Lexicon der Antike*, Stuttgart, 1964.

ZIMMER, H. *Pelagius in Irland: Texte und Untersuchungen zur Patristischen Litteratur*, Berlin, 1901.

—— *The Celtic Church in Britain and Ireland*, trans. A. Meyer, London, 1912.

Index

169

170

2. Other Writers Cited

171

3. General Index

173

175

Pelagius *(cont.)*
  on original sin   75f., 91
  on *posse, velle, esse*   35f.
  on 'sinlessness'   7f., 86, 93ff., 136
  personality   xii
  works   xii, 21, 83f., 133f.
  and *passim.*
Photinianism   26
Pike, James A., Bp   23
Pinianus, Melania and Albina   xii, 99
Pius XII,Pope   75
Plotinus   60
Praylius, Bp of Jerusalem   xii, 141
predestination   40ff., 50, 101ff., 103ff., 107,
  128
Priscillian, Priscillianism   16, 25ff., 86, 131
Proba   6
Prosper Tiro of Aquitaine, St   xiii, 21,
  103ff., 108ff., 110, 115, 118ff.

Quodvultdeus   16, 51

Reformers   73
reincarnation   16
Rhigyfarch (Ricemarch)   114ff.
Riparius   5
Rufinus the Syrian   9ff., 76, 86f., 89, 90, 140
Rufinus Tyrannius of Aquileia   2, 7, 9, 26,
  84ff., 93, 131

Sabellianism   10, 24
Sabinus   103
Saragossa, Council of, A.D. 380   25
Schleiermacher, F. D. E.   24, 57
Sedulius Scotus   122
'Semi-Augustinianism'   96, 106
Semi-Pelagianism   51, 73, 96, 98, 103ff.,
  106, 123f., 128
Severian, Bp   108, 123
Severinus, Pope, St   121
Severus of Trier   109
'Sicilian Briton'   11, 89, 111ff.
Simplicianus   30, 39, 42, 65
'sinlessness'/*impeccantia*   7f., 86, 136

Sixtus ('Xystus') II, Pope, St   84ff.
Sixtus III, Pope   51, 101ff., 107, 142
St Gall MS   122
Sulien, Bp of St Davids   114f.
Synergism   87, 96

Teilhard de Chardhin, Pierre   ix
Tertullian   30, 57, 62, 64, 78
Theodore, Bp of Mopsuestia   57, 86ff., 98,
  101, 142
Theodosius II, Emperor   25, 101
Theophilus, Patr. of Alexandria   7, 126
Thirty-Nine Articles   75
traducianism   16, 58
Turbantius   99
Tyconius   66

Uí Líathain   117

Valentinian III, Emperor   101
Valentinus   34, 102
Valerius, Count   99
Vandals   101
Venerius, Bp of Marseilles   106
Victoricus   119
Victorius of Aquitaine   122
'Victory, Synod of'   115
Victricius, Bp of Rouen, St   111, 114
Vincentian Canon   68f.
Vincentius Victor   60
Vincent of Lérins, St   ix, 106, 123
Vitalis, Bp of Carthage   51
Vitrier, Johan   131
Vortigern   106, 110, 113

Wesley, John   ix
Western Church   xv, 3, 26, 68, 127, 129
Whitehead, A. N.   47
William of Ockham   ix, 106, 124
William of St Thierry   123
Williams, Rowland   81
World Council of Churches   80
Wycliffites   42

Zimmer, Heinrich   121f.
Zosimus, Pope   xiv, 2f., 65, 90, 98f., 130, 141